√3.95

The Futurists

The Futurists

Edited with an introduction by

Alvin Toffler

Random House / New York

ISBN: 0–394–31713–0

Library of Congress Catalog Card Number: 70–39770

Manufactured in the United States of America
Composed by Cherry Hill Composition.
Printed and bound by Colonial Press, Clinton, Mass.

Typography by Hermann Strohbach

First Edition

987654321

11 - 1 - 72

54858

For Karen and Monica
to whom tomorrow belongs

Acknowledgments

No book, not even a relatively simple reader, is produced without considerable sweat and tears. This one is no exception. It could not have been completed in the allotted period without the collaborative efforts of my wife, Heidi, who helped me read and judge the massive pile of books, magazines, journals, and other documents from which it has been culled. Professor José Villegas, from whom I have learned much over the years, drew on his encyclopedic knowledge of futurist literature in many languages to suggest selections and help run down the more elusive items. A word of special thanks is also due Jim Smith, Stephanie Wald, and Hermann Strohbach of Random House, who piloted the resultant manuscript through its editorial, design, and production phases under unusually trying circumstances—and at unbelievably high speed.

Contents

Contents

Philosophers and Planners 233

Notes About the Authors

Daniel Bell. Sociologist . . . Harvard . . . Now completing work entitled *The Post-Industrial Society* . . . Born New York, 1919 . . . Former editor, the *New Leader, Fortune* . . . Author, *The End of Ideology, Work and Its Discontents* . . . Member, National Commission on Technology, Automation and Economic Progress, Chairman, Commission on the Year 2000 . . . Coeditor, the quarterly, *The Public Interest* . . .

I. Bestuzhev-Lada. Top Soviet futurist . . . In charge of Section for Social Forecasting, Institute of Concerted Social Research, U.S.S.R. Academy of Sciences . . . Also director, Social Forecasting Research Institute of Soviet Sociological Association . . . Author, *Outlines of the Future, If the World Disarms, Modern Problems of Social Forecasting* (all in Russian) . . . Charges that Western interest in futurism arose when capitalism needed a vision of the future with which to counter Marx . . .

Kenneth E. Boulding. Economist, University of Colorado . . . Born England, 1910, emigrated to U.S., 1937 . . . Former president, American Economic Association . . . Also winner of award by American Council of Learned Societies for distinguished scholarship in humanities . . . Worked with peace research groups . . . Author, *The Meaning of the Twentieth Century, Conflict and Defense, The Image,* and (with Emile Benoit) *Disarmament and the Economy, A Primer on Social Dynamics* . . .

Arthur C. Clarke. Author of science fiction and nonfiction . . . Has been auditor, technical editor, and underwater photographer . . . Former chairman, British Interplanetary Society . . . Forecast use of satellites for communication . . . Wrote story on which movie *2001* was based . . . Books include *Profiles of the Future, The Promise of Space, Childhood's End* . . . Winner, Kalinga Prize, UNESCO . . . Born England, 1917 . . . Lives in Ceylon . . .

Paul Ehrlich. Outspoken expert on population and ecology . . . Professor of biology, Stanford . . . Author, *The Population Bomb,* and, with Richard L. Harriman, *How to Be a Survivor* . . . Calls for strong controls on population growth, "de-development" of the technologically developed nations . . .

Ossip K. Flechtheim. Political scientist, Free University of Berlin . . . Invented concept of "futurology" and made important contributions to futures research . . . One of first to urge introduction of futures into education . . . Author, *History and Futurology, German Political Parties Since 1945, From Hegel to Kelsen, Between Yesterday and Tomorrow* . . . Editor, the journal, *Futurum* . . .

R. Buckminster Fuller. Born 1895, Massachusetts . . . Designer, engineer . . . created dramatically different 3-wheeled automobile, 1930s, invented geodesic dome, also new method of cartography . . . Professor, Southern Illinois University . . . Lectured at hundreds of universities . . . Author, *Nine Chains to the Moon, No More Second-Hand God, Ideas and Integrities, Operating Manual for Spaceship Earth* . . . Also poetry, *Unfinished Epic of Industrialization* . . . Sui generis . . .

Theodore J. Gordon. President, The Futures Group, private research firm . . . Former Director, Space Stations and Planetary Systems, Douglas Aircraft . . . Also former Senior Research Fellow, Institute for the Future . . . Author, *The Future, Ideas in Conflict* (about unconventional ideas in science) . . . codeveloper of "cross impact matrix analysis" forecasting technique . . .

Yujiro Hayashi. Professor, Social Technology . . . Tokyo Institute of Technology . . . Former chairman, Japan Society of Futurology . . . Former chief of Economic Research Institute . . . Coauthor of study of high diversity social systems—the "multi-channel" society . . .

Olaf Helmer. Director of Research, cofounder, Institute for the Future, a major futurist research center . . . Mathematician and logician . . . Formerly with RAND Corporation . . . Author, *Social Technology* . . . Primarily interested in gaming, simulation and other forecasting methods . . . Co-originator of Delphi technique . . .

M. S. Iyengar. Director, Regional Research Laboratory, Jorhat, India . . . Developing "micro-technology" for village-scale industrialization . . . Concerned with strategies for application of science and futurism to special problems of developing nations . . .

Erich Jantsch. Austrian astro-physicist and engineer . . . Consultant to Organization for Economic Co-operation and Development (OECD) . . . Taught, M.I.T. and Berkeley . . . Prepared influential report, *Technological Forecasting in Perspective* . . . Brings humanist outlook to scientific problems . . .

Bertrand de Jouvenel. Political economist, philosopher . . . Prime intellectual force in futurist movement . . . Born France, 1903 . . . Created Futuribles, international group of scholars involved in futurist research . . . President of SEDEIS (Société d'Études et de Documentation Economique, Industrielle et Sociale) . . . Author, *The Art of Conjecture, On Power, The Pure Theory of Politics, Sovereignty, The Ethics of Redistribution* . . .

Robert Jungk. Berlin-born writer . . . Key futurist organizer . . . Important link between futurism and European youth . . . Author, *Tomorrow Is Already Here, Children of the Ashes,* and *Brighter Than a Thousand Suns* . . . Founder, Mankind 2000 . . . Tireless proponent of social control of technology . . . Arrested Germany, anti-Nazi activities . . . Arrested and jailed war-time Switzerland for anti-Nazi writings . . . After war, Central European correspondent, London *Observer* . . . Created pioneer Institute for Future Research, Vienna . . . With the Norwegian futurist, Johan Galtung, edited *Mankind 2000* . . .

Herman Kahn. Director of the Hudson Institute, futurist "think tank" serving government and industry . . . Born New Jersey, 1922 . . . Former Senior physicist, RAND Corporation . . . Author, *On Thermonuclear War, Thinking About the Unthinkable, On Escalation,* and *The Year 2000* (with Anthony J. Wiener) . . .

John McHale. Sociologist . . . Director, Center for Integrative Studies, State University of New York at Binghamton . . . Widely exhibited artist and designer . . . Born Scotland . . . Past Executive Director, World Resources Inventory . . . Author, *The Future of the Future, The Ecological Context, World Facts and Trends 2* . . . Fellow of the World Academy of Art and Science, Royal Society of Arts (England) . . . Winner, Medaille d'Honneur en Vermeil, Société d'Encouragement au Progrès . . . Active member, Continuing Committee of the World Future Research Congress . . .

Marshall McLuhan. Communications theorist . . . Director, Center for Culture and Technology, University of Toronto . . . Born Canada, 1911 . . . Professor of English . . . Author, *The Mechanical Bride, The Gutenberg Galaxy, Understanding Media,* and *The Medium Is the Massage* (with

Quentin Fiore) . . . Argues that TV alters sensory responses and epistemological organization of the viewer . . . Fellow, Royal Society Canadian Roman Catholics . . .

Margaret Mead. Curator Emeritus of Ethnology, American Museum of Natural History, New York . . . Born Philadelphia, 1901 . . . At twenty-three, spent nine months on anthropological field trip to American Samoa . . . Returned repeatedly to various Pacific cultures . . . Author of anthropological classics: *Coming of Age in Samoa, New Lives for Old,* and *Male and Female* . . . Past president, American Anthropological Association and World Federation for Mental Health . . . Columnist, *Redbook* magazine . . .

Fred L. Polak. Leader of D-70, Dutch political party . . . Former personal advisor to Minister of Education . . . Professor of Sociology . . . Recipient of fellowships from UNESCO and Council of Europe . . . Author, *The Image of the Future* and *Prognostics* . . . Vice-president and cofounder, Erasmus Prize Foundation . . . Consultant on planning . . . Leading figure in Mankind 2000 and other international futurist committees . . .

Alvin Toffler. Author, social critic . . . Born New York, 1928 . . . Washington correspondent for various newspapers . . . Associate Editor *Fortune* . . . Taught first course in "sociology of the future" at New School for Social Research . . . Former Visiting Professor, Cornell University, Visiting Scholar, Russell Sage Foundation . . . Author, *The Culture Consumers, Future Shock* . . . Editor, *The Schoolhouse in the City* . . . Nominee: National Book Award . . . Winner: 1971 Prix du Meilleur Livre Étranger . . .

Arthur I. Waskow. Historian-futurist . . . Born Baltimore, 1933 . . . Former Legislative Assistant, House of Representatives, Washington . . . Senior Staff, Peace Research Institute . . . Fellow, Institute for Policy Studies . . . Author, *The Limits of Defense, Worried Man's Guide to World Peace, From Race Riot to Sit-In, Running Riot* . . .

Anthony J. Wiener. Chairman, Research Management Council, Hudson Institute . . . Former research associate, U.S. Joint Commission on Mental Illness and Health . . . Coauthor (with Herman Kahn) of *The Year 2000* . . . Contributor to many Hudson Institute projects and publications . . .

John Wren-Lewis. British Theologian . . . Scientist . . . Long-range planner . . . Formerly on planning staff, Imperial Chemical Industries . . . Religious correspondent, *The Guardian* . . . Regents Lecturer, University of California at Santa Barbara . . . Author, *God in a Technological Age, What Shall We Tell the Children?* . . . President, British Association for Humanistic Psychology . . . Chiefly concerned with links between science and religion, impact of scientific thought on society . . .

The Futurists

Introduction: Probing Tomorrow

Alvin Toffler

If we do not learn from history, we shall be compelled to relive it. True. But if we do not change the future, we shall be compelled to endure it. And that could be worse.

We cannot humanize the future until we draw it into our consciousness and probe it with all the intelligence and imagination at our command. This is what we are now just beginning to do.

Until a few years ago, the word "futurist" was virtually unknown in American intellectual life. When used at all, it referred to a school of poets, painters, and playwrights who flourished in Europe from 1909 to about 1925, then vanished into the library stacks and museum showcases. Today the term has leapt back into the language—but with a new meaning. The word now denotes a growing school of social critics, scientists, philosophers, planners, and others who concern themselves with the alternatives facing man as the human race collides with an onrushing future.

3

Futurism is the catch-all term applied in this country to "a considerable number of organizations, institutionalized programs and individual workers . . . whose *major,* and often sole, activity is concerned with the study of the future."[1] These range from planning teams armed with computers and vast data banks to students and scholars armed with vision and hope, from radical poets to conservative political scientists, from government think tanks to lonely communes of young people searching for new insights into tomorrow. Europeans prefer the terms "futurology" and "futurologist," since their languages are not freighted with the faintly negative and satiric connotations carried by the "ology" ending in English. But nomenclature aside, the phenomenon is by no means solely American.

Unlike the astrologers, necromancers, palm-readers, and oracles of the past, today's futurists, for the most part, lay no claim to the ability to predict. Wary of dogmatic statements about what "will" happen, they focus, rather, on the array of alternatives open to decision-makers, stressing that the future is fluid, not fixed or frozen.

Some are driven by a passionate wish to induce social change— to alter the future in specific ways. Others are more preoccupied by the methods with which we generate images of the future. They are less concerned with influencing change than they are with better forecasting techniques which, they believe, will help the rest of us pursue whatever our goals may be. Still other futurists are intellectually fascinated by questions having to do with time and knowledge: What can or cannot be known? How does information about the future contrast with information about the past or present? Some focus on possible futures, others on probable futures, still others on preferable futures.

A vast amount of imagination, energy, and skill has been released by this rediscovery, as it were, of the future. Institutes, seminars, conferences, clubs, and classes are springing up everywhere. It is becoming acceptable, in academic circles, to talk about the future. (Before now it seemed unscholarly, unscientific, even "unserious.") Some of the new energies flowing into "futuristic studies" are spilling over into and influencing the social sciences, the humanities, and other disciplines, forcing them again and again to ask "what are the hidden side effects, the long-range consequences of any action?" or "what are the value implications of our behavior?" or even "how should we define 'human' in the future?" And students, by the thousands, are responding to this new curiosity about tomorrow. I can scarcely recall a single American campus, of the scores I have visited in recent years, at which students have not come forward to ask about futurism and how they might become personally involved with it.

Given the widespread surge of interest, futurism has begun to take on some of the features of a movement. Like all movements, it has its faddist fringe and its violent critics. The latter argue that only the past or the present have meaning, yet even they, in their daily lives, cannot escape the need to make forecasts about the future. The issue is not whether we should devote attention to events that have not yet occurred, but whether we should be conscious of what we are doing and, through that consciousness, try to do it better. Despite the faddists and the critics, the futurist movement has spread rapidly around the globe. It is beginning to develop membership organizations like the World Future Society; journals like *The Futurist,* and *Futures;* an incipient division of labor; internal controversies over, for example, the role of quantification or intuition; it has a growing literature and even the beginnings of established leadership.

The purpose of this collection is to make accessible a few of the works of the best-known and, at the moment, most influential futurists. It makes no claim to completeness. Excellent and important work has been omitted for a variety of reasons—space limitations, technical language, and so forth. Nor will this collection stand as the "final" statement of the contributors or of the movement. Instead, it is a first attempt to bring together, out of a burgeoning hodgepodge of books, monographs, reports, mimeographed speeches, magazine articles, and other documents, an assemblage that will suggest the range of ideas, content, and sources of contemporary futurism.

To illustrate the diversity of the movement, I have drawn selections not merely from the United States, but also from Japan, France, the Netherlands, the U.S.S.R., India, Germany, and Canada. The diversity of the movement is also reflected in the personal and professional backgrounds of these authors. The futurists here brought together were trained in anthropology, biology, engineering, philosophy, mathematics, physics, astronomy, sociology, art, economics, history, journalism, and a dozen other disciplines.

Often a single writer is a magnificent product of intellectual crossbreeding, so that Ted Gordon, who was one of the key engineers on the Saturn Rocket—the power source that ultimately propelled the flight to the moon—has become an interesting social analyst whose findings touch on everything from drugs to religion. John Wren-Lewis, formerly a corporate long-range planner in Britain, is trained in physics, but actually is best known as a theologian. Kenneth Boulding is an economist. But to call him that is like calling Buckminster Fuller an engineer. Boulding is also a philosopher of the social sciences, an organization theorist, and a working pacifist, just as Fuller, among other things, is a visionary, the leader of something approaching a religious movement, and a poet as well. Fred Polak, the leader of a pivotally important Dutch political party, has been a top adviser to the Minister of Education, and has served as the cultural historian of the futurist movement. Robert Jungk has taught in Berlin, but he has also organized the anti-Nazi underground during World War II, and has been imprisoned for his opinions in, of all places, democratic Switzerland. Similarly, to term Margaret Mead an anthropologist is to ignore her impact as a mass communicator through the medium of television and her monthly column in *Redbook* magazine. John McHale is a card-carrying sociologist. But he has a close working knowledge of science and technology—and, more significantly, has been widely exhibited as an artist and designer. In short, most futurists defy easy occupational or professional classification.

By the same token, they defy the very categories in which they have been placed in this book. The division into social critics, scientists, and philosophers and planners was almost an act of desperation, since, at various times, many of the writers could have fit as easily into one classification as another. Some of the scientists have written rather philosophical material about the future; some of the philosophers have been social critics as well. The categories ought to be regarded as "throwaway containers," not permanent receptacles.

Because of this hybridization, the best futurist writing is characterized by the wide range of ideas and influences in it. The future does not come in packages neatly labeled "Economics" or

"Nineteenth Century Literature" or "Biology 212." Futurists pull their insights from extremely varied sources.

Not only do they start from different occupational subcultures and different political perspectives, their forecasts vary widely as well. For Daniel Bell, more conservative than most, the society of the year 2000 will be "more like the present than different"—an assumption of gradualism that other futurists would, and do, challenge, just as they differ with his contention that the university will be the central institution of the new society.[2] Some believe that the machine is likely to further centralize and bureaucratize our society, a position explicitly attacked by McLuhan and others in their work.

This diversity of origin and opinion only goes so far, however. For the fact is that, if we look at the movement in the United States, we quickly discover certain disturbing facts.

Not long ago two young community organizers from Columbus, Ohio, one black, one white, attended the First General Assembly of the World Future Society. This meeting in Washington drew more than 1,000 futurists from all over the United States, and a scattering from the rest of the world. Once again, on the surface, there was great diversity. But in a letter detailing their observations at that meeting, Lawrence Auls, black, and Ken Eye, white, wrote:

"We wanted to observe the tone, emphasis, thrust of our fellow futurists to judge whether futurists are talkers of the future or doers of the future, and either way, *whose* future. . . . We found . . . that most futurists are very busy, active people, . . . doers at heart." But, they noted, fewer than two per cent of those at the meeting who responded to a survey turned out to be nonwhite. Racism, while discussed occasionally at the meeting, did not emerge as a primary concern, leading Auls and Eye to ask whether, in fact, "most Americans are not aware that, without thinking about it at all, we are planning a white future."[3]

My own observations confirm their impressions. With a handful of exceptions—a long-range planner at General Electric, an urbanist at Harvard, an educational counselor in San Diego—the futurists I meet or talk to are uniformly white. (Outside the United States they also come from the dominant racial groups in their society, so that, in Japan, I know of no Korean futurist. The futurists I know in India are Hindu, not Moslem.)

If the faces one runs into at futurist meetings in the United States are white, they are also predominantly male. A woman sociologist, Mireya Caldera, works with the futures research group in Caracas. (She happens to be the daughter of the president of Venezuela.) A scattering of women are working in this field in other countries. In the United States, also, a fair number of women educators have begun to interest themselves in the movement. Nevertheless, it remains fair to say women are underrepresented.

An exception to the rule is provided by the wives of a number of well-known contributors to this volume. Madame de Jouvenel is an extremely influential organizing force behind the French, and indeed the whole European, branch of the movement. Magda Cordell, John McHale's wife, is a familiar face at futurist conferences and has collaborated with her husband on various research projects. Kenneth Boulding's wife, Elise, is responsible for the English translation of Fred Polak's magnum opus, *The Image of the Future,* and has written on her own. Paul Ehrlich lists his wife, Anne, as "virtually a co-author" of *The Population Bomb.* "Maggie" Helmer has been closely involved with her husband's work at the Institute for the Future. And my own wife, Heidi, works with me and has significantly shaped my views. I have heard futurists comment on this phenomenon and suggest that husband-wife professional collaboration may, indeed, turn out to be a common feature of the future.

The futurist movement, finally, also suffers from a disease now rampant in most of the high technology nations—what I call "middle-age imperialism." This is a state of affairs in which the young are kept out of the business-political-community decision-making apparatus for longer and longer periods (prolonged adolescence) while the elderly are extruded from the system at an earlier and earlier age (prolonged, enforced idleness). The result is that the basic power of the social order is concentrated in, and the day-to-day operating decisions are made by, people my own age—forty-three—give or take a dozen years. The overrepresentation of the middle-aged is present in the futurist movement, as well as in society at large. As for the contributors to this volume, with the exception of Mead and Fuller, both septuagenarians who have, luckily for us, escaped the curse of forced retirement, I would hazard a guess that their average age is on the high side of the range, perhaps fifty to fifty-five.

Given these facts, the reader is entitled to ask: What about this volume? Doesn't its list of contributors also tilt heavily on the side of the white male middle-aged intellectual?

The answer is Yes. With the exception of contributors from Japan and India, the rest are all white. With the exception of Margaret Mead, they are all male. And there is probably not a single author who is under thirty.

The reason for this is that I have deliberately chosen to reflect the movement approximately as it is right now, rather than as I think it ought to be. If the movement, warts and all, is held up to study, I think we shall see an infusion of new faces in it and begin to hear from urgent new voices. I believe that within the next three to five years, the average age in the movement will drop sharply, and that the racism and sexism present in it today will diminish.

Similarly, I believe that some of the names and ideas of the contributors to this volume will fade in importance. This is a strange thing to say. Normally, the editor of a collection advertises its contents as of "lasting value." In this collection we will find dramatic images of tomorrow, insights into art, education, and the so-called generation gap, attacks on technocracy, and a fascinating chronicle of the bloopers perpetrated by yesterdays' prophets of technology. We learn about some of the methods used by today's futurists in preparing their forecasts. We examine some of the political implications of futurism, and we are helped to understand the incredible social and ecological trap that we find ourselves in as the year 2000 speeds toward us. We probe into the very meaning of the word future and explore some of its cultural and psychological significance. Finally, we are treated to a poetic plea for the creation of a sane planetary environment for tomorrow. Yet permanence is relative. In today's swiftly changing world, even the best of today's insight runs the risk of rapid obsolescence. And this must be true of this book as well.

Finally, the book itself reflects what constitutes the emerging "establishment" within the futurist movement. Like everything else, even an "establishment" takes form at an accelerated pace these days. Even though the movement is hardly half a decade old, the time is already ripe for the appearance of a futurist "counter-establishment" which will challenge the assumptions put forth in these pages.

Oddly enough, I think most of the contributors to this volume, despite their presence in it, would welcome the rise of a "counter-establishment." The successive replacement of ideas, men, and institutions is nothing other than the future arriving. And that is what this book, in the end, is about.

Social Critics

Some futurists are content to explore
tomorrow. Others want to change it. In
this part we present seven futurists
whose work, whether explicitly labeled
"social criticism" or not, is inherently
change-oriented. Exhibiting sharply
different styles, attitudes, and political
postures, and ranging in concern from
ecology to art, from education to
anticipatory democracy, they share a
wish to shape the future. And each, in
his or her own way, already has!

Eco-Catastrophe!

Paul Ehrlich

One of the most disturbing images of tomorrow is evoked in this short, vivid essay by a leading ecologist. It is an example of one form of forecasting —the "scenario." The scenario writer chooses a single possible future, no matter how unlikely, then imaginatively traces a sequence of events that could combine to make it a reality.

[1] The end of the ocean came late in the summer of 1979, and it came even more rapidly than the biologists had expected. There had been signs for more than a decade, commencing with the discovery in 1968 that DDT slows down photosynthesis in marine plant life. It was announced in a short paper in the technical journal, *Science*, but to ecologists it smacked of doomsday. They knew that all life in the sea depends on photosynthesis, the chem-

 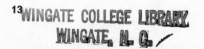

ical process by which green plants bind the sun's energy and make it available to living things. And they knew that DDT and similar chlorinated hydrocarbons had polluted the entire surface of the earth, including the sea.

But that was only the first of many signs. There had been the final gasp of the whaling industry in 1973, and the end of the Peruvian anchovy fishery in 1975. Indeed, a score of other fisheries had disappeared quietly from over-exploitation and various eco-catastrophes by 1977. The term "eco-catastrophe" was coined by a California ecologist in 1969 to describe the most spectacular of man's attacks on the systems which sustain his life. He drew his inspiration from the Santa Barbara offshore oil disaster of that year, and from the news which spread among naturalists that virtually all of the Golden State's seashore bird life was doomed because of chlorinated hydrocarbon interference with its reproduction. Eco-catastrophes in the sea became increasingly common in the early 1970s. Mysterious "blooms" of previously rare microorganisms began to appear in offshore waters. Red tides—killer outbreaks of a minute single-celled plant—returned to the Florida Gulf coast and were sometimes accompanied by tides of other exotic hues.

It was clear by 1975 that the entire ecology of the ocean was changing. A few types of phytoplankton were becoming resistant to chlorinated hydrocarbons and were gaining the upper hand. Changes in the phytoplankton community led inevitably to changes in the community of zooplankton, the tiny animals which eat the phytoplankton. These changes were passed on up the chains of life in the ocean to the herring, plaice, cod and tuna. As the diversity of life in the ocean diminished, its stability also decreased.

Other changes had taken place by 1975. Most ocean fishes that returned to fresh water to breed, like the salmon, had become extinct, their breeding streams so dammed up and polluted that their powerful homing instinct only resulted in suicide. Many fishes and shellfishes that bred in restricted areas along the coasts followed them as onshore pollution escalated.

By 1977 the annual yield of fish from the sea was down to 30 million metric tons, less than one-half the per capita catch of a decade earlier. This helped malnutrition to escalate sharply in a world where an estimated 50 million people per year were already dying of starvation. The United Nations attempted to get all chlorinated hydrocarbon insecticides banned on a worldwide basis, but the move was defeated by the United States. This opposition was generated primarily by the American petrochemical industry, operating hand in glove with its subsidiary, the United States Department of Agriculture. Together they persuaded the government to oppose the U.N. move—which was not difficult since most Americans believed that Russia and China were more in need of fish products than was the United States. The United Nations also attempted to get fishing nations to adopt strict and enforced catch limits to preserve dwindling stocks. This move was blocked by Russia, who, with the most modern electronic equipment, was in the best position to glean what was left in the sea. It was, curiously, on the very day in 1977 when the Soviet Union announced its refusal that another ominous article appeared in *Science.* It announced that incident solar radiation had been so reduced by worldwide air pollution that serious effects on the world's vegetation could be expected.

[2] Apparently it was a combination of ecosystem destabilization, sunlight reduction, and a rapid escalation in chlorinated hydrocarbon pollution from massive Thanodrin applications which triggered the ultimate catastrophe. Seventeen huge Soviet-financed Thanodrin plants were operating in underdeveloped countries by 1978. They had been part of a massive Russian "aid offensive" designed to fill the gap caused by the collapse of America's ballyhooed "Green Revolution."

It became apparent in the early '70s that the "Green Revolution" was more talk than substance. Distribution of high yield "miracle" grain seeds had caused temporary local spurts in agricultural production. Simultaneously, excellent weather had produced record harvests. The combination permitted bureaucrats, especially in the United States Department of Agriculture and the Agency for International Development (AID), to reverse their previous pessimism and indulge in an outburst of optimistic propaganda about staving off famine. They raved about the approaching transformation of agriculture in the underdeveloped countries (UDCs). The reason for the propaganda reversal was never made clear. Most historians agree that a combination of utter ignorance of ecology, a desire to justify past errors, and pressure from agro-industry (which was eager to sell pesticides, fertilizers, and farm machinery to the UDCs and agencies helping the UDCs) was behind the campaign. Whatever the motivation, the results were clear. Many concerned people, lacking the expertise to see through the Green Revolution drivel, relaxed. The population-food crisis was "solved."

But reality was not long in showing itself. Local famine persisted in northern India even after good weather brought an end to the ghastly Bihar famine of the mid-60s. East Pakistan was next, followed by a resurgence of general famine in northern India. Other foci of famine rapidly developed in Indonesia, the Philippines, Malawi, the Congo, Egypt, Colombia, Ecuador, Honduras, the Dominican Republic, and Mexico.

Everywhere hard realities destroyed the illusion of the Green Revolution. Yields dropped as the progressive farmers who had first accepted the new seeds found that their higher yields brought lower prices—effective demand (hunger plus cash) was not sufficient in poor countries to keep prices up. Less progressive farmers, observing this, refused to make the extra effort required to cultivate the "miracle" grains. Transport systems proved inadequate to bring the necessary fertilizer to the fields where the new and extremely fertilizer-sensitive grains were being grown. The same systems were also inadequate to move produce to markets. Fertilizer plants were not built fast enough, and most of the underdeveloped countries could not scrape together funds to purchase supplies, even on concessional terms. Finally, the inevitable happened, and pests began to reduce yields in even the most carefully cultivated fields. Among the first were the famous "miracle rats" which invaded Philippine "miracle rice" fields early in 1969. They were quickly followed by many insects and viruses, thriving on the relatively pest-susceptible new grains, encouraged by the vast and dense plantings, and rapidly acquiring resistance to the chemicals used against them. As chaos spread until even the most obtuse agriculturists and economists realized that the Green Revolution had turned brown, the Russians stepped in.

In retrospect it seems incredible that the Russians, with the American mistakes known to them, could launch an even more incompetent program of aid to the underdeveloped world. Indeed, in the early 1970s there were cynics in the United States who claimed that outdoing the stupidity of American foreign aid would be physically impossible. Those critics were, however, obviously unaware that the Russians had been busily destroying their own environment for many years. The virtual disappearance of sturgeon from Russian rivers caused a great shortage of caviar by 1970. A standard joke among Russian scientists at that time was that they had created an artificial caviar which was indistinguishable from the real thing—except by taste. At any rate the Soviet Union, observing with interest the progressive deterioration of relations between the UDCs and the United States, came up with a solution. It had recently developed what it claimed was the ideal insecticide, a highly lethal chlorinated hydrocarbon complexed with a special agent for penetrating the external skeletal armor of insects. Announcing that the new pesticide, called Thanodrin, would truly produce a Green Revolution, the Soviets entered into negotiations with various UDCs for the construction of massive Thanodrin factories. The USSR would bear all the costs; all it wanted in return were certain trade and military concessions.

It is interesting now, with the perspective of years, to examine in some detail the reasons why the UDCs welcomed the Thanodrin plan with such open arms. Government officials in these countries ignored the protests of their own scientists that Thanodrin would not solve the problems which plagued them. The governments now knew that the basic cause of their problems was overpopulation, and that these problems had been exacerbated by the dullness, daydreaming, and cupidity endemic to all governments. They knew that only population control and limited development aimed primarily at agriculture could have spared them the horrors they now faced. They knew it, but they were not about to admit it. How much easier it was simply to accuse the Americans of failing to give them proper aid; how much simpler to accept the Russian panacea.

And then there was the general worsening of relations between the United States and the UDCs. Many things had contributed to this. The situation in America in the first half of the 1970s deserves our close scrutiny. Being more dependent on imports for raw materials than the Soviet Union, the United States had, in the early 1970s, adopted more and more heavy-handed policies in order to insure continuing supplies. Military adventures in Asia and Latin America had further lessened the international credibility of the United States as a great defender of freedom—an image which had begun to deteriorate rapidly during the pointless and fruitless Viet-Nam conflict. At home, acceptance of the carefully manufactured image lessened dramatically, as even the more romantic and chauvinistic citizens began to understand the role of the military and the industrial system in what John Kenneth Galbraith had aptly named "The New Industrial State."

At home in the U.S.A. the early '70s were traumatic times. Racial violence grew and the habitability of the cities diminished, as nothing substantial was done to ameliorate either racial inequities or urban blight. Welfare rolls grew as automation and general technological progress forced more and more people into the category of "unemployable." Simultaneously a taxpayers' revolt occurred. Although there was not enough money to build the schools, roads, water systems, sewage systems, jails, hospitals, urban transit lines, and all the other amenities needed to support a burgeoning population, Americans refused to tax themselves more heavily. Starting in Youngstown, Ohio in 1969 and followed closely by Richmond, California, community after community was forced to close its schools or curtail educational operations for lack of funds. Water supplies, already marginal in quality and quantity in many places by 1970, deteriorated quickly. Water rationing occurred in 1,723 municipalities in the summer of 1974, and hepatitis and epidemic dysentery rates climbed about 500 per cent between 1970–1974.

[3] Air pollution continued to be the most obvious manifestation of environmental deterioration. It was, by 1972, quite literally in the eyes of all Americans. The year 1973 saw not only the New York and Los Angeles smog disasters, but also the publication of the Surgeon General's massive report on air pollution and health. The public had been partially prepared for the worst by the publicity given to the U.N. pollution conference held in 1972. Deaths in the late '60s caused by smog were well known to scientists, but the public had ignored them because they mostly involved the early demise of the old and sick rather than people dropping dead on the freeways. But suddenly our citizens were faced with nearly 200,000 corpses and massive documentation that they could be the next to die from respiratory disease. They were not ready for that scale of disaster. After all, the U.N. conference had not predicted that

accumulated air pollution would make the planet uninhabitable until almost 1990. The population was terrorized as TV screens became filled with scenes of horror from the disaster areas. Especially vivid was NBC's coverage of hundreds of unattended people choking out their lives outside of New York's hospitals. Terms like nitrogen oxide, acute bronchitis and cardiac arrest began to have real meaning for most Americans.

The ultimate horror was the announcement that chlorinated hydrocarbons were now a major constituent of air pollution in all American cities. Autopsies of smog disaster victims revealed an average chlorinated hydrocarbon load in fatty tissue equivalent to 26 parts per million of DDT. In October, 1973, the Department of Health, Education and Welfare announced studies which showed unequivocally that increasing death rates from hypertension, cirrhosis of the liver, liver cancer and a series of other diseases had resulted from the chlorinated hydrocarbon load. They estimated that Americans born since 1946 (when DDT usage began) now had a life expectancy of only 49 years, and predicted that if current patterns continued, this expectancy would reach 42 years by 1980, when it might level out. Plunging insurance stocks triggered a stock market panic. The president of Velsicol, Inc., a major pesticide producer, went on television to "publicly eat a teaspoonful of DDT" (it was really powdered milk) and announce that HEW had been infiltrated by Communists. Other giants of the petrochemical industry, attempting to dispute the indisputable evidence, launched a massive pressure campaign on Congress to force HEW to "get out of agriculture's business." They were aided by the agro-chemical journals, which had decades of experience in misleading the public about the benefits and dangers of pesticides. But by now the public realized that it had been duped. The Nobel Prize for medicine and physiology was given to Drs. J. L. Radomski and W. B. Deichmann, who in the late 1960s had pioneered in the documentation of the long-term lethal effects of chlorinated hydrocarbons. A Presidential Commission with unimpeachable credentials directly accused the agro-chemical complex of "condemning many millions of Americans to an early death." The year 1973 was the year in which Americans finally came to understand the direct threat to their existence posed by environmental deterioration.

And 1973 was also the year in which most people finally comprehended the indirect threat. Even the president of Union Oil Company and several other industrialists publicly stated their concern over the reduction of bird populations which had resulted from pollution by DDT and other chlorinated hydrocarbons. Insect populations boomed because they were resistant to most pesticides and had been freed, by the incompetent use of those pesticides, from most of their natural enemies. Rodents swarmed over crops, multiplying rapidly in the absence of predatory birds. The effect of pests on the wheat crop was especially disastrous in the summer of 1973, since that was also the year of the great drought. Most of us can remember the shock which greeted the announcement by atmospheric physicists that the shift of the jet stream which had caused the drought was probably permanent. It signaled the birth of the Midwestern desert. Man's air-polluting activities had by then caused gross changes in climate patterns. The news, of course, played hell with commodity and stock markets. Food prices skyrocketed, as savings were poured into hoarded canned goods. Official assurances that food supplies would remain ample fell on deaf ears, and even the government showed signs of nervousness when California migrant field workers went out on strike again in protest against the continued use of pesticides by growers. The strike burgeoned into farm burning and riots. The workers, calling themselves "The Walking Dead," demanded immediate compensation for their shortened lives, and crash research programs to attempt to lengthen them.

It was in the same speech in which President Edward Kennedy, after much delay, finally declared a national emergency and called out the National Guard to harvest California's crops, that the first mention of population control was made. Kennedy pointed out that the United States would no longer be able to offer any food aid to other nations and was likely to suffer food shortages herself. He suggested that, in view of the manifest failure of the Green Revolution, the only hope of the UDCs lay in population control. His statement, you will recall, created an uproar in the underdeveloped countries. Newspaper editorials accused the United States of wishing to prevent small countries from becoming large nations and thus threatening American hegemony. Politicians asserted that President Kennedy was a "creature of the giant drug combine" that wished to shove its pills down every woman's throat.

Among Americans, religious opposition to population control was very slight. Industry in general also backed the idea. Increasing poverty in the UDCs was both destroying markets and threatening supplies of raw materials. The seriousness of the raw material situation had been brought home during the Congressional Hard Resources hearings in 1971. The exposure of the ignorance of the cornucopian economists had been quite a spectacle—a spectacle brought into virtually every American's home in living color. Few would forget the distinguished geologist from the University of California who suggested that economists be legally required to learn at least the most elementary facts of geology. Fewer still would forget that an equally distinguished Harvard economist added that they might be required to learn some economics, too. The overall message was clear: America's resource situation was bad and bound to get worse. The hearings had led to a bill requiring the Departments of State, Interior, and Commerce to set up a joint resource procurement council with the express purpose of "insuring that proper consideration of American resource needs be an integral part of American foreign policy."

Suddenly the United States discovered that it had a national consensus: population control was the only possible salvation of the underdeveloped world. But that same consensus led to heated debate. How could the UDCs be persuaded to limit their populations, and should not the United States lead the way by limiting its own? Members of the intellectual community wanted America to set an example. They pointed out that the United States was in the midst of a new baby boom: her birth rate, well over 20 per thousand per year, and her growth rate of over one per cent per annum were among the very highest of the developed countries. They detailed the deterioration of the American physical and psychic environments, the growing health threats, the impending food shortages, and the insufficiency of funds for desperately needed public works. They contended that the nation was clearly unable or unwilling to properly care for the people it already had. What possible reason could there be, they queried, for adding any more? Besides, who would listen to requests by the United States for population control when that nation did not control her own profligate reproduction?

Those who opposed population controls for the U.S. were equally vociferous. The military-industrial complex, with its all-too-human mixture of ignorance and avarice, still saw strength and prosperity in numbers. Baby food magnates, already worried by the growing nitrate pollution of their products, saw their market disappearing. Steel manufacturers saw a decrease in aggregate demand and slippage for that holy of holies, the Gross National Product. And military men saw, in the growing population-food-environment crisis, a serious threat to their carefully nurtured Cold War. In the end, of course, economic arguments held sway, and the "inalienable right of every American couple to determine the size of its family," a freedom invented for the occasion in the early '70s, was not compromised.

The population control bill, which was passed by Congress early in 1974, was quite a document, nevertheless. On the domestic front, it authorized an increase from 100 to 150 million dollars in funds for "family planning" activities. This was made possible by a general feeling in the country that the growing army on welfare needed family planning. But the gist of the bill was a series of measures designed to impress the need for population control on the UDCs. All American aid to countries with overpopulation problems was required by law to consist in part of population control assistance. In order to receive any assistance each nation was required not only to accept the population control aid, but also to match it according to a complex formula. "Overpopulation" itself was defined by a formula based on U.N. statistics, and the UDCs were required not only to accept aid, but also to show progress in reducing birth rates. Every five years the status of the aid program for each nation was to be re-evaluated.

The reaction to the announcement of this program dwarfed the response to President Kennedy's speech. A coalition of UDCs attempted to get the U.N. General Assembly to condemn the United States as a "genetic aggressor." Most damaging of all to the American cause was the famous "25 Indians and a dog" speech by Mr. Shankarnarayan, Indian Ambassador to the U.N. Shankarnarayan pointed out that for several decades the United States, with less than six per cent of the people of the world, had consumed roughly 50 per cent of the raw materials used every year. He described vividly America's contribution to worldwide environmental deterioration, and he scathingly denounced the miserly record of United States foreign aid as "unworthy of a fourth-rate power, let alone the most powerful nation on earth."

It was the climax of his speech, however, which most historians claim once and for all destroyed the image of the United States. Shankarnarayan informed the assembly that the average American family dog was fed more animal protein per week than the average Indian got in a month. "How do you justify taking fish from protein-starved Peruvians and feeding them to your animals?" he asked. "I contend," he concluded, "that the birth of an American baby is a greater disaster for the world than that of 25 Indian babies." When the applause had died away, Mr. Sorensen, the American represen-tative, made a speech which said essentially that "other countries look after their own self-interest, too." When the vote came, the United States was condemned.

[4] This condemnation set the tone of U.S.–UDC relations at the time the Russian Thanodrin proposal was made. The proposal seemed to offer the masses in the UDCs an opportunity to save themselves and humiliate the United States at the same time; and in human affairs, as we all know, biological realities could never interfere with such an opportunity. The scientists were silenced, the politicians said yes, the Thanodrin plants were built, and the results were what any beginning ecology student could have pre-dicted. At first Thanodrin seemed to offer excellent control of many pests. True, there was a rash of human fatalities from improper use of the lethal chemical, but, as Russian technical advisors were prone to note, these were more than compensated for by increased yields. Thanodrin use skyrocketed throughout the underdeveloped world. The Mikoyan design group developed a dependable, cheap agricultural aircraft which the Soviets donated to the effort in large numbers. MIG sprayers became even more common in UDCs than MIG interceptors.

Then the troubles began. Insect strains with cuticles resistant to Thanodrin penetration began to appear. And as streams, rivers, fish culture ponds and onshore waters became rich in Thanodrin, more fisheries began to disappear. Bird populations were decimated. The sequence of events was standard for broadcast use of a synthetic pesticide: great success at first, followed by removal of natural enemies and development of resistance by the pest. Populations of crop-eating insects in areas treated with Thanodrin made steady comebacks and soon became more abundant than ever. Yields plunged, while farmers in their desperation increased the Thanodrin dose and shortened the time between treatments. Death from Thanodrin poisoning became common. The first violent incident occurred in the Canete Valley of Peru, where farmers had suffered a similar chlorinated hydrocarbon disaster in the mid-'50s. A Russian advisor serving as an agricultural pilot was assaulted and killed by a mob of enraged farmers in January, 1978. Trouble spread rapidly during 1978, especially after the word got out that two years earlier Russia herself had banned the use of Thanodrin at home because of its serious effects on ecological systems. Suddenly Russia, and not the United States, was the *bête noir* in the UDCs. "Thanodrin parties" became epidemic, with farmers, in their ignorance, dumping carloads of Thanodrin concentrate into the sea. Russian advisors fled, and four of the Thanodrin plants were leveled to the ground. Destruction of the plants in Rio and Calcutta leds to hundreds of thousands of gallons of Thanodrin concentrate being dumped directly into the sea.

Mr. Shankarnarayan again rose to address the U.N., but this time it was Mr. Potemkin, representative of the Soviet Union, who was on the hot seat. Mr. Potemkin heard his nation described as the greatest mass killer of all time as Shankarnarayan predicted at least 30 million deaths from crop failures due to overdependence on Thanodrin. Russia was accused of "chemical aggression," and the General Assembly, after a weak reply by Potemkin, passed a vote of censure.

It was in January, 1979, that huge blooms of a previously unknown variety of diatom were reported off the coast of Peru. The blooms were accompanied by a massive die-off of sea life and of the pathetic remainder of the birds which had once feasted on the anchovies of the area. Almost immediately another huge bloom was reported in the Indian ocean, centering around the Seychelles, and then a third in the South Atlantic off the African coast. Both of these were accompanied by spectacular die-offs of marine animals. Even more ominous were growing reports of fish and bird kills at oceanic points where there were no spectacular blooms. Biologists were soon able to explain the phenomena: the diatom had evolved an enzyme which broke down Thanodrin; that enzyme also produced a breakdown product which interfered with the transmission of nerve impulses, and was therefore lethal to animals. Unfortunately, the biologists could suggest no way of repressing the poisonous diatom bloom in time. By September, 1979, all important animal life in the sea was extinct. Large areas of coastline had to be evacuated, as windrows of dead fish created a monumental stench.

But stench was the least of man's problems. Japan and China were faced with almost instant starvation from a total loss of the seafood on which they were so dependent. Both blamed Russia for their situation and demanded immediate mass shipments of food. Russia had none to send. On October 13, Chinese armies attacked Russia on a broad front. . . .

[5] A pretty grim scenario. Unfortunately, we're a long way into it already. Everything mentioned as happening before 1970 has actually occurred; much of the rest is based on projections of trends already appearing. Evidence that pesticides have long-term lethal effects on human beings has started to accumulate, and recently Robert Finch, Secretary of the Department of Health, Education and Welfare expressed his extreme apprehension about the pesticide situation. Simultaneously the petrochemical industry continues its unconscionable poison-peddling. For instance, Shell Chemical has been carrying on a high-pressure campaign to sell the insecticide Azodrin to farmers as a killer of cotton pests. They continue their program even though they know that Azodrin is not only ineffective, but often *increases* the pest density. They've covered themselves nicely in an advertisement which states, "Even if an overpowering migration [sic] develops, the flexibility of Azodrin lets you regain control fast. Just increase the dosage according to label recommendations." It's a great game—get people to apply the poison and kill the natural enemies of the pests. Then blame the increased pests on "migration" and sell even more pesticide!

Right now fisheries are being wiped out by over-exploitation, made easy by modern electronic equipment. The companies producing the equipment know this. They even boast in advertising that only their equipment will keep fishermen in business until the final kill. Profits must obviously be maximized in the short run. Indeed, Western society is in the process of completing the rape and murder of the planet for economic gain. And, sadly, most of the rest of the world is eager for the opportunity to emulate our behavior. But the underdeveloped peoples will be denied that opportunity —the days of plunder are drawing inexorably to a close.

Most of the people who are going to die in the greatest cataclysm in the history of man have already been born. More than three and a half billion people already populate our moribund globe, and about half of them are hungry. Some 10 to 20 million will starve to death *this year*. In spite of this, the population of the earth will increase by 70 million souls in 1969. For mankind has artificially lowered the death rate of the human population, while in general birth rates have remained high. With the input side of the population system in high gear and the output side slowed down, our fragile planet has filled with people at an incredible rate. It took several million years for the population to reach a total of two billion people in 1930, while a *second two billion will have been added by 1975*! By that time some experts feel that food shortages will have escalated the present level of world hunger and starvation into famines of unbelievable proportions. Other experts, more optimistic, think the ultimate food-population collision will not occur until the decade of the 1980s. Of course more massive famine may be avoided if other events cause a prior rise in the human death rate.

Both worldwide plague and thermonuclear war are made more probable as population growth continues. These, along with famine, make up the trio of potential "death rate solutions" to the population problem—solutions in which the birth rate–death rate imbalance is redressed by a rise in the death rate rather than by a lowering of the birth rate. Make no mistake about it, *the imbalance will be redressed*. The shape of the population growth curve is one familiar to the biologist. It is the outbreak part of an outbreak-crash sequence. A population grows rapidly in the presence of abundant resources, finally runs out of food or some other necessity, and crashes to a low level or extinction. Man is not only running out of food, he is also destroying the life support systems of the Spaceship Earth. The situation was recently summarized very succinctly: "It is the top of the ninth inning. Man, always a threat at the plate, has been hitting Nature hard. It is important to remember, however, that **Nature bats last.**"

The Future: Prefigurative Cultures and Unknown Children

Margaret Mead

In this striking chapter from her book *Culture and Commitment,* the famed anthropologist argues that we have shifted from a culture that is "postfigurative" (one in which the young learn from the old) to one that is "cofigurative" (one in which both children and adults learn chiefly from their peers). She appeals for a "prefigurative" culture in which, as the future explodes into the present, the old learn to learn from the young. Her voice, crossing generational and academic lines, has been influential in preparing the soil for the futurists.

Our present crisis has been variously attributed to the overwhelming rapidity of change, the collapse of the family, the decay of capitalism, the triumph of a soulless technology, and, in wholesale repudiation, to the final breakdown of the Establishment. Behind these attributions there is a more basic conflict between those for whom the present represents no more than an intensification of our existing cofigurative culture, in which peers are more than ever replacing parents as the significant models of behavior, and those who contend that we are in fact entering a totally new phase of cultural evolution.

Most commentators, in spite of their differences in viewpoint, still see the future essentially as an extension of the past. Teller can still speak of the outcome of a nuclear war as a state of destruction relatively no more drastic than the ravages wrought by Genghis Khan. Writing about the present crisis, moralists refer to the decay of religious systems in the past and historians point out that time and again civilization has survived the crumbling of empires.

Similarly, most commentators treat as no more than an extreme form of adolescent rebellion the repudiation of present and past by the dissident youth of every persuasion in every kind of society in the world. So Max Lerner can say "Every adolescent must pass through two crucial periods: one when he identifies with a model— a father, an older brother, a teacher—the second when he disassociates himself from his model, rebels against him, reasserts his own selfhood." There is little substantial difference between Lerner's view and that of David Riesman in his delineation of the autonomous man, who emerges from the present without too sharp a break with the past.

Perhaps the most extraordinary response to youthful rebellion has been that of Mao, who has attempted to turn the restive young against their parents as a way of preserving the momentum of the revolution made by the grandparent generation. Little as we understand the details of what has been going on in China, what we do know suggests a tremendous effort to transform the desire to destroy, which characterizes the attitudes of young activists all around the world, into an effective instrument for the preservation of the recently established Chinese Communist regime. If the Maoists succeed in this attempt, they will have made the most dramatic use of the techniques of temporary cofiguration to bring about a return to a postfigurative culture of which we have any record. There are indications that the modern Chinese may treat such new Western technologies as electronics as parallel to processes of assimilation that have occurred many times in the long history of Chinese civilization—no more significant than a new form of metallurgy.

Theorists who emphasize the parallels between past and present in their interpretations of the generation gap ignore the irreversibility of the changes that have taken place since the beginning of the industrial revolution. This is especially striking in their handling of modern technological development, which they treat as comparable in its effects to the changes that occurred as one civilization in the past took over from another such techniques as agriculture, script, navigation, or the organization of labor and law.

It is, of course, possible to discuss both postfigurative and cofigurative cultures in terms of slow or rapid change without specifying the nature of the process. For example, when the children of agricultural and handicraft workers entered the first factories, this marked the beginning of an irreversible change. But the fact that accommodation to this new way of living was slow, since it was spread out over several generations, meant that the changes were not necessarily perceived to be more drastic than those experienced by the peoples who were incorporated by conquest into the Roman Empire. So also, when attention is focused on generation relationships and on the type of modeling through which a culture is transmitted, it is possible to treat as fully comparable a past situation, as when a formerly land-bound people learned the techniques of fishing, and a present situation, as when the children of emigrant Haitians learn computer programming.

It is only when one specifies the nature of the process that the contrast between past and present change becomes clear. One urgent problem, I believe, is the delineation of the nature of change in the modern world, including its speed and dimensions, so that we can better understand the distinctions that must be made between change in the past and that which is now ongoing.

The primary evidence that our present situation is unique, without any parallel in the past, is that the generation gap is world wide. The particular events taking place in any country—China, England, Pakistan, Japan, the United States, New Guinea, or elsewhere—are not enough to explain the unrest that is stirring modern youth everywhere. Recent technological change or the handicaps imposed by its absence, revolution or the suppression of revolutionary activities, the crumbling of faith in ancient creeds or the attraction of new creeds—all these serve only as partial explanations of the particular forms taken by youth revolt in different countries. Undoubtedly, an upsurge of nationalism is more likely in a country like Japan, which is recovering from a recent defeat, or in countries that have newly broken away from their colonial past than it is, for example, in the United States. It is easier for the government of a country as isolated as China to order vast changes by edict than it is for the government of the Soviet Union, acting on a European stage, to subdue Czechoslovakian resistance. The breakdown of the family is more apparent in the West than in the East. The speed of change is more conspicuous and more consciously perceived in the least and in the most industrialized countries than it is in countries occupying an intermediate position. But all this is, in a sense, incidental when the focus of attention is on youthful dissidence, which is world wide in its dimensions.

Concentration on particularities can only hinder the search for an explanatory principle. Instead, it is necessary to strip the occurrences in each country of their superficial, national, and immediately temporal aspects. The desire for a liberated form of communism in Czechoslovakia, the search for "racial" equality in the United States, the desire to liberate Japan from American military influence, the support given to excessive conservatism in Northern Ireland and Rhodesia or to the excesses of communism in Cuba—all these are particularistic forms. Youthful activism is common to them all.

It was with the hope of turning anthropological analysis to this use that I tried to describe the essential characteristics of the postfigurative model and some of the forms taken by the cofigurative model under certain conditions of rapid change. It is my belief that the delineation of these models, as we have come to understand them through the study of older cultures, can help to clarify what is happening in the contemporary world.

The key question is this: What are the new conditions that have brought about the revolt of youth right around the world?

The first of these is the emergence of a world community. For the first time human beings throughout the world, in their information about one another and responses to one another, have become a community that is united by shared knowledge and danger. We cannot say for certain now that at any period in the past there was a single community made up of many small societies whose members were aware of one another in such a way that consciousness of what differentiated one small society from another heightened the self-consciousness of each constituent group. But as far as we know, no such single, interacting community has existed within archaeological time. The largest clusters of interacting human groups were fragments of a still larger unknown whole. The greatest empires pushed their borders outward into regions where there were peoples whose languages, customs and very appearance were unknown. In the very partially charted world of the past the idea that all men were, in the same sense, human beings was either unreal or a mystical belief. Men could think about the fatherhood of God and the brotherhood of man and biologists could argue the issue of monogenesis versus polygenesis; but what all men had in common was a matter of continuing speculation and dispute.

The events of the last twenty-five years changed this drastically. Exploration has been complete enough to convince us that there are no humanoid types on the planet except our own species. World-wide rapid air travel and globe-encircling television satellites have turned us into one community in which events taking place on one side of the earth become immediately and simultaneously available to peoples everywhere else. No artist or political censor has time to intervene and edit as a leader is shot or a flag planted on the moon. The world is a community though it still lacks as yet the forms of organization and the sanctions by which a political community can be governed.

The nineteenth-century industrial revolution replaced the cruder forms of energy. The twentieth-century scientific revolution has made it possible to multiply agricultural production manyfold but also drastically and dangerously to modify the ecology of the entire planet and destroy all living things. Science has made possible, through the use of computers, a new concentration of intellectual efforts that allows men to begin the exploration of the solar system, and opens the way to simulations by means of which men, especially men working in organized groups, can transcend earlier intellectual accomplishments.

The revolution in the development of food resources is on a world-wide scale. Up to the present, in many parts of the world, the medical revolution has so increased the population that the major effect of increased, efficient food production has been to stave off famine. But if we are able to bring the human population into a new balance, all of humanity can be, for the first time, well nourished. The medical revolution by reducing the pressure for population increase has begun, in turn, to release women from the age-old necessity of devoting themselves almost completely to reproductivity and, thus, will profoundly alter women's future and the future rearing of children.

Most importantly, these changes have taken place almost simultaneously—within the lifetime of one generation—and the impact of knowledge of the change is world wide. Only yesterday, a New Guinea native's only contact with modern civilization may have been a trade knife that was passed from hand to hand into his village or an airplane seen in the sky; today, as soon as he enters the smallest frontier settlement, he meets the transistor radio. Until yesterday, the village dwellers everywhere were cut off from the urban life of their own country; today radio and television bring them sounds and sights of cities all over the world.

Men who are the carriers of vastly different cultural traditions are entering the present at the same point in time. It is as if, all around the world, men were converging on identical immigration posts, each with its identifying sign: "You are now about to enter the post-World War II world at Gate 1 (or Gate 23 or Gate 2003, etc.)." Whoever they are and wherever their particular point of entry may be, all men are equally immigrants into the new era— some come as refugees and some as castaways.

They are like the immigrants who came as pioneers to a new land, lacking all knowledge of what demands the new conditions of life would make upon them. Those who came later could take their peer groups as models. But among the first comers, the young adults had as models only their own tentative adaptations and innovations. Their past, the culture that had shaped their understanding—their thoughts, their feelings, and their conceptions of the world—was no sure guide to the present. And the elders among them, bound to the past, could provide no models for the future.

Today, everyone born and bred before World War II is such an immigrant in time—as his forebears were in space—struggling to grapple with the unfamiliar conditions of life in a new era. Like all immigrants and pioneers, these immigrants in time are the bearers of older cultures. The difference today is that they represent all the cultures of the world. And all of them, whether they are sophisticated French intellectuals or members of a remote New Guinea tribe, land-bound peasants in Haiti or nuclear physicists, have certain characteristics in common.

Whoever they are, these immigrants grew up under skies across which no satellite had ever flashed. Their perception of the past was an edited version of what had happened. Whether they were wholly dependent on oral memory, art, and drama or also had access to print and still photography and film, what they could know had been altered by the very act of preservation. Their perception of the immediate present was limited to what they could take in through their own eyes and ears and to the edited versions of other men's sensory experience and memories. Their conception of the future was essentially one in which change was incorporated into a deeper changelessness. The New Guinea native, entering the complex modern world, followed cultural models provided by Europeans and expected in some way to share their future. The industrialist or military planner, envisaging what a computer, not yet constructed, might make possible, treated it as another addition to the repertoire of inventions that have enhanced man's skills. It expanded what men could do, but did not change the future.

It is significant that mid-twentieth-century science fiction, written by young writers with little experience of human life, rang untrue to the sophisticated and experienced ear and was less interesting to most well-educated men than such myths as those of Icarus and Daedalus, which include men and gods as well as the mechanisms of flight. Most scientists shared the lack of prescience of other members of their generation and failed to share the dreams of modern science fiction writers.

When the first atom bomb was exploded at the end of World War II, only a few individuals realized that all humanity was entering a new age. And to this day the majority of those over twenty-five have failed to grasp emotionally, however well they may grasp intellectually, the difference between any war in which, no matter how terrible the casualties, mankind will survive, and one in which there will be no survivors. They continue to think that a war, fought with more lethal weapons, would just be a worse war; they still do not grasp the implications of scientific weapons of extinction. Even scientists, when they form committees, are apt to have as their goal not the total abolition of war, but the prevention of the particular kinds of warfare for which they themselves feel an uncomfortable special responsibility—such as the use of pesticides in Vietnam.

In this sense, then, of having moved into a present for which none of us was prepared by our understanding of the past, our interpretations of ongoing experience or our expectations about the future, all of us who grew up before World War II are pioneers, immigrants in time who have left behind our familiar worlds to live in a new age under conditions that are different from any we have known. Our thinking still binds us to the past—to the world as it existed in our childhood and youth. Born and bred before the electronic revolution, most of us do not realize what it means.

We still hold the seats of power and command the resources and the skills necessary to keep order and organize the kinds of societies we know about. We control the educational systems, the apprenticeship systems, the career ladders up which the young must climb, step by step. The elders in the advanced countries control the resources needed by the young and less advanced countries for their development. Nevertheless, we have passed the point of no return. We are committed to life in an unfamiliar setting; we are making do with what we know. We are building makeshift dwellings in old patterns with new and better understood materials.

The young generation, however, the articulate young rebels all around the world who are lashing out against the controls to which they are subjected, are like the first generation born into a new country. They are at home in this time. Satellites are familiar in their skies. They have never known a time when war did not threaten annihilation. Those who use computers do not anthropomorphize them; they know that they are programmed by human beings. When they are given the facts, they can understand immediately that continued pollution of the air and water and soil will soon make the planet uninhabitable and that it will be impossible to feed an indefinitely expanding world population. They can see that control of conception is feasible and necessary. As members of one species in an underdeveloped world community, they recognize that invidious distinctions based on race and caste are anachronisms. They insist on the vital necessity of some form of world order.

They live in a world in which events are presented to them in all their complex immediacy; they are no longer bound by the simplified linear sequences dictated by the printed word. In their eyes the killing of an enemy is not qualitatively different from the murder of a neighbor. They cannot reconcile our efforts to save our own children by every known means with our readiness to destroy the children of others with napalm. Old distinctions between peacetime and wartime, friend and foe, "my" group and "theirs"—the outsiders, the aliens—have lost their meaning. They know that the people of one nation alone cannot save their own children; each holds the responsibility for the others' children.

Although I have said *they know* these things, perhaps I should say that this is *how they feel.* Like the first generation born in a new country, they listen only half-comprehendingly to their parents' talk about the past. For as the children of pioneers had no access to the landscapes, memories of which could still move their parents to tears, the young today cannot share their parents' responses to events that deeply moved them in the past. But this is not all that separates the young from their elders. Watching, they can see that their elders are groping, that they are managing clumsily and often unsuccessfully the tasks imposed on them by the new conditions. They have no firsthand knowledge of the way their parents lived far across the seas, of how differently wood responded to tools, or land to hoe. They see that their elders are using means that are inappropriate, that their performance is poor, and the outcome very uncertain. The young do not know what must be done, but they feel that there must be a better way.

Just how they do feel was expressed in an essay by Shannon Dickson, a fifteen-year-old Texan boy:

There is a mass confusion in the minds of my generation in trying to find a solution for ourselves and the world around us.

We see the world as a huge rumble as it swiftly goes by with wars, poverty, prejudice, and the lack of understanding among people and nations.

Then we stop and think: there must be a better way and we have to find it.

We see the huge rat race of arguing people trying to beat their fellow man out. All of this builds up, causing unrest between nations and in the home. My generation is being used almost like a machine. We are to learn set standards, strive for better education so we can follow in our elders' footsteps. But why? If we are to be a generation of repetition, the situation will be worse. But how shall we change? We need a great deal of love for everyone, we need a universal understanding among people, we need to think of ourselves and to express our feelings, but that is not all. I have yet to discover what else we need, nor have I practiced these things as fully as I should. Because when I try I'm sneered at by my elders and those who do not hear, or look at it with a closed mind. Computers take the place of minds; electronics are taking over, only confusing things more.

I admit we should follow some basic rules but first you should look at who is making the rules.

Sometimes I walk down a deserted beach listening to the waves and birds and I hear them forever calling and forever crying and sometimes we feel that way but everyone goes on with his own little routines, afraid to stop and listen for fear of cracking their nutshell.

The answer is out there somewhere. We need to search for it.

They feel that there must be a better way and that they must find it.

Today, nowhere in the world are there elders who know what the children know, no matter how remote and simple the societies are in which the children live. In the past there were always some elders who knew more than any children in terms of their experience of having grown up within a cultural system. Today there are none. It is not only that parents are no longer guides, but that there are no guides, whether one seeks them in one's own country or abroad. There are no elders who know what those who have been reared within the last twenty years know about the world into which they were born.

The elders are separated from them by the fact that they, too, are a strangely isolated generation. No generation has ever known, experienced, and incorporated such rapid changes, watched the sources of power, the means of communication, the definition of humanity, the limits of their explorable universe, the certainties of a known and limited world, the fundamental imperatives of life and death—all change before their eyes. They know more about change than any generation has ever known and so stand, over, against, and vastly alienated, from the young, who by the very nature of their position, have had to reject their elders' past.

Just as the early Americans had to teach themselves not to day-dream of the past but concentrate on the present, and so in turn taught their children not to daydream but to act, so today's elders have to treat their own past as incommunicable, and teach their children, even in the midst of lamenting that it is so, not to ask, because they can never understand. We have to realize that no other generation will ever experience what we have experienced. In this sense we must recognize that we have no descendants, as our children have no forebears.

The elders are a strangely isolated generation. No other generation has ever known, experienced, and struggled to incorporate such massive and rapid change—has watched while the sources of energy, the means of communication, the certainties of a known world, the limits of the explorable universe, the definition of humanity, and the fundamental imperatives of life and death have changed before their eyes. Adults today know more about change than any previous generation. So we are set apart both from earlier generations and from the young who have rejected the past and all that their elders are making of the present.

At this breaking point between two radically different and closely related groups, both are inevitably very lonely, as we face each other knowing that they will never experience what we have experienced, and that we can never experience what they have experienced.

This sense of distance, this feeling of lacking a living connection with members of the other generation, sometimes takes bizarre forms. In the summer of 1968 a group of American clergy who were meeting in Uppsala talked with some of the young American conscientious objectors who had taken refuge in Sweden, and in a written report they said: "We are persuaded that these are our children." They could not take their cultural paternity for granted, but had to persuade themselves that it was so—after long discussion. So incredible it seemed—to believe that any of their children could leave the United States, where, in the past, the persecuted of Europe had taken refuge. They spoke almost as if a process of blood typing had had to be introduced to prove their spiritual paternity.

In most discussions of the generation gap, the alienation of the young is emphasized, while the alienation of their elders may be wholly overlooked. What the commentators forget is that true communication is a dialogue and that both parties to the dialogue lack a vocabulary.

We are familiar with the problems of communication between speakers of two languages who have been reared in radically different cultures, one, for example, in China and the other in the United States. Not only language, but also the incommensurability of their experience prevents them from understanding each other. Yet a willingness to learn the other's language and to explore the premises of both cultures can open the way to conversation. It can be done, but it is not often done.

The problem becomes more difficult, because it is more subtle, when speakers from two different cultures share what is regarded as a common tongue, such as English for Americans and Englishmen, Spanish for Spaniards and Latin Americans. Then true communication becomes possible only when both realize that they speak not one, but two languages in which the "same" words have divergent, sometimes radically different meanings. Then, if they are willing to listen and to ask, they can begin to talk and talk with delight.

This is also the problem of the two generations. Once the fact of a deep, new, unprecedented world-wide generation gap is firmly established, in the minds of both the young and the old, communication can be established again. But as long as any adult thinks that he, like the parents and teachers of old, can become introspective, invoke his own youth to understand the youth before him, then he is lost.

But this is what most elders are still doing. The fact that they delegate authority—that the father sends his sons away to school to learn new ideas and the older scientist sends his pupils to other laboratories to work on newer problems—changes nothing. It only means that parents and teachers are continuing to use the mechanisms of cofiguration characteristic of a world in which parents, having given up the right to teach their own children, expect their children to learn from other adults and their more knowledgeable age mates. Even in science, where we have tried to build in the expectation of discovery and innovations, students learn from old models, and normal young scientists work to fill in blank spaces in accepted paradigms. In today's accelerating rate of scientific discovery, the old are outmoded rapidly and replaced by near peers, but still within a framework of authority.

In the deepest sense, now as in the past, the elders are still in control. And partly because they are in control, they do not realize that the conditions for beginning a new dialogue with the young do not yet exist.

Ironically, it is often those who were, as teachers, very close to former generations of students, who now feel that the generation gap cannot be bridged and that their devotion to teaching has been betrayed by the young who cannot learn in the old ways.

From one point of view the situation in which we now find ourselves can be described as a crisis in faith, in which men, having lost their faith not only in religion but also in political ideology and in science, feel they have been deprived of every kind of security. I believe this crisis in faith can be attributed, at least in part, to the fact that there are now no elders who know more than the young themselves about what the young are experiencing. C. H. Waddington has hypothesized that one component of human evolution and the capacity for choice is the ability of the human child to accept on authority from elders the criteria for right and wrong. The acceptance of the distinction between right and wrong by the child is a consequence of his dependence on parental figures who are trusted, feared, and loved, who hold the child's very life in their hands. But today the elders can no longer present with certainty moral imperatives to the young.

True, in many parts of the world the parental generation still lives by a postfigurative set of values. From parents in such cultures children may learn that there have been unquestioned absolutes, and this learning may carry over into later experience as an expectation that absolute values can and should be re-established. Nativistic cults, dogmatic religious and political movements flourish most vigorously at the point of recent breakdown of postfigurative cultures and least in those cultures in which orderly change is expected to occur within a set of stable values at higher levels of abstraction.

The older industrialized countries of the West have incorporated in their cultural assumptions the idea of change without revolution through the development of new social techniques to deal with the conditions brought about by economic change and technological advances. In these same countries, obsolescence tends to be treated as survival, loved or deprecated as the case may be. In England, the messenger who carried a dispatch case to France was retained long after the dispatches were sent by post; there, too, the pageantry of the throne exists side by side with the parliamentary government that has long superseded the throne as the source of power. In Sweden the most modern laws about sex behavior coexist with the most uncompromising orthodox religious support of an absolute morality.

Similarly, in the United States there is both a deep commitment to developmental change, which is interpreted as progress, and a continuing resort to absolutism, which takes many forms. There are the religious sects and minor political groups, the principal appeal of which is their dogmatism with regard to right and wrong. There are the Utopian communities that have been a constant feature of our social, political, and intellectual development. And there is the tacit acceptance of a color caste system that exists in violation of our declared belief in the fundamental equality of all men.

Elsewhere in the world where change has been rapid, abrupt and often violent, where the idea of orderly processes of change has not taken hold, there is a continuing possibility of sudden eruptions that may take the form of revolutions and counterrevolutions—as in most Latin American countries—or may bring about, in sudden reversal—even though in a new form—the re-establishment of an archaic orthodoxy in which nonbelievers may be persecuted, tortured, and burned alive. The young people, today, who turn themselves into living torches mirror in very complex ways both the attitudes of orthodox absolutism and reactions to it. They follow the example of Buddhists who responded to the dogmatisms of communism and reactive anticommunism with an extreme violation of their own permissive and unabsolute religious values. But their acts also represent, implicitly, the treatment accorded heretics and nonbelievers by any absolutist system that allows no appeal from its dogmas.

There are still parents who answer a child's questions—why must I go to bed? or eat my vegetables? or stop sucking my thumb?

or learn to read?—with simple assertions: Because it is *right* to do so, because *God* says so, or because *I* say so. These parents are preparing the way for the re-establishment of postfigurative elements in the culture. But these elements will be far more rigid and intractable than in the past because they must be defended in a world in which conflicting points of view, rather than orthodoxies, are prevalent and accessible.

Most parents, however, are too uncertain to assert old dogmatisms. They do not know how to teach these children who are so different from what they themselves once were, and most children are unable to learn from parents and elders they will never resemble. In the past, in the United States, the children of immigrant parents pleaded with them not to speak their foreign language in public and not to wear their outlandish, foreign clothes. They knew the burning shame of being, at the same time, unable to repudiate their parents and unable to accept simply and naturally their way of speaking and doing things. But in time they learned to find new teachers as guides, to model their behavior on that of more adapted age mates, and to slip in, unnoticed, among a group whose parents were more bearable.

Today the dissident young discover very rapidly that this solution is no longer possible. The breach between themselves and their parents also exists between their friends and their friends' parents and between their friends and their teachers. There are no bearable answers in the old books or in the brightly colored, superficially livened-up new textbooks they are asked to study.

Some look abroad for models. They are attracted by Camus, who, in his conflict between his Algerian birth and his intellectual allegiance to France, expressed some of the conflict they feel; but he is dead. They try to adapt to their own purposes the words of an aging Marxist, Marcuse, or the writings of the existentialists. They develop cultist attitudes of desperate admiration for the heroes of other young revolutionary groups. White students ally themselves with the black separatists. Black students attempt to restructure the past in their struggle to restructure the present.

These young dissidents realize the critical need for immediate world action on problems that affect the whole world. What they want is, in some way, to begin all over again. The idea of orderly, developmental change is lost for this generation of young, who cannot take over the past from their elders, but can only repudiate what their elders are doing now. The past for them is a colossal, unintelligible failure and the future may hold nothing but the destruction of the planet. Caught between the two, they are ready to make way for something new by a kind of social bulldozing—like the bulldozing in which every tree and feature of the landscape is destroyed to make way for a new community. Awareness of the reality of the crisis (which is, in fact, perceived most accurately not by the young, but by their discerning and prophetic elders) and the sense the young have that their elders do not understand the modern world, because they do not understand the modern world, because they do not understand rebellion in which planned reformation of the present system is almost inconceivable.

Nevertheless those who have no power also have no routes to power except through those against whom they are rebelling. In the end, it was men who gave the vote to women; and it will be the House of Lords that votes to abolish the House of Lords, and those over eighteen who must agree if those under eighteen are to vote, as also, in the final analysis, nations will act to limit national sovereignty. Effective, rapid evolutionary change, in which no one is guillotined and no one is forced into exile, depends on the co-operation of a large number of those in power with the dispossessed who are seeking power. The innovating idea may come from others, but the initiative for successful action must come from those whose privileges, now regarded as obsolete, are about to be abolished.

There are those among the dissident young who recognize this. Significantly, they want their parents or those who represent their parents—deans and college presidents and editorial writers—to be on their side, to agree with them or at least to give them a blessing. Behind their demands is their hope that, even as they demonstrate against the college administration, the college president will come and talk with them—and bring his children. But there are also some who entertain no such hope.

I have spoken mainly about the most articulate young people, those who want to drop out of the whole system and those who want to take the system apart and start over. But the feeling that nothing out of the past is meaningful and workable is very much more pervasive. Among the less articulate it is expressed in such things as the refusal to learn at school, co-operate at work, or follow normal political paths. Perhaps most noncompliance is of this passive kind. But the periodic massing of students behind their more active peers suggests that even passive noncompliance is highly inflammable.

Resistance among the young is also expressed by an essentially uninvolved and exploitative compliance with rules that are regarded as meaningless. Perhaps those who take this stand are the most frightening. Going through the forms by which men were educated for generations, but which no longer serve to educate those who accept them, can only teach students to regard all social systems in terms of exploitation.

But whatever stand they take, none of the young, neither the most idealistic nor the most cynical, is untouched by the sense that there are no adults anywhere in the world from whom they can learn what the next steps should be.

These, in brief, are the conditions of our time. These are the two generations—pioneers in a new era and their children, who have as yet to find a way of communicating about the world in which both live, though their perceptions of it are so different. No one knows what the next steps should be. Recognizing that this is so is, I submit, the beginning of an answer.

For I believe we are on the verge of developing a new kind of culture, one that is as much a departure in style from cofigurative cultures, as the institutionalization of cofiguration in orderly—and disorderly—change was a departure from the postfigurative style. I call this new style *prefigurative*, because in this new culture it will be the child—and not the parent and grandparent—that represents what is to come. Instead of the erect, white-haired elder who, in postfigurative cultures, stood for the past and the future in all their grandeur and continuity, the unborn child, already conceived but still in the womb, must become the symbol of what life will be like. This is a child whose sex and appearance and capabilities are unknown. This is a child who is a genius or suffers from some deep impairment, who will need imaginative, innovative, and dedicated adult care far beyond any we give today.

About the unborn child little can be known with certainty. We can tell with delicate instruments that supplement the ear that the child is alive, that its heart is beating. Other instruments, still more delicate, can give some clues as to the child's well-being. We can predict the approximate time when it will be born. We know that unless the mother is protected, nourished, and cared for, the child's chance for life will sink with her own; should she sicken and die, the child's life will also flicker out. But all else is promise.

No one can know in advance what the child will become—how swift his limbs will be, what will delight his eye, whether his tempo will be fast or slow, whether he will waken ready to cope with the world or only reach his best hours when the day people are tiring. No one can know how his mind will work—whether he will learn best from sight or sound or touch or movement. But knowing what we do not know and cannot predict, we can construct an environment in which a child, still unknown, can be safe and can grow and discover himself and the world.

In a safe and flexible environment there must be skilled care, anesthetics, oxygen, and blood on hand to protect the mother and the child in a difficult birth. There must be supportive care for the mother who becomes depressed or frightened. There must be artificial food for the infant who cannot be breast-fed. For the child who cannot sleep in the dark, there must be soft light. For the child who is sensitive to sound, there must be ways of muting noise.

As the child begins to reach out to people, he must be carried—held or propped or cradled—into company. As his eyes respond to color, there must be many colors, differing in hue, saturation, and brightness, for him to choose among. There must be many kinds of objects for him to classify, many rhythms and melodies to start him dancing. And as he begins to form an image of the world, he must have examples of the worlds other men have made and crayons and paints and clay so he can give form to the world of his own imagination.

Even so simple an enumeration of ways of meeting a child's needs makes us conscious of how much children have been bound to the ways of their forebears through love and dependence and trust. It also makes us conscious of how little flexibility there is in the child's dependence on adults as compared to the great flexibility that can be developed in the adult's succoring care. Without adult care, the infant will die in a few hours. Without adult care, the child will never learn to speak. Without the experience of trust, the child will never become a trusting member of society, who is able to love and care for others. The child is wholly dependent, and it is on this dependency that human culture has been built as, generation after generation for hundreds of thousands of years, adults have imposed on children, through their care for them, their vision of what life should be. Dependency has made conscience possible and, as both Julian Huxley and C. H. Waddington have argued so eloquently, ethics are not external to nature but are crucial to human evolution.

The continuity of culture and the incorporation of every innovation depended on the success of the postfigurative system by which the young were taught to replicate the lives of their ancestors. Then, as men learned to live in many different environments and as they traveled and traded with one another, contrasts among different postfigurative cultures began to provide the necessary conditions for change and for the development of cofigurative cultures in which people who had been reared to one form of commitment learned to adapt themselves to other forms but with the same absolute commitment.

Later, as the idea of change became embodied as a postfigurative element in many cultures, the young could learn from their elders that they should go beyond them—achieve more and do different things. But this beyond was always within the informed imagination of their elders; the son might be expected to cross the seas his father never crossed, study nuclear physics when his father had only an elementary school education, fly in the plane which his father watched from the ground. The peasant's son became a scholar; the poor man's son crossed the ocean his father had never seen; the teacher's son became a scientist.

Love and trust, based on dependency and answering care, made it possible for the individual who had been reared in one culture to move into another, transforming without destroying his earlier learning. It is seldom the first generation of voluntary immigrants and pioneers who cannot meet the demands of a new environment. Their previous learning carries them through. But unless they embody what is new postfiguratively, they cannot pass on to their children what they themselves had acquired through their own early training—the ability to learn from others the things their parents could not teach them.

Now, in a world in which there are no more knowledgeable others to whom parents can commit the children they themselves cannot teach, parents feel uncertain and helpless. Still believing that there should be answers, parents ask: How can we tell our children what is right? So some parents try to solve the problem by advising their children, very vaguely: You will have to figure that out for yourselves. And some parents ask: What are the others doing? But this resource of a cofigurative culture is becoming meaningless to parents who feel that the "others"—their children's age mates—are moving in ways that are unsafe for their own children to emulate and who find that they do not understand what their children figure out for themselves.

It is the adults who still believe that there is a safe and socially approved road to a kind of life they themselves have not experienced who react with the greatest anger and bitterness to the discovery that what they had hoped for no longer exists for their children. These are the parents, the trustees, the legislators, the columnists, and commentators who denounce most vocally what is happening in schools and colleges and universities in which they had placed their hopes for their children.

Today, as we are coming to understand better the circular processes through which culture is developed and transmitted, we recognize that man's most human characteristic is not his ability to learn, which he shares with many other species, but his ability to teach and store what others have developed and taught him. Learning, which is based on human dependency, is relatively simple. But human capacities for creating elaborate teachable systems, for understanding and utilizing the resources of the natural world, and for governing society and creating imaginary worlds, all these are very complex. In the past, men relied on the least elaborate part of the circular system, the dependent learning by children, for continuity of transmission and for the embodiment of the new. Now, with our greater understanding of the process, we must cultivate the most flexible and complex part of the system—the behavior of adults. We must, in fact, teach ourselves how to alter adult behavior so that we can give up postfigurative upbringing, with its tolerated cofigurative components, and discover prefigurative ways of teaching and learning that will keep the future open. We must create new models for adults who can teach their children not what to learn, but how to learn and not what they should be committed to, but the value of commitment.

Postfigurative cultures, which focused on the elders—those who had learned the most and were able to do the most with what they had learned—were essentially closed systems that continually replicated the past. We must now move toward the creation of open systems that focus on the future—and so on children, those whose capacities are least known and whose choices must be left open.

In doing this we explicitly recognize that the paths by which we came into the present can never be traversed again. The past is the road by which we have arrived where we are. Older forms of culture have provided us with the knowledge, the techniques, and the tools necessary for our contemporary civilization. Coming by different roads out of the past, all the peoples of the earth are now arriving in the new world community. No road into the present need be repudiated and no former way of life forgotten. But all these different pasts, our own and all others, must be treated as precursors.

It is significant how extremely difficult it has been even for the prophetic writers of science fiction to imagine and accept an unknown future. At the close of *Childhood's End,* Arthur Clarke wrote: "The stars are not for men."

Space operas picture the return of the last broken spaceship from imagined galactic societies to the "hall of the beginning" on Terra of Sol. In the *Midwich Cuckoos,* John Wyndham killed off the strange golden-eyed, perceptive children bred by earth women to visitors from outer space. The film, *2001: A Space Odyssey,* ended in failure. This deep unwillingness to have children go too far into the future suggests that the adult imagination, acting alone, remains fettered to the past.

So the freeing of men's imagination from the past depends, I believe, on the development of a new kind of communication with those who are most deeply involved with the future—the young who were born in the new world. That is, it depends on the direct participation of those who, up to now, have not had access to power and whose nature those in power cannot fully imagine. In the past, in cofigurational cultures, the elders were gradually cut off from limiting the future of their children. Now, as I see it, the development of prefigurational cultures will depend on the existence of a continuing dialogue in which the young, free to act on their own initiative, can lead their elders in the direction of the unknown. Then the older generation will have access to the new experiential knowledge, without which no meaningful plans can be made. It is only with the direct participation of the young, who have that knowledge, that we can build a viable future.

Instead of directing their rebellion toward the retrieval of a grandparental Utopian dream, as the Maoists seem to be doing with the young activists in China, we must learn together with the young how to take the next steps. Out of their new knowledge—new to the world and new to us—must come the questions to those who are already equipped by education and experience to search for answers.

Archibald MacLeish wrote in *The Hamlet of A. MacLeish,*

> We have learned the answers, all the answers:
> It is the question that we do not know.

His book was sent to me in 1928 while I was in the Admiralties, studying the Manus. At that time it seemed almost certain that the Manus, a people still proudly adapted to their stone-age culture, whose only experience of another kind of civilization was with the dehumanizing and degrading contact-culture, would eventually become poorly educated proletarians in a world they could neither understand nor influence.

Today, forty years later, the Manus people have skipped thousands of years and been able to take their destiny in their own hands, as they could not in the days when, locked within the stone age, they bullied and ravished the villages of their less aggressive neighbors. Today they are preparing their children for college, for law schools and medical schools, and transferring the leadership they once exercised, fitfully and with poor organization, in a tiny archipelago, as a tribe, into the wider world of a developing nation. And today, when the quotation came back to me, I phrased it differently because now we can say that we *do* know at least who must ask the questions if we, who have a long heritage of answers at our disposal, are to be able to answer them. The children, the young, must ask the questions that we would never think to ask, but enough trust must be re-established so that the elders will be permitted to work with them on the answers. As in a new country with makeshift shelters adapted hastily from out-of-date models, the children must be able to proclaim that they are cold and where the drafts are coming from. Father is still the man who has the skill and the strength to cut down the tree to build a different kind of house.

During the last few years, I have been exposed to something that I at first branded as a temptation. Young people sometimes turn to me, when we have been co-operating vividly in a goal we share, and say, "You belong to us." This I felt to be a temptation which must be resisted at all costs, especially in a country where youth, in every form, is a tempting refuge for the middle-aged and aging. So I used to reply, "No, I do not belong to your generation. You think I do because you are currently in favor of things that I have been working on for forty years. But that does not make me a member of your generation. And how do I know that you will not, in fact, be opposing these very goals ten years from now?" But I think that this reply was another example of our insistence that the future will be like the past, that most people go through cycles of revolt and reaction, that experience in the past can be applied to the future. Because I made that assumption I failed to see that perhaps they may have been saying something different. I was reared, as they wish they had been, by a grandmother and parents who did not think they could set their children's feet on any given path. I was reared almost seven decades ahead of my time, as today's twenty-year-olds proclaim they will rear their children, leaving them free to grow, straight and tall, into a future that must be left open and free. It is in a sense as a tribute to such a childhood that I am able to insist that we can change into a pre-figurative culture, consciously, delightedly, and industriously, rearing unknown children for an unknown world.

But to do this we, the peoples of the world, must relocate the future. For the West the future has lain ahead of us, sometimes only a few hours ahead, sometimes a thousand years ahead, but always ahead, not here yet, beyond our reach. For many Oceanic peoples, the future lies behind, not before. For the Balinese the future is like an exposed but undeveloped film, slowly unrolling, while men stand and wait for what will be revealed. It is seen catching up with them, a figure of speech that we, too, use when we speak of hearing time's relentless footsteps behind us.

If we are to build a prefigurative culture in which the past is instrumental rather than coercive, we must change the location of the future. Here again we can take a cue from the young who seem to want instant Utopias. They say: The Future Is Now. This seems unreasonable and impetuous, and in some of the demands they make it is unrealizable in concrete detail; but here again, I think they give us the way to reshape our thinking. We must place the future, like the unborn child in the womb of a woman, within a community of men, women, and children, among us, already here, already to be nourished and succored and protected, already in need of things for which, if they are not prepared before it is born, it will be too late. So, as the young say, The Future Is Now.

The Plastic Parthenon

John McHale

The Scottish-born author of this short, classic essay is a brilliant blend of scientist, sociologist, and ecologist. But he is also a widely exhibited artist and designer whose writing reveals an intense concern with the aesthetics of the future. Here he explores the subtle impact of technology on our imagery and our arts.

Our emergent world society, with its particular qualities of speed, mobility, mass production and consumption, rapidity of change and innovation, is the latest phase of an ongoing cultural and social revolution. It has few historical precedents as a cultural context. Industrial technologies, now approaching global scale, linked to an attendant multiplicity of new communications channels, are producing a planetary culture whose relation to earlier forms is as Vostok or Gemini to a wheeled cart.

World communications, whose latest benchmark is Telstar, diffuse and interpenetrate local cultural tradition, providing commonly shared cultural experience in a manner which is unparalleled in human history. Within this global network, the related media of cinema, t.v., radio, pictorial magazine and newspaper *are* a common cultural environment sharing and transmuting man's symbolic needs and their expression on a world scale.

Besides the enlargement of the *physical* world now available to our direct experience, these media virtually extend our psychical environment, providing a constant stream of moving, fleeting images of the world for our daily appraisal. They provide *psychical* mobility for the greater mass of our citizens. Through these devices we can telescope time, move through history and span the world in a great variety of unprecedented ways.

The expansion of swift global transportation, carrying around the world the diverse products of mass production technology, provides common cultural artifacts which engender, in turn, shared attitudes in their requirements and use. Packaged foods are as important a cultural change agent as packaged "culture" in a book or play! The inhabitant of any of the world's large cities—London, Tokyo, Paris, New York—is more likely to find himself "at home" in any of them, than in the rural parts of his own country; the international cultural milieu which sustains him will be more evident.

So-called "mass" culture, both agent and symptom of this transformation, is yet hardly understood by the intellectual establishments.

Past traditional canons of literary and artistic judgment, which still furnish the bulk of our critical apparatus, are approximately no guide to its evaluation. They tend to place high value on permanence, uniqueness and the enduring universal value of chosen artifacts. Aesthetic pleasure was associated with conditions of socio-moral judgment—"beauty is truth," and the truly beautiful of ageless appeal!

Such standards worked well with the "one-off" products of handcraft industry and the fine and folk arts of earlier periods. They in no way enable one to relate adequately to our present situation in which astronomical numbers of artifacts are mass produced, circulated and consumed. These products may be identical, or only marginally different. In varying degrees, they are expendable, replaceable and lack any unique "value" or intrinsic "truth" which might qualify them within previous artistic canons.

Where previously creation and production were narrowly geared to relatively small tastemaking elites, they are now directed to the plurality of goals and preferences of a whole society. Where previous cultural messages traveled slowly along restricted routes to their equally restricted, local audiences, the new media broadcast to the world in a lavish diversity of simultaneous modes.

The term "mass" applied to such cultural phenomena is indicative only of its circulation and distribution. Common charges of "standardized taste" and "uniformity" confuse the mass provision of items with their individual and selective consumption. The latter remains more than ever, and more widely, within the province of personal choice—less dictated than ever formerly by tradition, authority and scarcity. The denotably uniform society was the primitive enclave or preindustrial peasant community, with its limited repertoire of cultural forms and possible "life style" strategies.

We have, then, few critical precedents with which to evaluate our present cultural milieu. Most of the physical facilities which render it possible have not previously existed. Their transformative capacities pose more fundamental questions regarding cultural values than may be more than hinted at here.

What are the principal characteristics which differentiate the new continuum from earlier and more differentiated forms? The brief comments, offered below, are only notes towards the development of a more adequately descriptive and evaluative schema. As pragmatic and contextual they relate performance to process in a given situation.

Limiting ourselves to three main aspects, we may consider: one, expendability and permanence; two, mass replication and circulation; and three, the swift transference of cultural forms across and through multicommunication channels. All are associated with varying degrees of accelerated stylistic change and with the co-existence of a huge number of available and unconditional choices open to the participant or consumer, i.e., there is no inherent value contradiction implied in enjoying Bach *and* the Beatles. The situation is characteristically *"both/and"* rather than "either/or."

We may consider such expendability and "mass" replication as concomitant aspects of the same process—the application of industrial technologies to human requirements.

Man has only recently emerged from the "marginal" survival of a preindustrial society based on the economics of scarcity values; one in which laboriously made products were unique and irreplaceable. In such conditions, "wealth" and "value" resided in material goods and property, as representing survival value—as ideal and enduring beyond individual man.

World society need no longer be based on the economics of scarcity. There is a revolutionary shift to a society in which the only unique and irreplaceable element is man. This is one of the main points about automation. In previous periods, objects, products, resources, etc., tended to have more importance in sustaining the societal group than individual man. Man was, in a sense, used most prodigally in order that the idea of man might survive. The material object was unique. Man was expendable. Now, through developed industrialization the object may be produced prodigally. The product is expendable—only man is unique. In fully automated process the only unique resource input is information—organized human knowledge. Automation returns value into man.

Intrinsic value becomes, then, a function of the human use-cycle of an object or process. Use value is now largely replacing ownership value. We note this, for example, in the growth of rental and service—not only in automobiles and houses, but in a range from skis to bridal gowns—to "heirloom" silver, castles and works of art. The vast range of our personal and household objects may, also, when worn out, lost or destroyed, be replaced by others exactly similar. Also, and importantly, when worn out symbolically, i.e., no longer fashionable, they may be replaced by another item, of identical function but more topical form. Swift obsolescence whilst indefensible, or impossible, in earlier scarcity economies is a natural corollary of technological culture.

Within this process, there are relative time scales of use and consumption. A paper napkin, a suit, a chair or an automobile are, variously, single and multiple use items with possible identical replacement. A building and a painting may be respectively unique and irreplaceable. The latter have different time scales of "consumption," but the terms of style change still limit them to more or less given periods of currency. How long does an art work remain viable—before it is "museumized" into a different category? What is the status of the original with facsimile multicolor reproduction? Most of Europe's main cathedrals, if destroyed, may now be reconstructed from their detailed photogrammetric records.

Then there are also the cycles of use and re-use of materials. In creating or producing we, in effect, only re-arrange some local material resource in a quite temporal sense. The metals in a cigarette lighter today may be, variously, within a month or a year, part of an auto, a lipstick case or an orbiting satellite. Such accelerated turnover of materials in manufacture underlines the relative temporality of all "permanent" artifacts.

The capacity of the industrial process to replicate exactly by machine process, not only new products, but also, and with equal success, old products from earlier traditions, is a quality which has bothered aesthetes from the onset of the industrial revolution. They have tried to overcome this, mainly, by restricting the scope of machine process through various idea systems—like "beauty as the promise of function," "truth to materials," "form follows function," etc. The loose amalgam of such ideas is often called the "machine aesthetic." Although claiming moral relevance this remains a "visual" aesthetic criterion, dependent on taste. When new materials may be synthesized with any particular "truth," surface, texture or performance characteristics required, and when their strengths and functions are at the molecular level and quite subvisible, such criteria are no more moral or true than any other *stylistic* preference.

The success of much so-called "industrial" design has been largely through its acceptance as symbol—as conveying the image of functional modernity rather than its actuality. One might trace this from the "Bauhaus-International" style to ergonomic tableware, streamlined typewriters and the "contemporary" chair. Acceptance is related more to symbolic "status" than to any rationale of increased efficiency via improved design.

Generalizing broadly on this aspect of the difference between the physical use-function and the symbolic status-function of cultural objects, one may indicate two associated trends. On the one hand, the swift growth of the museum, devoted to the permanent preservation of cultural artifacts of past and present; and, on the other, the corresponding trend towards more expendable artifacts in the present environment. We seem to reconstruct and "permanentize" the past as swiftly as we move forward into a more materially "ephemeral" present and future.

Linking these two trends is an interesting preoccupation with the "image of permanence past" which is evinced in various modes. For example, in fine art, sheer size as substitute monumentality lends an aura of permanence, or the expendable "junk trouve" is immortalized in bronze. Timestopping, as in Segal's figure groups or Kienholz's full-size replica of "The Beanery," shares a certain affinity with reconstructed Williamsburg. In the general media-continuum, the past vies with the present and future for the most lavish treatment. *Life* magazine covers the Bible; the movie spectacular, "Genesis"; and at European "son et lumière," or Disneyland or Freedomland, USA, you have, ". . . a chance to live through those past moments that made our nation(s) great. See Old Chicago burn down—every twenty minutes—even help put out the fire! Visit the Civil War, and escape narrowly as the blue and gray shells just miss your wagon!"

The replication of "permanence past" may be seen to operate in a variety of ways. Often the more ephemeral the product, e.g., fashion, cosmetics, etc., the more its symbolic context is "ennobled by time" and by the appropriate mythological or antique image. The Venus de Milo, the Parthenon, the eighteenth century as the "Age of Elegance" are used in a manner which differs from simpler Victorian eclecticism, but depends on a reliable grammar of common symbols to evoke responses of "dignity, permanence and worth."

The "Plastic Parthenon" is a metaphorical question about the ikonic function of sacred and secular symbols. How may we now regard the expendable replicas of permanent and unique objects? How may we evaluate the ways in which symbolic "value" may be transferred in different forms, materials and at different size and time scales in quite different media?

The transference of symbolic "affect" through replication has always worked for sacred objects. Replicas of gods and saints, and of their relics, carried the same magical powers as the originals.[1]

This question of "value" is one of the central dialogues of our period. We may approach it from another viewpoint in the ikon-making function. Without lengthy discussion we may note that such ikons or "ideal referent" images were earlier provided by local fine/folk arts, in relation to prevailing religious belief and ritual. Today, as human consciousness is expanded electronically to global inter-linkage, we may see, hear, experience more in a single life-span than ever before.

Such rapid frequency changes in the human condition generate, in turn, a rich profusion of symbolic images which enable man to locate in, learn and adapt to his evolving society. These are now conveyed in the multiple-mass communication channels, within which we may include the marginally differentiated fine and folk arts. The constant re-creation and renewal of such images matches up to the requirements of a highly mobile and plastic environ— providing a replaceable, expendable series of ikons. These referent images of human action and experience take their character from the processes and channels which carry them, requiring no act of faith for their acceptance. Though individually fleeting, they achieve ikonic status by enormous concurrent circulation of typically repeated themes and configurations.

Secular by definition, but mythological in function, such ikons are typically of man (woman) associated with specific symbolic objects and contexts. . . . All the extremities of the human condition, the significant gestures and socio-cultural rhetorics, are encapsulated in a stream of ephemeral ikons whose only constant in a pragmatic performance-relation is to immediate or projected human experience.

The speed, range and visual immediacy of such images enables them to diffuse swiftly through local cultural tradition—causing equally swift changes in social attitudes and cultural forms. Two recent and extreme examples may be of interest here: one, the influence of a dime store Halloween mask as engendering a new mask-making ritual among primitive Eskimos,[2] and the other, a sociological comment on how the t.v. Western movie "has become in Asia the vehicle of an optimistic philosophy of history,"[3] in reversing the classic ritual drama in which the good were so often masochistically defeated.

This interpenetration, rapid diffusion and replication is most evident in the position of fine art in the new continuum. Transference through various modes changes both form and content—the new image can no longer be judged in the previous canon. The book, the film of the book, the book of the film, the musical of the film, the book, the t.v. or comic strip version of the musical—or however the cycle may run—is, at each stage, a transmutation which alters subtly the original communication. These transformative changes and diffusions occur with increasing rapidity. Now, in the arts, an avant-garde may only be "avant" until the next t.v. news broadcast or issue of *"Time/Life/Espresso."* Not only pop but op, camp and super-camp styles and "sub-styles" have an increasingly immediate circulation, acceptance and "usage" whose feedback directly influences their evolution. We might formally say that they become "academic" almost as they emerge, but this notion of academy versus avant-garde elites is no longer tenable, and may take its place with the alienated artist and other myths.

The position seems more clearly one in which the fine arts as institution may no longer be accorded the prime role in conveying the myths or defining the edge of innovation in society. The visionary "poetry" of technology or its "symphonic" equivalent is as likely to be found on t.v., or in the annual report of an aerospace company, as in the book, art gallery or concert hall. The arts, as traditionally regarded, are no longer a *"canonical"* form of communication. Their canonizing elites and critical audiences are only one sector of a network of ingroups who variously award an Oscar, Golden Disc or Prix de Venise to their choices.

Such comment on fine art as institution in no way denigrates the personally innovative role of the artist. At best, in presently destroying the formal divisions between art forms, and in their now casual moves from one expressive medium to another, individual artists demonstrate new attitudes towards art and life. Theirs is, ". . . in effect, a denial of specialization by an insistence on the fusion of all arts but one . . . an erasure of all boundaries between arts and experience."[4]

Various intuitive jumps in art may anticipate not only new institutional art forms, but also new social possibilities, e.g., Duchamp's isolation of *choice* as the status giving, creative gesture; the development of works involving the spectator in creative interaction.[5] These presage electronic advances towards a more directly participative form of society, e.g., computerized voting, t.v. forums, polls, etc.

As the apparatus of cultural diffusion becomes increasingly

technological, its "products" became less viewable as discrete, individual events, but rather more as related elements in a continuous contextual flow, i.e., the book-novel as compared to t.v. The artwork, as, for example, in Rauschenberg-type "Combines," moves towards a continuous format, juxtaposing "still" images with live radio and t.v. sets in the same piece, which characteristically spill out of the frame into the general environment.

The future of art seems no longer to lie with the creation of enduring masterworks but with defining alternative cultural strategies, through series of communicative gestures in multi-media forms. As art and non-art become interchangeable, and the masterwork may only be a reel of punched or magnetized tape, the artist defines art less through any intrinsic value of art object than by furnishing new conceptualities of life style and orientation. Generally, as the new cultural continuum underlines the expendability of the material artifact, life is defined as art—as the only contrastingly permanent and continuously unique experience.

Automation: Learning a Living

Marshall McLuhan

The startling prognostications and offbeat insights of this Canadian communications theorist have been praised and damned loudly. Yet there is no controversy about one point: his basically optimistic probe into the future has forced us all to think in new ways about tomorrow. Here he flatly challenges the view that machines will regiment and homogenize the human race.

A newspaper headline recently read, "Little Red Schoolhouse Dies When Good Road Built." One-room schools, with all subjects being taught to all grades at the same time, simply dissolve when better transportation permits specialized spaces and specialized teaching. At the extreme of speeded-up movement, however, specialism of space and subject disappears once more. With automation, it is not only jobs that disappear, and complex roles that reappear. Centuries of specialist stress in pedagogy and in the arrangement of data now end with the instantaneous retrieval of information made possible by electricity. Automation is information and it not only ends jobs in the world of work, it ends subjects in the world of learning. It does not end the world of learning. The future of work consists of learning a living in the automation age. This is a familiar pattern in electric technology in general. It ends the old dichotomies between culture and technology, between art and commerce, and between work and leisure. Whereas in the mechanical age of fragmentation leisure had been the absence of work, or mere idleness, the reverse is true in the electric age. As the age of information demands the simultaneous use of all our faculties, we discover that we are most at leisure when we are most intensely involved, very much as with the artists in all ages.

In terms of the industrial age, it can be pointed out that the difference between the previous mechanical age and the new electric age appears in the different kinds of inventories. Since electricity, inventories are made up not so much of goods in storage as of materials in continuous process of transformation at spatially removed sites. For electricity not only gives primacy to *process,* whether in making or in learning, but it makes independent the source of energy from the location of the process. In entertainment media, we speak of this fact as "mass media" because the source of the program and the process of experiencing it are independent in space, yet simultaneous in time. In industry this basic fact causes the scientific revolution that is called "automation" or "cybernation."

In education the conventional division of the curriculum into subjects is already as outdated as the medieval trivium and quadrivium after the Renaissance. Any subject taken in depth at once relates to other subjects. Arithmetic in grade three or nine, when taught in terms of number theory, symbolic logic, and cultural history, ceases to be mere practice in problems. Continued in their present patterns of fragmented unrelation, our school curricula will insure a citizenry unable to understand the cybernated world in which they live.

Most scientists are quite aware that since we have acquired

some knowledge of electricity it is not possible to speak of atoms as pieces of matter. Again, as more is known about electrical "discharges" and energy, there is less and less tendency to speak of electricity as a thing that "flows" like water through a wire, or is "contained" in a battery. Rather, the tendency is to speak of electricity as painters speak of space; namely, that it is a variable condition that involves the special positions of two or more bodies. There is no longer any tendency to speak of electricity as "contained" in anything. Painters have long known that objects are not contained in space, but that they generate their own spaces. It was the dawning awareness of this in the mathematical world a century ago that enabled Lewis Carroll, the Oxford mathematician, to contrive *Alice in Wonderland,* in which times and spaces are neither uniform nor continuous, as they had seemed to be since the arrival of Renaissance perspective. As for the speed of light, that is merely the speed of total causality.

It is a principal aspect of the electric age that it establishes a global network that has much of the character of our central nervous system. Our central nervous system is not merely an electric network, but it constitutes a single unified field of experience. As biologists point out, the brain is the interacting place where all kinds of impressions and experiences can be exchanged and translated, enabling us to *react to the world as a whole.* Naturally, when electric technology comes into play, the utmost variety and extent of operations in industry and society quickly assume a unified posture. Yet this organic unity of interprocess that electromagnetism inspires in the most diverse and specialized areas and organs of action is quite the opposite of organization in a mechanized society. Mechanization of any process is achieved by fragmentation, beginning with the mechanization of writing by movable types, which has been called the "monofracture of manufacture."

The electric telegraph, when crossed with typography, created the strange new form of the modern newspaper. Any page of the telegraph press is a surrealistic mosaic of bits of "human interest" in vivid interaction. Such was the art form of Chaplin and the early silent movies. Here, too, an extreme speed-up of mechanization, an assembly line of still shots on celluloid, led to a strange reversal. The movie mechanism, aided by the electric light, created the illusion of organic form and movement as much as a fixed position had created the illusion of perspective on a flat surface five hundred years before.

The same thing happens less superficially when the electric principle crosses the mechanical lines of industrial organization. Automation retains only as much of the mechanical character as the motorcar kept of the forms of the horse and the carriage. Yet people discuss automation as if we had not passed the oat barrier, and as if the horse-vote at the next poll would sweep away the automation regime.

Automation is not an extension of the mechanical principles of fragmentation and separation of operations. It is rather the invasion of the mechanical world by the instantaneous character of electricity. That is why those involved in automation insist that it is a way of thinking, as much as it is a way of doing. Instant synchronization of numerous operations has ended the old mechanical pattern of setting up operations in lineal sequence. The assembly line has gone the way of the stag line. Nor is it just the lineal and sequential aspect of mechanical analysis that has been erased by the electric speed-up and exact synchronizing of information that is automation.

Automation or cybernation deals with all the units and components of the industrial and marketing process exactly as radio or TV combine the individuals in the audience into new interprocess. The new kind of interrelation in both industry and entertainment is the result of the electric instant speed. Our new electric technology now extends the instant processing of knowledge by interrelation that has long occurred within our central nervous system. It is that same speed that constitutes "organic unity" and ends the mechanical age that had gone into high gear with Gutenberg. Automation brings in real "mass production," not in terms of size, but of an instant inclusive embrace. Such is also the character of "mass media." They are an indication, not of the size of their audiences, but of the fact that everybody becomes involved in them at the same time. Thus commodity industries under automation share the same structural character of the entertainment industries in the degree that both approximate the condition of instant information. Automation affects not just production, but every phase of consumption and marketing; for the consumer becomes producer in the automation circuit, quite as much as the reader of the mosaic telegraph press makes his own news, or just *is* his own news.

But there is a component in the automation story that is as basic as tactility to the TV image. It is the fact that, in any automatic machine, or galaxy of machines and functions, the generation and transmission of power is quite separate from the work operation that uses the power. The same is true in all servomechanist structures that involve feedback. The source of energy is separate from the process of translation of information, or the applying of knowledge. This is obvious in the telegraph, where the energy and channel are quite independent of whether the written code is French or German. The same separation of power and process obtains in automated industry, or in "cybernation." The electric energy can be applied indifferently and quickly to many kinds of tasks.

Such was never the case in the mechanical systems. The power and the work done were always in direct relation, whether it was hand and hammer, water and wheel, horse and cart, or steam and piston. Electricity brought a strange elasticity in this matter, much as light itself illuminates a total field and does not dictate what shall be done. The same light can make possible a multiplicity of tasks, just as with electric power. Light is a nonspecialist kind of energy or power that is identical with information and knowledge. Such is also the relation of electricity to automation, since both energy and information can be applied in a great variety of ways.

Grasp of this fact is indispensable to the understanding of the electronic age, and of automation in particular. Energy and production now tend to fuse with information and learning. Marketing and consumption tend to become one with learning, enlightenment, and the intake of information. This is all part of the electric *implosion* that now follows or succeeds the centuries of *explosion* and increasing specialism. The electronic age is literally one of illumination. Just as light is at once energy and information, so electric automation unites production, consumption, and learning in an inextricable process. For this reason, teachers are already the largest employee group in the U.S. economy, and may well become the *only* group.

The very same process of automation that causes a withdrawal of the present work force from industry causes learning itself to become the principal kind of production and consumption. Hence the folly of alarm about unemployment. Paid learning is already becoming both the dominant employment and the source of new wealth in our society. This is the new *role* for men in society, whereas the older mechanistic idea of "jobs," or fragmented tasks and specialist slots for "workers," becomes meaningless under automation.

It has often been said by engineers that, as information levels rise, almost any sort of material can be adapted to any sort of use. This principle is the key to the understanding of electric automation. In the case of electricity, as energy for production becomes independent of the work operation, there is not only the speed that makes for total and organic interplay, but there is, also, the fact that electricity is sheer information that, in actual practice, illuminates all it touches. Any process that approaches instant interrelation of a total field tends to raise itself to the level of conscious awareness, so that computers seem to "think." In fact, they are highly specialized at present, and quite lacking in the full process of interrelation that makes for consciousness. Obviously, they can be made to simulate the process of consciousness, just as our electric global networks now begin to simulate the condition of our central nervous system. But a conscious computer would still be one that was an extension of our consciousness, as a telescope is an extension of our eyes, or as a ventriloquist's dummy is an extension of the ventriloquist.

Automation certainly assumes the servomechanism and the computer. That is to say, it assumes electricity as store and expediter of information. These traits of store, or "memory," and accelerator are the basic features of any medium of communication whatever. In the case of electricity, it is not corporeal substance that is stored or moved, but perception and information. As for technological acceleration, it now approaches the speed of light. All nonelectric media had merely hastened things a bit. The wheel, the road, the ship, the airplane, and even the space rocket are utterly lacking in the character of instant movement. Is it strange, then, that electricity should confer on all previous human organization a completely new character? The very toil of man now becomes a kind of enlightenment. As unfallen Adam in the Garden of Eden was appointed the task of the contemplation and naming of creatures, so with automation. We have now only to name and program a process or a product in order for it to be accomplished. Is it not rather like the case of Al Capp's Schmoos? One had only to look at a Schmoo and think longingly of pork chops or caviar, and the Schmoo ecstatically transformed itself into the object of desire. Automation brings us into the world of the Schmoo. The custom-built supplants the mass-produced.

Let us, as the Chinese say, move our chairs closer to the fire and see what we are saying. The electric changes associated with automation have nothing to do with ideologies or social programs. If they had, they could be delayed or controlled. Instead, the technological extension of our central nervous system that we call the electric media began more than a century ago, subliminally. Subliminal have been the effects. Subliminal they remain. At no period in human culture have men understood the psychic mechanisms involved in invention and technology. Today it is the instant speed of electric information that, for the first time, permits easy recognition of the patterns and the formal contours of change and development. The entire world, past and present, now reveals itself to us like a growing plant in an enormously accelerated movie. Electric speed is synonymous with light and with the understanding of causes. So, with the use of electricity in previously mechanized situations, men easily discover causal connections and patterns that were quite unobservable at the slower rates of mechanical change. If we play backward the long development of literacy and printing and their effects on social experience and organization, we can easily see how these forms brought about that high degree of social uniformity and homogeneity of society that is indispensable for mechanical industry. Play them backward, and we get just that shock of unfamiliarity in the familiar that is necessary for the understanding of the life of forms. Electricity compels us to play our mechanical development backward, for it reverses much of that development. Mechanization depends on the breaking up of processes into homogenized but unrelated bits. Electricity unifies these fragments once more because its speed of operation requires a high degree of interdependence among all phases of any operation. It is this electric speed-up and interdependence that has ended the assembly line in industry.

This same need for organic interrelation, brought in by the electric speed of synchronization, now requires us to perform, industry-by-industry, and country-by-country, exactly the same organic inter-relating that was first effected in the individual automated unit. Electric speed requires organic structuring of the global economy quite as much as early mechanization by print and by road led to the acceptance of national unity. Let us not forget that nationalism was a mighty invention and revolution that, in the Renaissance, wiped out many of the local regions and loyalties. It was a revolution achieved almost entirely by the speed-up of information by means of uniform movable types. Nationalism cut across most of the traditional power and cultural groupings that had slowly grown up in various regions. Multi-nationalisms had long deprived Europe of its economic unity. The Common Market came to it only with the Second War. War is accelerated social change, as an explosion is an accelerated chemical reaction and movement of matter. With electric speeds governing industry and social life, explosion in the sense of crash development becomes normal. On the other hand, the old-fashioned kind of "war" becomes as impracticable as playing hopscotch with bulldozers. Organic inter-dependence means that disruption of any part of the organism can prove fatal to the whole. Every industry has had to "rethink through" (the awkwardness of this phrase betrays the painfulness of the process), function by function, its place in the economy. But automation forces not only industry and town planners, but government and even education, to come into some relation to social facts.

The various military branches have had to come into line with automation very quickly. The unwieldy mechanical forms of military organization have gone. Small teams of experts have replaced the citizen armies of yesterday even faster than they have taken over the reorganization of industry. Uniformly trained and homogenized citizenry, so long in preparation and so necessary to a mechanized society, is becoming quite a burden and problem to an automated society, for automation and electricity require depth approaches in all fields and at all times. Hence the sudden rejection of standard-ized goods and scenery and living and education in America since the Second War. It is a switch imposed by electric technology in general, and by the TV image in particular.

Automation was first felt and seen on a large scale in the

chemical industries of gas, coal, oil, and metallic ores. The large changes in these operations made possible by electric energy have now, by means of the computer, begun to invade every kind of white-collar and management area. Many people, in consequence, have begun to look on the whole of society as a single unified machine for creating wealth. Such has been the normal outlook of the stockbroker, manipulating shares and information with the cooperation of the electric media of press, radio, telephone, and teletype. But the peculiar and abstract manipulation of information as a means of creating wealth is no longer a monopoly of the stockbroker. It is now shared by every engineer and by the entire communications industries. With electricity as energizer and synchronizer, all aspects of production, consumption, and organization become incidental to communications. The very idea of communication as interplay is inherent in the electrical, which combines both energy and information in its intensive manifold.

Anybody who begins to examine the patterns of automation finds that perfecting the individual machine by making it automatic involves "feedback." That means introducing an information loop or circuit, where before there had been merely a one-way flow or mechanical sequence. Feedback is the end of the lineality that came into the Western world with the alphabet and the continuous forms of Euclidean space. Feedback or dialogue between the mechanism and its environment brings a further weaving of individual machines into a galaxy of such machines throughout the entire plant. There follows a still further weaving of individual plants and factories into the entire industrial matrix of materials and services of a culture. Naturally, this last stage encounters the entire world of policy, since to deal with the whole industrial complex as an organic system affects employment, security, education, and politics, demanding full understanding in advance of coming structural change. There is no room for witless assumptions and subliminal factors in such electrical and instant organizations.

As artists began a century ago to construct their works backward, *starting with the effect*, so now with industry and planning. In general, electric speed-up requires complete knowledge of ultimate effects. Mechanical speed-ups, however radical in their reshaping of personal and social life, still were allowed to happen sequentially. Men could, for the most part, get through a normal life span on the basis of a single set of skills. That is not at all the case with electric speed-up. The acquiring of new basic knowledge and skill by senior executives in middle age is one of the most common needs and harrowing facts of electric technology. The senior executives, or "big wheels," as they are archaically and ironically designated, are among the hardest pressed and most persistently harassed groups in human history. Electricity has not only demanded ever deeper knowledge and faster interplay, but has made the harmonizing of production schedules as rigorous as that demanded of the members of a large symphony orchestra. And the satisfactions are just as few for the big executives as for the symphonists, since a player in a big orchestra can hear nothing of the music that reaches the audience. He gets only noise.

The result of electric speed-up in industry at large is the creation of intense sensitivity to the interrelation and interprocess of the whole, so as to call for ever-new types of organization and talent. Viewed from the old perspectives of the machine age, this electric network of plants and processes seems brittle and tight. In fact, it is not mechanical, and it does begin to develop the sensitivity and pliability of the human organism. But it also demands the same varied nutriment and nursing as the animal organism.

With the instant and complex interprocesses of the organic form, automated industry also acquires the power of adaptability to multiple uses. A machine set up for the automatic production of electric bulbs represents a combination of processes that were previously managed by several machines. With a single attendant, it can run as continuously as a tree in its intake and output. But, unlike the tree, it has a built-in system of jigs and fixtures that can be shifted to cause the machine to turn out a whole range of products from radio tubes and glass tumblers to Christmas-tree ornaments. Although an automated plant is almost like a tree in respect to the continuous intake and output, it is a tree than can change from oak to maple to walnut as required. It is part of the automation or electric logic that specialism is no longer limited to just one specialty. The automatic machine may work in a specialist way, but it is not limited to one line. As with our hands and fingers that are capable of many tasks, the automatic unit incorporates a power of adaptation that was quite lacking in the pre-electric and mechanical stage of technology. As *any*thing becomes more complex, it becomes less specialized. Man is more complex and less specialized than a dinosaur. The older mechanical operations were designed to be more efficient as they became larger and more specialized. The electric and automated unit, however, is quite otherwise. A new automatic machine for making automobile tailpipes is about the size of two or three office desks. The computer control panel is the size of a lectern. It has in it no dies, no fixtures, no settings of any kind, but rather certain general-purpose things like grippers, benders, and advancers. On this machine, starting with lengths of ordinary pipe, it is possible to make eighty different kinds of tailpipe in succession, as rapidly, as easily, and as cheaply as it is to make eighty of the same kind. And the characteristic of electric automation is all in this direction of return to the general-purpose handicraft flexibility that our own hands possess. The programming can now include endless changes of program. It is the electric feedback, or dialogue pattern, of the automatic and computer-programmed "machine" that marks it off from the older mechanical principle of one-way movement.

This computer offers a model that has the characteristics shared by all automation. From the point of intake of materials to the output of the finished product, the operations tend to be independently, as well as interdependently, automatic. The synchronized concert of operations is under the control of gauges and instruments that can be varied from the control-panel boards that are themselves electronic. The material of intake is relatively uniform in shape, size, and chemical properties, as likewise the material of the output. But the processing under these conditions permits use of the highest level of capacity for any needed period. It is, as compared with the older machines, the difference between an oboe in an orchestra and the same tone on an electronic music instrument. With the electronic music instrument, any tone can be made available in any intensity and for any length of time. Note that the older symphony orchestra was, by comparison, a machine of separate instruments that *gave the effect of organic unity.* With the electronic instrument, one *starts* with organic unity as an immediate fact of perfect synchronization. This makes the attempt to create the effect of organic unity quite pointless. Electronic music must seek other goals.

Such is also the harsh logic of industrial automation. All that we had previously achieved mechanically by great exertion and coordination can now be done electrically without effort. Hence the specter of joblessness and propertylessness in the electric age. Wealth and work become information factors, and totally new structures are needed to run a business or relate it to social needs and markets. With the electric technology, the new kinds of instant interdependence and interprocess that take over production also enter the market and social organizations. For this reason, markets and education designed to cope with the products of servile toil and mechanical production are no longer adequate. Our education has long ago acquired the fragmentary and piece-meal character of mechanism. It is now under increasing pressure to acquire the depth and interrelation that are indispensable in the all-at-once world of electric organization.

Paradoxically, automation makes liberal education mandatory. The electric age of servomechanisms suddenly releases men from the mechanical and specialist servitude of the preceding machine age. As the machine and the motorcar released the horse and projected it onto the plane of entertainment, so does automation with men. We are suddenly threatened with a liberation that taxes our inner resources of self-employment and imaginative participation in society. This would seem to be a fate that calls men to the role of artist in society. It has the effect of making most people realize how much they had come to depend on the fragmentalized and repetitive routines of the mechanical era. Thousands of years ago man, the nomadic food-gatherer, had taken up positional, or relatively sedentary, tasks. He began to specialize. The development of writing and printing were major stages of that process. They were supremely specialist in separating the roles of knowledge from the roles of action, even though at times it could appear that "the pen is mightier than the sword." But with electricity and automation, the technology of fragmented processes suddenly fused with the human dialogue and the need for over-all consideration of human unity. Men are suddenly nomadic gatherers of knowledge, nomadic as never before, informed as never before, free from fragmentary specialism as never before—but also involved in the total social process as never before; since with electricity we extend our central nervous system globally, instantly interrelating every human experience. Long accustomed to such a state in stock-market news or front-page sensations, we can grasp the meaning of this new dimension more readily when it is pointed out that it is possible to "fly" unbuilt airplanes on computers. The specifications of a plane can be programmed and the plane tested under a variety of extreme conditions before it has left the drafting board. So with new products and new organizations of many kinds. We can now, by computer, deal with complex social needs with the same architectural certainty that we previously attempted in private housing. Industry as a whole has become the unit of reckoning, and so with society, politics, and education as wholes.

Electric means of storing and moving information with speed and precision make the largest units quite as manageable as small ones. Thus the automation of a plant or of an entire industry offers a small model of the changes that must occur in society from the same electric technology. Total interdependence is the starting fact. Nevertheless, the range of choice in design, stress, and goal within that total field of electromagnetic interprocess is very much greater than it ever could have been under mechanization.

Since electric energy is independent of the place or kind of work-operation, it creates patterns of decentralism and diversity in the work to be done. This is a logic that appears plainly enough in the difference between firelight and electric light, for example. Persons grouped around a fire or candle for warmth or light are less able to pursue independent thoughts, or even tasks, than people supplied with electric light. In the same way, the social and educational patterns latent in automation are those of self-employment and artistic autonomy. Panic about automation as a threat of uniformity on a world scale is the projection into the future of mechanical standardization and specialism, which are now past.

Evolution and
Revolution
in the West

Robert Jungk

If one man can be regarded as the organizing force
of the worldwide futurist movement, it is a
German author whose pessimistic 1954 book,
Tomorrow is Already Here, created a sensation
in Europe. Robert Jungk has crisscrossed the globe
encouraging the formation of "prognostic cells,"
passionately urging the control of technology, and
working for the humanization of futurism itself.
Here he discusses the revolt of the young and
calls for the creation of a democratic "world brain."

Of all the events which have happened on our planet Earth during
the last two or three years, the most interesting and most baffling
one has been the continuing mood of protest and revolt, which

has taken hold of the young in East and West. The deepest reason for this unrest is a growing dissatisfaction with the way the older generations have misdirected evolution ever since mankind has been able to influence and—to a certain degree—guide its own development. I feel that these demonstrations go deeper than the well-known political upheavals of the past. They ask: what will man do with his god-like new powers? Will he at last recognise the immense responsibilities and creative challenge they present to him? In [the pages that follow] I try to point out the role that *information* might have to play in this new stage of evolution, and plead for a "seeing progress," to replace the "blind progress" which has led us into the present crisis.

To many observers it has been a surprise, that the most active elements of the protest movement do not come from the same class of population as the revolutionaries of the past. They are mostly children of reasonably well-to-do families, and therefore are not driven by their own immediate material needs. This has led some observers to the conclusion that the student movement is nothing but a vast prank, or—as a lifelong professional revolutionary put it—"the silly noises of pampered brats."

He could not have been more wrong. The young men and women in Paris and Prague, Warsaw and Mexico City, Berlin and Chicago, London and Tokyo may not suffer from hunger and other immediate physical miseries, their grief is of a different nature. They hunger for justice, they are pained by the contradictions of our age, they feel insulted by the gap between man's new possibilities and the wrong use made of them.

They are touched and grieved by brutality and repression even if it happens thousands of kilometers away from their homes, because they are the first "Planetarians." For them there exists no "Far East" on a globe where every point is only hours away by plane, and not even seconds away by TV or radio. So the notion of "Foreign Policy" has ceased to exist for them. Everything political is "Domestic Policy" to them, and they feel as responsible for the cruel pranks of a Latin American Prime Minister as if he were their own chief of government.

Having mentally conquered the spatial distances between man and his fellow man, this new and deeply changed generation has also begun to transcend the bonds of time: they live in a closer dialogue with the future than any generation before them. When I asked one of them why he, a genuine pacifist for a number of years, had supported violent actions against the Embassy of a certain country, he answered: "Because that might help to stop the more terrible violence of tomorrow, which a government of that particular nation might, if it had had no warning, let loose upon mankind."

It is true these young "troublemakers" shout, but how else can their alert be heard? They smash and they burn, but how else can they push through the walls of indifference, how can they otherwise shed light on their justified fears of things to come? Their acute awareness of a new reality, which has abolished the old frontiers of space and time, turns the young into strangers in our midst. But are not we the "unadjusted" ones, are not we the strangers in the world we have brought about? The young have—thank God!—developed a turn of mind, which my great friend the Austrian historian Friedrich Heer has called *"zeitadaequates Bewusstsein,"* that is a way of feeling and thinking, which is "up to the times."

Why did this happen to them rather than to those who, in earlier revolutionary hagiography, have been called the "avant-garde of mankind"—the proletarians? Why have the workers all over the world from the United States via France to Soviet Russia become the supporters of the *status quo* or even the enemies of innovation? The answer is disarmingly simple. Because they have become partners in the misdevelopment of the industrial society, and because they lack the information to see, behind their apparent affluence, the misery already existing, and the catastrophes which threaten them, which threaten all of us.

I will develop this point a little further, because—as I mentioned before—I feel that information, its lack and availability, its use and misuse, its treatment and transfer and, last but not least, its possession, may well be a crucial factor in our evolutionary crisis. Probably most people would agree with me, that scientific and technological achievements have been the driving force of our most recent evolutionary phase, which started in the seventeenth century. By now we all have become weary of the facile optimism, which greeted this era of progress in its earlier phases, because we all know and have been made to feel some of the most harrowing results of it. We have begun to ask: Why did mankind devastate its environment and why does it continue to do so? Why were millions of people killed in the most cruel and destructive wars of history? Why was the so-called "population explosion" set into motion before we knew how to feed the excess millions? Why did we squander our raw materials in only two or three generations? I submit to you the hypothesis, that these things happened not so much as a series of deliberately nasty acts, but because a disastrous neglect of information made some of the most intelligent and in some cases even the most benevolent men make short-sighted or criminal decisions.

This does not mean that they were entirely without knowledge about the new forces at their disposal. The men who decided to build and drop an atom bomb, for instance, had a fair amount of information at hand. But it concerned mostly the direct and immediate effect of their new weapon. When some of the scientists tried to draw their attention to the biological, political and psycho-sociological consequences of the bomb, they did not want to listen.

Not even the possibly negative consequences of beneficial innovations were clear to those who brought them about. Who would have thought in the beginning, that penicillin and other antibiotics, by prolonging the life of millions, might upset the economic and demographic balance of mankind? Who could have seen that the motorcar, when it first appeared in our midst, was anything but an agreeable improvement of our mobility, or that the bulldozer was anything more than an effective and forceful substitute for human toil? Only recently have we begun to discover in the automobile the villain who destroys the "quality of life," and, in the mechanised arsenal of the modern roadbuilder, a weight which tilts the ecological balance.

If we analyse the methods of handling and presenting information which have prevailed in the last three hundred years, we find that information—especially information about new events!—tends to be too narrow, too one-sided, too particular. What mankind lacked—and is still lacking—is cohesive and complementary information, which will not stop at single facts and particular facets, at isolated incidents and one-sided descriptions. What is needed (and I do not talk here as a "Teilhardian thinker" but as a newsman, who has become dissatisfied with the way news is handled) is more synthesis, perspective, comparison and critical evaluation of so-called "facts." We see some of this nowadays in a number of newspapers, in radio hook-ups and TV round-tables. But how little of it really. It is—just to give one example—quite normal that political or diplomatic correspondents, and even writers of "leaders" in the best papers, should have almost no inkling of science or technology despite that fact that political news is more and more deeply influenced by events on test grounds and in laboratories. On the other hand—how many "science writers" give much thought to the social implications of the research work they report about?

So the average citizen, living with an ever growing avalanche of specialised, atomised, single news items, rarely gets an idea how they connect and how they act upon each other. Only here and there does he get glimpses of the "larger picture," and is able to perceive the more complex pattern of the times he is part of. To this is added the even greater problem of evaluating the possible or probable effects of daily events upon the years ahead. Future-oriented journalism is still largely dominated by sensationalism. It reports possible extraordinary events in years to come rather than the more general trends, which may deeply affect our lives.

Yet a change in the information pattern has already begun to emerge at the university, administration and management levels, and it may one day trickle down to the information media. Interdisciplinary studies have been started on many subjects and in many countries. These "generalist" efforts will at last recreate a fuller and truer picture of reality than we have been able to see in the era of "specialisation." So far these attempts to study "wholes" by assembling a group of specialists have not been too successful. It takes some time for these men to understand each other, to find the way back from the babel of scientific jargon to a common language. It will probably take years before a deeper mutual understanding can be reached. A few weekend sessions, monthly seminars, or one conference in a year, will hardly be sufficient. What is really needed is a new type of intellectual institution: an interdisciplinary department on top of all the faculties. It is quite conceivable that in a not too distant future, students will complete their curriculum in a given speciality by visiting a postgraduate school specialising in "non specialisation," an academic institution devoted to "the whole."

The developments in the new field of "future-research" point precisely in that direction. "Futurologists" see their work as an effort based on interdisciplinary co-operation. The American "think factories" with their teams of researchers coming from the most diverse fields may in fact represent the beginnings of those new intellectual institutions I mentioned.

These "think factories" were founded after World War II with a rather narrow objective: to look into the future of military and political warfare, that is into the evolution of weaponry and propaganda. The approaches and methods of information analysis developed in these places proved so convincing to the American "power élite" that they were copied by other government departments and notably by "Big Business," not only in the United States but also in other parts of the Western world. Nowadays it is estimated that U.S. industries spend as much as one per cent of their considerable research budgets on such "forecasting activities" in the hope that they "can provide information about the kinds of future development which are possible."[1]

But the implications of these activities go deeper, the aims of "technological forecasters" are higher and have great relevance to the subject we are discussing here: evolution. Erich Jantsch, a scientist educated in a number of disciplines and now working as a consultant for the Organisation for Economic and Cultural Development, who has been a very able chronicler of these new developments, has described them as follows:

Modern Technological Forecasting can provide a probabilistic assessment of the likelihood of each development, given the urgency with which it is desired. . . . But modern technological forecasting is concerned with more than this. It is also carried out to influence the direction and pace of technological development. A passive or even fatalistic attitude towards technological development has dominated planning in many parts of the globe until fairly recently—and it still does govern a great deal of European thinking. That man should have considered himself the slave of technological development, and not have recognised to what extent it is his own creation, may come as a surprise in a period of general emancipation of the human spirit. But it was only some twenty-five years ago, when opportunities for technological development started drastically to outgrow our ability to tackle them in an indiscriminate manner, that we were forced to select projects which seemed desirable, and to drop others which seemed less so. It was primarily this which led to the necessity of evaluating the future benefits that might accrue from research programmes. With the successful "crash programmes" of war and post-war research and development there came a new confidence in technological forward planning. At the same time it began to be realised how important technology was shortly to become in transforming society by bringing it into the scientific and technological age.

What is spelled out here is nothing less than a programme for the guided evolution of mankind. Another prominent "futurist," Olaf Helmer, of the RAND Corporation and a founding member of the new "Institute of the Future" in Connecticut, offered an even more generalised and provocative formula, when he proclaimed: "We must cease to be mere spectators in our own ongoing history and participate with determination in moulding the future."[2]

So we have begun, in the West, to travel on a road which so far has only been chosen by Marxists: the conscious effort of man to shape his own history, to dominate his fate, to guide his own evolution. The fact that "technological forecasting" is not "hardware," is neither a machine nor a weapon, gives it a rather innocuous appearance. But Jantsch is quite right, when he sees in it a "powerful means of directing and concentrating human energy and of interfering with the movement of history. He (Man) will have to guard against consequences of the sort Goethe's 'sorcerer's apprentice' experienced."

I feel it is high time that the activities of "future researchers" which have so far escaped real public scrutiny should become a topic of common concern. We can see these efforts, which started out with design of future weapons systems, and now aim at the design of future societal systems, not only as an opportunity to escape from the former conditions of blindness and passivity, but also as a possible threat to a free and humanistically oriented evolution.

Such a threat is indeed at this very moment a distinct possibility. There is one passage in the survey of Jantsch I have mentioned, which has worried me ever since I read it. Here it is: "It should be clearly understood that normative technological forecasting is meaningful only if two conditions obtain: If the levels to which it is applied are characterised by constraints; normative forecasting can be applied to the impact levels (goals, objectives, missions) only if these levels are sufficiently 'closed' by natural or artificial forces, or by consensus (for example an agreed set of values or ethical directives, etc.); *fully integrated forecasting is applicable only to a 'closed' society.*

"If more opportunities exist and are recognized on these levels than can be exploited under given constraints, normative forecasting is essentially an attempt to optimise, *which implies selection.*"[3]

These passages seem to point to a type of totalitarian, technocratic society, to societies dominated by an élite, which "selects its goals." The élite defines its aims much more clearly than can other more complex and contradictory social units. Their linear autocratic command structure is built to assure the fast, smooth and undisputed execution of planned objectives. And if we have a look at "technological forecasting" as it is used at present we find —with very few exceptions—precisely this style of authoritarian decision-making at work! Small managerial groups in the higher echelons of the Defence Departments for instance, or the directing boards of large corporations, helped by their staff of medium range or long range planning experts, invent and prepare the future according to their views and their best interests.

Neither the "man in the street," nor the parliamentarian supposed to represent him, takes part in this decisive stage of the process, when analyses of future developments based on synthesis and extrapolation of information are presented, and concepts of future strategies, future weapons, future products are formulated. They may be called in later—if at all!—but what happens then can be illustrated by the case of the Supersonic Transport Plane, which is forced upon society despite the fact that its costs are enormous and its side effects dangerous (the famous supersonic boom, which threatens not only the sleep of thousands of people but also older structures like cathedrals, castles, etc.). In this case "prognosis" by eminent experts is used as propaganda, which tries to persuade the public that such a development is necessary or even inevitable for a technically advanced nation. The existence of such a plane becomes a fixed item in more and more published anticipations of things to come, so that in the end fewer and fewer people dare to oppose it, because that would mean that they are "against the future."*

As forecasting activities with normative intentions increase within the administrative and economic executive branches of most Western democracies they gain a decisive influence on further development, which could be checked by the legislatures or by the consumer only if they are in possession of:

1. as much, or even more complete information as the "power élites";
2. the means of evaluating and extrapolating this information;
3. the means of formulating alternative goals or models based on a mass of information.

How can this be achieved? One distinct possibility points to an international and inter-ideological institution like UNESCO, under whose authority information banks and "forecasting units" might be formed, which would be dedicated to the guided evolution of mankind as a whole and not to the service of determined power groups. Kenneth Boulding has proposed such an institution, which in his words should try "to develop a more systematic apparatus of information, collection and processing for the international system as a whole." He writes: "The next great step forward should be the establishment of a world-wide system of social-data collecting stations, much as we have meteorological stations, which would collect information regarding the social system to be centrally processed in much the same way that the information collected at meteorological stations is processed into weather maps and predictions. The sociosphere like the atmosphere encircles the globe in a complex web of persons, organisations, exchanges, transactions, relationships and events. Every element in it is located in time and space. It is possible to sample and quantify many important elements in it, and to process this information in a form which is readily available and comprehensible. If we could see incomes rising and falling on the world map the way we do barometric pressure, if we could trace the rise and fall of sentiments, hostilities, attitudes and ideologies, the concept of the world social, economic and political climate might then become a statistical reality."[4]

* This article was written before the SST program was decisively beaten in the United States. In Europe, plans for the production and commercial application of the Concorde continue. [Ed.]

Another international project, which implies such a data collecting base, but goes a few steps further, has recently been submitted by me to the Council of Europe at the request of its director general Peter Smithers. In proposing a "European Look-Out Institution"[5] I have postulated:

1. an "Intelligence Unit," which largely corresponds to Boulding's "system of social data collecting stations";
2. a "Model Unit," which would design "models" of alternative and desirable futures in answer to the warnings of a social warning system;
3. a "Feedback Unit," which would give its attention to the impact of the warnings and proposed solutions on the decision makers, the citizens and public opinion;
4. a "Research Unit," which would try to refine methods of looking into the future and further research into new ones, thus guiding evolution. This unit would also be entrusted with keeping a critical eye on the rest of the institution. It should present at least once a year a pointedly self-critical evaluation of all activities of the institution.[6]

The main functions of such an international "think factory" would be to: provide a larger picture; set up a social warning system; stimulate workshops of social invention; inform and educate the public; initiate and support research into the methods of "futurology"; think about the higher social goals, beyond technological achievement and the fulfillment of material needs.

It will probably be some time before such international "Look-Out Institutions" come into being. Meanwhile it is of the greatest importance that smaller "prognostic cells" and "future-creating workshops" should be started by those groups and interests which are not yet represented, or are under-represented, in this new and increasingly important field of "future creation."

How could this be done? The first and most obvious model of forecasting in a democratic framework has been described by Nigel Calder, who thinks that each political party should compile its own portfolio of technical and other trends, which match its political intentions. Bertrand de Jouvenel has proposed a "surmising forum" as a kind of second parliament, where qualified people from the most different spheres of interest might discuss "possible and desirable futures."

But who will be considered to be "qualified"? The opening-up of a sphere of debate and speculation, which has up to now been the almost exclusive domain of the scientific and technological expert, must evoke objections and raise doubts reminiscent of the debates which raged in the transition period from feudal to democratic forms of government. The "aristocrats of knowledge" will be afraid the barbarian laymen might vulgarise and destroy their "kingdoms." The level of discourse, they will let us know, would suffer, and crude manners, cross words become the rule.

Such fears are not unjustified. But nevertheless, the doors of the lecture-halls, seminars, laboratories and institutes will have to be opened much wider. How can such a "democratisation" be made to work? I think it will demand a continuous mutual learning process between the "haves" (in specialised and highly qualified information) and the "have-nots," and this implies the creation of institutions where laymen and experts can meet and discuss, and the education of sufficient intermediaries and "interpreters" between them.

Such a democratisation of knowledge would be the most important precondition for a democratisation of "forecasting" and its use in guiding the evolutionary process. It would probably lengthen the time spent on deliberation and decision, but that would be time well-employed, because it would restore to millions of people the feeling that the civilisation growing out of such debates is partly their work, that it is a creation to which they have been able to contribute or at least been asked to do so.

The democratisation of forecasting implies a pluralism of forecasting institutions. We would need groups who would concentrate their energies on the hitherto badly neglected biological, psychological and aesthetic possibilities of the future, while others would devote special attention to the future of their professions. It is particularly most important that "prognostic cells" should speculate about the future of religion and the future of philosophy. All these "future workshops" should be linked in a vast network. The quality of such a "world brain" would increase with its ability to develop a very high degree of differentiation. In order to assure the survival of humanity it will also have to perform heuristic functions and acquire the ability to develop and correct itself by experience through its human "cells."

It is particularly important that in this family of "look-out institutions" there should be a number of experimental units trying continually to re-examine, change and improve their own styles and methods. More advanced prognostic cells might be devised, which would be more open to the unpredictable, more flexible, and readier to up-date and correct; such cells should experiment with methods of escape from the "prison of the present" by standing certain anticipations on their heads or enriching them with "impossible" or "crazy" parameters. Also these experimental forecasting groups should try to get a mental grip on qualitative phenomena, which are harmed or killed by quantification. They might study the nature and role of processes, images, perspectives, "wholes" (which implies more than systems)—phenomena which can be felt but not yet expressed in any existing form of language. They would be ready to use and develop intuitive, imaginative and visionary approaches.

This points in the direction of a new, not yet developed, branch of forecasting, which I would call "human forecasting." It would try to draw an "envelope curve" of man, that is the ever-widening limits of the ability of man on his never-ending way to God.

Let me at the end . . . return to [my] beginning. I have discussed the ideas contained here with students in different European countries. They agreed that the "establishment" had become more "intelligent" by using the information sciences and the new forecasting techniques growing out of them. But they were pessimistic about the chances of establishing neutral institutions dedicated to the goal of guided evolution, and they doubted whether data-banks and look-out institutions in the service of the non-ruling groups would ever be as complete, as strong, and as efficient as the "think factories" of the armed forces and of "Big Business."

Therefore they feel that only revolution can open the way to an evolution guided by humanistic aims. I do not think that these non-conformistic groups can be integrated into the existing organisations. Nor do I believe in their ability to "takeover." They are just not powerful enough, nor sufficiently well organised. They will continue to clamour, to rebel, to fight, and by doing so they might perhaps force a more rational power élite to steer a different course. They will be "the pain" in mankind's body. But this is only a hope, no certainty at all. Still: the possibility of "evolution by unsuccessful revolutions" seems worth considering.

Towards a Democratic Futurism

Arthur I. Waskow

The radical youth movement has often been attacked for its failure to put forward coherent images of a preferable future. Here a participant in that movement answers the charge. He classifies futurists into elitist-technocrats, humanist–social democrats, and youthful radicals. He argues that it is the task of the radical not merely to explore and describe, but to create the future in the present.

When the Foreign Policy Association celebrated its fifty years of history last fall in a New York Hilton dinner chaired by Charlie "Goldfinger" Engelhard and addressed by Dean Rusk, the movement met the dinner with a quasi-military assault. Frightened that it might be losing the generation that will guide the next 50 years,

85

FPA turned to a convocation it was planning on the year 2018, as the appropriate moment to invite the movement to negotiate. Did not the mysterious young, after all, believe at least in imagining the future?

Well, they do and they don't. It depends on how, by whom, and for what—in short, on the politics of the imagining. And this the FPA could never grasp, for it was sunk so deep in the assumptions of its own politics that it could not believe they were political at all—just "neutral education." So it spent over $150,000 on a convocation at the New York Hilton, May 27–29, 1968, that turned off hundreds more of the younger generation.

The FPA's recipe for a disaster:

1. Invite 500 people over 35 years old and 500 under (including about 50 of the more intellectual New Left and another 50 new-liberal leaders— such as Peace Corps returned volunteers and insurgent Pennsylvania assemblymen).
2. Circulate a dreadful little book of 13 chapters by such people as Ithiel de Sola Pool (who takes public-opinion surveys on how much the Vietnamese love Americans), Herman Kahn (on economics this year), and Najeeb Halaby (senior vice-president of PanAm, writing on transportation), each celebrating some new "inevitable" gadget and deducing all social "change"—that is, no major change at all—from a kind of gadgetary determinism.
3. Invite 22 speakers, of whom the only one under 35 is Bill Moyers— whose power base and sense of life scarcely come from the youth.
4. Have the meeting chaired by a colorless ex-professor (and State Department, of course, consultant) who trembles at the sight of a beard, tells jokes nobody laughs at, and thinks letting John Kenneth Galbraith speak is a concession to the New Left.

Without the radicals this would simply have been the recipe for a crashing bore. But they translated yawns into irreverent rebellion, forced some of their number to be accepted as commentators and speakers, held some unauthorized teach-ins, and laid bare to a large number of liberals, moderates, and FPA staff both how biased and how boring the FPA was.

The radicals tried to make a more basic point: not simply that radicals should have been invited to speak, but that even if they had been, no convocation of the kind FPA put together could have led to a democratic futurism. Not chiefly because of its content—the pro-military views of almost all the speakers, the assumption that technological development would necessarily follow precisely the same lines it had over the past 50 years (as if these were "natural" rather than politically chosen and politically changeable), the focus on how economic development could be done by the rich for (maybe) the poor, instead of by the poor for themselves. Much more crucial was the very process of the convocation: bringing the future "leaders" of America together to share the delights of contemplating their future leadership. The notion that the future of America should be constructed by the people of America—school teachers, welfare mothers, auto workers, shopkeepers, high-school dropouts—would have dictated quite a different format.

The format FPA adopted was closely connected with the emergence in the last few years of a "profession" of the study of the future. In the American Academy of Arts and Sciences, there is a Commission on the Year 2000, headed by Daniel Bell of Columbia University. (He was a major figure at the Hilton.) The Commission very much regarded itself as a panel of the priesthood: to whom the mysteries were revealed and who could guide the people, but would not open those mysteries to the people. (When one member of the Commission proposed inviting a number of young people to join it on the ground that they might actually live till the year 2000, he was told that mere youth could not make them experts— and only experts could do the requisite planning.)

In the RAND Corporation, there has grown out of concern with the future of military strategy a group with a wider interest in the future of American policy generally; but that interest remains oriented to the group of people that run the government of the United States and is still based on the assumption that this need not, could not, ought not, be in any sense the property of the American public. (The RAND group helped bring into being an Institute on the Future which opened its doors on Carnegie and Ford Foundation grants.)

The new élite futurologists of course deny that élitism is a problem at all, saying that just as astronomy is a matter for the professional, so the study of the future has to be. These experts— and their overseas analogues like the *Futuribles* group in France— relay their "findings" to the public through books, pamphlets, top-down conferences, and so on. And usually they take the "public" to mean a somewhat larger circle of experts, administrators, and politicians. Very few of the élite futurists ever respond to a challenge that is democratically couched: Who does the future belong to? Is it indeed a subject like astronomy, or something quite different in that the future of the world presumably belongs to all the people of the world—who should therefore understand and decide it?

One possible response of democrats to the emergence of this highly professionalized, élitist study of the future is to shrug it off, saying that this makes little difference; that politics comes from quite different sources—not from intellectual analysis of what might be done and should be done, either on the part of the haves or the have-nots, but from much more visceral responses of people to the place they hold in society and the way that society is treating them: in short, that change comes from revulsion and anger at the present, so far as the excluded are concerned, and from an urgent desire to protect their holdings, on the part of the powerful.

That may well be true; but it does not gainsay the old fact that knowledge is power, and that in a super-industrial (some people have even said a "post-industrial") society, knowledge of the future is enormous power and ignorance of the future may prevent one from feeling revulsion and anger until it is too late. Decisions on research and development of weapon systems made today will affect what the world looks like twenty years from now. They will affect, for example, whether it is even *possible* to achieve a disarmed world twenty years hence. Decisions on seemingly less crucial matters like the supersonic transport will affect the way our cities develop ten years hence. And very few people know this—only the experts with an "interest" in the matter, with an established political or economic interest which they already know about. The rest of the public is not ready to worry, not trained to worry; it won't get angry about sonic booms till the SSTs are already there, and that will be too late. In an era of very swift technological change, it has to be possible for the whole public to be able to understand the possible futures confronting their society 20, 25, 30 years from now, in order to be able to insist on the decision to be made now that would enable the kind of society to emerge 20 or 30 years from now that they want.

In response to these conflicting values and interests of the public and private good, there have emerged various and conflicting styles of futurism. At the First International Future Research Congress, held in September 1967, in Oslo, the futurists divided into these groups. One might be called the techno-planners—concerned chiefly with technological forecasting. They had frequently been involved in systems-analysis kinds of work; they saw the future as buildable through governments and similar large-scale institutions with very considerable power. Most of these people were from the United States; many of them came out of the RAND Corporation or similar kinds of institutions. And they were vigorously putting forward their images of how one might construct pieces of the twenty-first century, and describing ways in which they have worked with governments in the super-industrial or in the underdeveloped world, to try to construct those pieces. For them, "planning" was clearly a way of helping those who now hold power to know what they must do in order to keep holding power thirty or fifty years hence. What must they change, where should they beat a strategic retreat, what new organizations and technologies should they invent, when can they hold the line?

The second major group at Oslo might be called the humanist social democrats. They included both a great number of the western Europeans and a great number of the eastern Europeans, plus a couple of Americans. They were typically in their mid-50s, about a decade older than the techno-planners. They were quite distressed at technocratic planning. The eastern Europeans tended to be very fearful of the way it had gone in eastern Europe, for example. They tended to be very critical of the way central planning had operated in the twenty years from 1946 or 1947 until fairly recently and were concerned about the ignoring of human values that had resulted from pressure from a central planning source for technological advance and swift economic development. They tended to see the western, especially American, technocrats as very similar to the state planners with whom they'd had to cope in Poland and Czechoslovakia. And they feared that human values would similarly get lost. There was considerable horror, for example, over an attempt to plan a 700 million megalopolis on the Bay of Bengal for the middle of the twenty-first century—the second group feeling horrified that this could not possibly be a *human* social system and that planning it and getting the Indian government to begin building it was the same kind of process that they had gone through in eastern Europe. They were very frightened of that, and most of the western Europeans agreed with them.

In reaction against the "expert" orientation of the élitist technological planners, the social democrats at their best have tried to move one step beyond "planning" towards teaching the general public the art of thinking in a 30-to-40-year span. For example, the discussions of the "Mankind 2000" project, involving an international group of scholars, centering in western Europe and Britain but including some Americans and east Europeans, have focused on how to involve large numbers of the public in planning the future. Robert Jungk of the Mankind 2000 group has suggested a permanent (perhaps mobile) exposition on the future, in which larger numbers of visitors than those usually oriented to books would be exposed to vivid exhibitions of the possible social realities of the future. Charles Osgood of the Mankind 2000 group is exploring, through Project PLATO at the University of Illinois, the possibilities of using computer and teaching machine technology to make available complex sets of branching choices, leading to various futures, so that participants could play through certain choices in the present to see how they might open up and close off various possible futures.

Both of these experimental efforts move in the direction of involving large sections of the public in future-thinking, but both still present the public with *faits accomplis* and leave little room for the invention of new forms or parts of the future, on the local and personal levels, that would mesh with large-scale change and make it viable.

Finally, there was at Oslo a third group, made up of several young North Americans and several young western Europeans, especially a couple of Englishmen and some Scandinavians—typically in their early thirties. They might be called the participatory futurists. They were equally distressed by top-down technocratic planning and by what many of them felt was a kind of literary fuzziness in the humanist social democrats. They criticized the social democrats from the standpoint that they were not able to make anything real out of their fears or their hopes, and that the literary and philosophical musings with which they seemed to confront top-down planning, whether the Eastern or Western variety, was not an effective way of building the kind of future which they seemed to want to build.

The typical methodology of this third group of people could be called one of "creative disorder": that is, attempting to project a decent and workable vision of the future over a one-generation-hence time period, *and then attempting to build chunks of that future in the present.* But not to build them with the help of presently powerful institutions; to build them from the bottom, without the permission of the powerful and often against the laws or the mores of the present "order."

Some of the participatory futurists were working on such unorthodox projects, chunks of a possible future, as neighborhood-level quasi-governments in metropolitan centers—democratically run and oriented partly to such traditional issues as schools or housing, but also involved in imagining alternative futures for the neighborhood. Others at Oslo were working on putting together transnational groups of scholars and students interested in projecting visions of world order—which those groups of people, by their very existence and action as transnational bodies, would help to bring into existence.

And the methodology of this third group was, therefore, quite different from the methodology of both the first two. They did not tend to do any technological forecasting; most of them were not technologically trained; and they were deeply skeptical about involvement with governments as the way of bringing about a decent future.

At the New York Hilton, it became clear the Foreign Policy Association had never imagined any kind of futurists but the first: the élite, technologically oriented "planners." The conference was intended to tell the future second-level leaders of America what to plan for. The shock of confrontation with the movement came from the movement's demand for participatory futurism. And though the movement was not yet ready to specify how to go about *doing* participatory futurism, it was ready to draw upon its own experience. Although the movement has been unwilling to develop detailed images of what the future decent society might look like, it has in a very narrow and *ad hoc* way (a way that we should recognize, mull over, and deliberately turn into a conscious method) been focusing on images of the future. The neatest case is the sit-ins, where the civil rights movement said:

Our desirable-achievable future is that we want to be able to eat in integrated restaurants. We will not petition legislatures to require integration, we will not petition the owners of the restaurants to integrate, *we will simply create the future.* That is, *we* will integrate the restaurants, and it will rest upon those who have the power of law and the power of ownership in their hands, to decide how to respond to that creation. So we will build *now* what it is we want to exist in the future, and the powerful will have to react to that. They will have to let us build it, or punish us for trying. If they punish us, we believe we can build support around that vision of the future, and can therefore mobilize even more people into action to achieve it.

So also the draft-resistance movement, whose imagined future was one without conscription; and the Quaker medical-aid-to-North-Vietnam program, whose imagined future was one where national enmities and even boundaries had dissolved in the face of need; and the student-power movement, whose imagined future was one where students always had access to Administration files because they shared control over the Administration.

All these efforts assume the creation of strains and tensions between imagined future and the existing present. Creating and judging the strain is crucial. If it is not done well, the possibilities are these: One might create something so utterly out of relation with the present, and so challenging to it, that it is smashed immediately beyond repair, in which case one is unlikely to have created much change. On the other hand, one can import into the present something so irrelevant that it is simply encapsulated and allowed to go its own way without creating any tension and therefore any change at all. Both those poles have to be avoided if one can, and one way to avoid them is simply to keep experimenting and to discover at what point one is neither smashed nor ignored, but creates enough change to move the society. *That* is creative disorder; disorder because it obeys the "law and order" of some more or less distant future, and is therefore likely to be "unlawful" or "disorderly" by the standards of the present.

One who uses this approach should not expect that his picture of the future will be achieved. That is, one does not expect that sitting in 1967, one can draw a 1999 which world society will, in fact, be like in 1999. We must expect exactly the opposite: that along the way the process of imagination and creation will lead one to change his imagination. If all goes well, the process will engage wholly new people in imagining the future who do not now imagine it, and by doing that will engage them in creation of a kind of future which was not imagined by the ones who began the process. That is one of the major goals, and therefore one should expect to move in the direction of it; one should expect perhaps to move in some quite different direction after moving part way, but never *to* it. And indeed, it might be wise to set a deadline, a five- or ten-year deadline, at the end of which we throw the old image away and start over again. In a sense this is like the process of science at its best: hypothesis, experiment, new hypothesis—always knowing that no theory is "the truth," but only a useful and beautiful way of understanding and reshaping the complex reality. And this process never ends: not only is the process itself always open-ended, but so is the result.

Thus one begins with a mythical vision, a provisional vision, of the future as an open-ended future: a future which is free to decide on *its* own future: a society in which politics can happen, in which different groups of people are able to press towards change in the society.

To get this process started, what the participatory futurist needs is a medium for the presentation of practicable desirable futures that offers human beings a chance to "work" the futures, to test them out and to invent parts of them or work out new solutions for problems that emerge from them. For the possibility of participatory futurism depends on the availability to the whole public of images of the future on which they can practice creative disorder in the present.

One way of doing this might be to cross-fertilize the simulation games used by Establishment strategists like RAND with the role-playing and highly schematic guerrilla theater used by many movement organizations to politicize their constituents or train their activists. For instance, let us imagine the creation of Future Gaming Centers—perhaps alongside radical community-organizing projects that are focused on present discontents and revulsions. Such Future Gaming Centers could offer experience in "living" alternative futures to Americans who are fed up with the present but have no feel for a workable or desirable society. They could be the first step towards broad popular involvement in the process of "creative disorder": for they would encourage the invention of model futures that could then be attempted in the present.

Such "future games" could focus on several different kinds of situations. One might project, for example, a particular sort of school system of the year 2000 in an American city: perhaps a highly automated high school whose students frequently use euphoria-creating drugs, are politically organized, and carry on political and social action with deprived groups in the community as part of training for a Peace Corps ROTC. Participants in this "game" might play the roles of parent, student, teacher, principal, city councilman, and local taxpayer, each confronted with the crisis created by the sudden advent of a powerful intelligence-enhancing drug.

Another game might pose the problem of a revolution in South Africa, in a world in which total national disarmament was being enforced by a minimal, non-governmental world police force. How would American and Soviet cabinet members, UN officials, Chinese revolutionary propagandists, and similar persons respond to the crisis and to each other's responses?

Or again, in an Indian village of the year 2000, how would the American Farm Corpsman, the Chinese revolutionary organizer, the French teacher, the Russian engineer, the Yugoslavian syndicalist labor leader, the UN development economist, the Indian government official, and the local villagers react to and upon each other?

The movement is not the only institution that could be encouraged to develop such future gaming; or, to put it another way, as the energy and appeal of the movement begin to transform particular schools, recreation centers, and private associations, these "mainstream" groups could well begin to offer alternative futures to scrutiny and testing out by their members and publics.

Nor is the neighborhood Future Gaming Center the only possible approach to participatory futurism. Public-opinion surveys that now offer people only the narrowest of choices within the present social system could be broadened to present (and vividly so that they do not seem ridiculous) possible futures or alternatives that lie outside present assumptions. The mass media might begin to show people "real" worlds that *might* be as well as the fake world that already is, and might create new audience-feedback processes. There may be many other places in which "taking a trip" not on the latest psychedelic but on political imagination could expand the social consciousness of large numbers of people formerly imprisoned in a disastrous present.

Such efforts would require amounts of money and time that the movement does not now have available. It would also require the movement itself to shift (at least in part) from "revulsion organizing" to "attraction organizing"—a change it does not often feel emotionally able to make, under the pressure of horrors daily piled on horrors. But in the absence of such efforts, the field is almost certain to be left to the anti-democratic futurism of the present; and there can be no surer way to guarantee an undemocratic future.

The Strategy of Social Futurism

Alvin Toffler

Future shock, the disorientation produced by
super-change, has important political implications.
We cannot create a sane social system until
technology is tamed, the educational system totally
revolutionized, and future-consciousness injected
into our political lives. This chapter from
Future Shock attacks the bankruptcy of technocratic
planning and calls for a new politics built around
"anticipatory democracy."

Can one live in a society that is out of control? That is the question
posed for us by the concept of future shock. For that is the situation we find ourselves in. If it were technology alone that had
broken loose, our problems would be serious enough. The deadly
fact is, however, that many other social processes have also begun

to run free, oscillating wildly, resisting our best efforts to guide them.

Urbanization, ethnic conflict, migration, population, crime—a thousand examples spring to mind of fields in which our efforts to shape change seem increasingly inept and futile. Some of these are strongly related to the breakaway of technology; others partially independent of it. The uneven, rocketing rates of change, the shifts and jerks in direction, compel us to ask whether the techno-societies, even comparatively small ones like Sweden and Belgium, have grown too complex, too fast to manage?

How can we prevent mass future shock, selectively adjusting the tempos of change, raising or lowering levels of stimulation, when governments—including those with the best intentions—seem unable even to point change in the right direction?

Thus a leading American urbanologist writes with unconcealed disgust: "At a cost of more than three billion dollars, the Urban Renewal Agency has succeeded in materially reducing the supply of low cost housing in American cities." Similar debacles could be cited in a dozen fields. Why do welfare programs today often cripple rather than help their clients? Why do college students, supposedly a pampered elite, riot and rebel? Why do expressways add to traffic congestion rather than reduce it? In short, why do so many well-intentioned liberal programs turn rancid so rapidly, producing side effects that cancel out their central effects? No wonder Raymond Fletcher, a frustrated Member of Parliament in Britain, recently complained: "Society's gone random!"

If random means a literal absence of pattern, he is, of course, overstating the case. But if random means that the outcomes of social policy have become erratic and hard to predict, he is right on target. Here, then, is the political meaning of future shock. For just as individual future shock results from an inability to keep pace with the rate of change, governments, too, suffer from a kind of collective future shock—a breakdown of their decisional processes.

With chilling clarity, Sir Geoffrey Vickers, the eminent British social scientist, has identified the issue: "The rate of change increases at an accelerating speed, without a corresponding acceleration in the rate at which further responses can be made; and this brings us nearer the threshold beyond which control is lost."

The Death of Technocracy

What we are witnessing is the beginning of the final breakup of industrialism and, with it, the collapse of technocratic planning. By technocratic planning, I do not mean only the centralized national planning that has, until recently, characterized the USSR, but also the less formal, more dispersed attempts at systematic change management that occur in all the high technology nations, regardless of their political persuasion. Michael Harrington, the socialist critic, arguing that we have rejected planning, has termed ours the "accidental century." Yet, as Galbraith demonstrates, even within the context of a capitalist economy, the great corporations go to enormous lengths to rationalize production and distribution, to plan their future as best they can. Governments, too, are deep into the planning business. The Keynesian manipulation of post-war economies may be inadequate, but it is not a matter of accident. In France, *Le Plan* has become a regular feature of national life. In Sweden, Italy, Germany and Japan, governments actively intervene in the economic sector to protect certain industries, to capitalize others, and to accelerate growth. In the United States and Britain, even local governments come equipped with what are at least *called* planning departments.

Why, therefore, despite all these efforts, should the system be spinning out of control? The problem is not simply that we plan too little; we also plan too poorly. Part of the trouble can be traced to the very premises implicit in our planning.

First, technocratic planning, itself a product of industrialism, reflects the values of that fast-vanishing era. In both its capitalist and communist variants, industrialism was a system focused on the maximization of material welfare. Thus, for the technocrat, in Detroit as well as Kiev, economic advance is the primary aim; technology the primary tool. The fact that in one case the advance redounds to private advantage and in the other, theoretically, to the public good, does not alter the core assumptions common to both. Technocratic planning is *econocentric*.

Second, technocratic planning reflects the time-bias of industrialism. Struggling to free itself from the stifling past-orientation of previous societies, industrialism focused heavily on the present. This meant, in practice, that its planning dealt with futures near at hand. The idea of a five-year plan struck the world as insanely futuristic when it was first put forward by the Soviets in the 1920s. Even today, except in the most advanced organizations on both sides of the ideological curtain, one- or two-year forecasts are regarded as "long-range planning." A handful of corporations and government agencies, as we shall see, have begun to concern themselves with horizons ten, twenty, even fifty years in the future. The majority, however, remain blindly biased toward next Monday. Technocratic planning is *short-range.*

Third, reflecting the bureaucratic organization of industrialism, technocratic planning was premised on hierarchy. The world was divided into manager and worker, planner and plannee, with decisions made by one for the other. This system, adequate while change unfolds at an industrial tempo, breaks down as the pace reaches super-industrial speeds. The increasingly unstable environment demands more and more non-programmed decisions down below; the need for instant feedback blurs the distinction between line and staff; and hierarchy totters. Planners are too remote, too ignorant of local conditions, too slow in responding to change. As suspicion spreads that top-down controls are unworkable, plannees begin clamoring for the right to participate in the decision-making. Planners, however, resist. For like the bureaucratic system it mirrors, technocratic planning is essentially *undemocratic.*

The forces sweeping us toward super-industrialism can no longer be channeled by these bankrupt industrial-era methods. For a time they may continue to work in backward, slowly moving industries or communities. But their misapplication in advanced industries, in universities, in cities—wherever change is swift—cannot but intensify the instability, leading to wilder and wilder swings and lurches. Moreover, as the evidences of failure pile up, dangerous political, cultural and psychological currents are set loose.

One response to the loss of control, for example, is a revulsion against intelligence. Science first gave man a sense of mastery over his environment, and hence over the future. By making the future seem malleable, instead of immutable, it shattered the opiate religions that preached passivity and mysticism. Today, mounting evidence that society is out of control breeds disillusionment with science. In consequence, we witness a garish revival of mysticism. Suddenly astrology is the rage. Zen, yoga, seances, and witchcraft become popular pastimes. Cults form around the search for Dionysian experience, for non-verbal and supposedly non-linear communication. We are told it is more important to "feel" than to "think," as though there were a contradiction between the two. Existentialist oracles join Catholic mystics, Jungian psychoanalysts, and Hindu gurus in exalting the mystical and emotional against the scientific and rational.

This reversion to pre-scientific attitudes is accompanied, not surprisingly, by a tremendous wave of nostalgia in the society. Antique furniture, posters from a bygone era, games based on the remembrance of yesterday's trivia, the revival of Art Nouveau, the spread of Edwardian styles, the rediscovery of such faded pop-cult celebrities as Humphrey Bogart or W. C. Fields, all mirror a psychological lust for the simpler, less turbulent past. Powerful fad machines spring into action to capitalize on this hunger. The nostalgia business becomes a booming industry.

The failure of technocratic planning and the consequent sense of lost control also feeds the philosophy of "now-ness." Songs and advertisements hail the appearance of the "now generation," and learned psychiatrists, discoursing on the presumed dangers of repression, warn us not to defer our gratifications. Acting out and a search for immediate payoff are encouraged. "We're more oriented to the present," says a teen-age girl to a reporter after the mammoth Woodstock rock music festival. "It's like do what you want to do now. . . . If you stay anywhere very long you get into a planning thing. . . . So you just move on." Spontaneity, the personal equivalent of social planlessness, is elevated into a cardinal psychological virtue.

All this has its political analog in the emergence of a strange coalition of right wingers and New Leftists in support of what can only be termed a "hang loose" approach to the future. Thus we hear increasing calls for anti-planning or non-planning, sometimes euphemized as "organic growth." Among some radicals, this takes on an anarchist coloration. Not only is it regarded as unnecessary or unwise to make long-range plans for the future of the institution or society they wish to overturn, it is sometimes even regarded as poor taste to plan the next hour and a half of a meeting. Planlessness is glorified.

Arguing that planning imposes values on the future, the anti-planners overlook the fact that non-planning does so, too—often with far worse consequence. Angered by the narrow, econo-centric character of technocratic planning, they condemn systems analysis, cost benefit accounting, and similar methods, ignoring the fact that, used differently, these very tools might be converted into powerful techniques for humanizing the future.

When critics charge that technocratic planning is anti-human, in the sense that it neglects social, cultural and psychological values in its headlong rush to maximize economic gain, they are usually right. When they charge that it is shortsighted and undemocratic, they are usually right. When they charge it is inept, they are usually right.

But when they plunge backward into irrationality, anti-scientific attitudes, a kind of sick nostalgia, and an exaltation of now-ness, they are not only wrong, but dangerous. Just as, in the main, their alternatives to industrialism call for a return to pre-industrial insti-tutions, their alternative to technocracy is not post-, but pre-technocracy.

Nothing could be more dangerously maladaptive. Whatever the theoretical arguments may be, brute forces are loose in the world. Whether we wish to prevent future shock or control population, to check pollution or defuse the arms race, we cannot permit deci-sions of earth-jolting importance to be taken heedlessly, witlessly, planlessly. To hang loose is to commit collective suicide.

We need not a reversion to the irrationalisms of the past, not a passive acceptance of change, not despair or nihilism. We need, instead, a strong new strategy. For reasons that will become clear, I term this strategy "social futurism." I am convinced that, armed with this strategy, we can arrive at a new level of competence in the management of change. We can invent a form of planning more humane, more far-sighted, and more democratic than any so far in use. In short, we can transcend technocracy.

The Humanization of the Planner

Technocrats suffer from econo-think. Except during war and dire emergency, they start from the premise that even non-economic problems can be solved with economic remedies.

Social futurism challenges this root assumption of both Marxist and Keynesian managers. In its historical time and place, industrial society's single-minded pursuit of material progress served the human race well. As we hurtle toward super-industrialism, however, a new ethos emerges in which other goals begin to gain parity with, and even supplant those of economic welfare. In personal terms, self-fulfillment, social responsibility, aesthetic achievement, hedonistic individualism, and an array of other goals vie with and often overshadow the raw drive for material success. Affluence serves as a base from which men begin to strive for varied post-economic ends.

At the same time, in societies arrowing toward super-industrialism, economic variables—wages, balance of payments, productivity—grow increasingly sensitive to changes in the non-economic environment. Economic problems are plentiful, but a whole range of issues that are only secondarily economic break into prominence. Racism, the battle between the generations, crime, cultural autonomy, violence—all these have economic dimensions; yet none can be effectively treated by econocentric measures alone.

The move from manufacturing to service production, the psychologization of both goods and services, and ultimately the shift toward experiential production all tie the economic sector much more tightly to non-economic forces. Consumer preferences turn over in accordance with rapid life style changes, so that the coming and going of subcults is mirrored in economic turmoil. Super-industrial production requires workers skilled in symbol manipulation, so that what goes on in their heads becomes much more important than in the past, and much more dependent upon cultural factors.

There is even evidence that the financial system is becoming more responsive to social and psychological pressures. It is only in an affluent society on its way to super-industrialism that one witnesses the invention of new investment vehicles, such as mutual funds, that are consciously motivated or constrained by non-economic considerations. The Vanderbilt Mutual Fund and the Provident Fund refuse to invest in liquor or tobacco shares. The giant Mates Fund spurns the stock of any company engaged in munitions production, while the tiny Vantage 10/90 Fund invests part of its assets in industries working to alleviate food and population problems in developing nations. There are funds that invest only, or primarily, in racially integrated housing. The Ford Foundation and the Presbyterian Church both invest part of their sizeable portfolios in companies selected not for economic payout alone, but for their potential contribution to solving urban problems. Such developments, still small in number, accurately signal the direction of change.

In the meantime, major American corporations with fixed investments in urban centers, are being sucked, often despite themselves, into the roaring vortex of social change. Hundreds of companies are now involved in providing jobs for hard-core unemployed, in organizing literacy and job-training programs, and in scores of other unfamiliar activities. So important have these new involvements grown that the largest corporation in the world, the American Telephone and Telegraph Company, recently set up a Department of Environmental Affairs. A pioneering venture, this agency has been assigned a range of tasks that include worrying about air and water pollution, improving the aesthetic appearance of the company's trucks and equipment, and fostering experimental preschool learning programs in urban ghettos. None of this necessarily implies that big companies are growing altruistic; it merely underscores the increasing intimacy of the links between the economic sector and powerful cultural, psychological and social forces.

While these forces batter at our doors, however, most technocratic planners and managers behave as though nothing had happened. They continue to act as though the economic sector were hermetically sealed off from social and psychocultural influences. Indeed, econocentric premises are buried so deeply and held so widely in both the capitalist and communist nations, that they distort the very information systems essential for the management of change.

For example, all modern nations maintain elaborate machinery for measuring economic performance. We know virtually day by day the directions of change with respect to productivity, prices, investment, and similar factors. Through a set of "economic indicators" we gauge the overall health of the economy, the speed at which it is changing, and the overall directions of change. Without these measures, our control of the economy would be far less effective.

By contrast, we have no such measures, no set of comparable "social indicators" to tell us whether the society, as distinct from the economy, is also healthy. We have no measures of the "quality of life." We have no systematic indices to tell us whether men are more or less alienated from one another; whether education is more effective; whether art, music and literature are flourishing; whether civility, generosity or kindness are increasing. "Gross National Product is our Holy Grail," writes Stewart Udall, former United States Secretary of the Interior, ". . . but we have no environmental index, no census statistics to measure whether the country is more livable from year to year."

On the surface, this would seem a purely technical matter—something for statisticians to debate. Yet it has the most serious political significance, for lacking such measures it becomes difficult to connect up national or local policies with appropriate long-term social goals. The absence of such indices perpetuates vulgar technocracy.

Little known to the public, a polite, but increasingly bitter battle over this issue has begun in Washington. Technocratic planners and economists see in the social indicators idea a threat to their entrenched position at the ear of the political policy maker. In contrast, the need for social indicators has been eloquently argued by such prominent social scientists as Bertram M. Gross of Wayne State University, Eleanor Sheldon and Wilbert Moore of the Russell Sage Foundation, Daniel Bell and Raymond Bauer of Harvard. We are witnessing, says Gross, a "widespread rebellion against what has been called the 'economic philistinism' of the United States government's present statistical establishment."

This revolt has attracted vigorous support from a small group of politicians and government officials who recognize our desperate need for a post-technocratic social intelligence system. These include Daniel P. Moynihan, a key White House adviser; Senators Walter Mondale of Minnesota and Fred Harris of Oklahoma, and several former Cabinet officers. In the near future, we can expect the same revolt to break out in other world capitals as well, once again drawing a line between technocrats and post-technocrats.

The danger of future shock, itself, however, points to the need for new social measures not yet even mentioned in the fast-burgeoning literature on social indicators. We urgently need, for example, techniques for measuring the level of transience in different communities, different population groups, and in individual experience. It is possible, in principle, to design a "transience index" that could disclose the rate at which we are making and breaking relationships with the things, places, people, organizations and informational structures that comprise our environment.

Such an index would reveal, among other things, the fantastic differences in the experiences of different groups in the society —the static and tedious quality of life for very large numbers of people, the frenetic turnover in the lives of others. Government policies that attempt to deal with both kinds of people in the same way are doomed to meet angry resistance from one or the other— or both.

Similarly, we need indices of novelty in the environment. How often do communities, organizations or individuals have to cope with first-time situations? How many of the articles in the home of the average working-class family are actually "new" in function or appearance; how many are traditional? What level of novelty— in terms of things, people or any other significant dimension—is required for stimulation without over-stimulation? How much more novelty can children absorb than their parents—if it is true that they can absorb more? In what way is aging related to lower novelty tolerances, and how do such differences correlate with the political and intergenerational conflict now tearing the techno-societies apart? By studying and measuring the invasion of newness, we can begin, perhaps, to control the influx of change into our social structures and personal lives.

And what about choice and overchoice? Can we construct measures of the degree of significant choice in human lives? Can any government that pretends to be democratic not concern itself with such an issue? For all the rhetoric about freedom of choice, no government agency in the world can claim to have made any attempt to measure it. The assumption simply is that more income or affluence means more choice and that more choice, in turn, means freedom. Is it not time to examine these basic assumptions of our political systems? Post-technocratic planning must deal with precisely such issues, if we are to prevent future shock and build a humane super-industrial society.

A sensitive system of indicators geared to measuring the achievement of social and cultural goals, and integrated with economic indicators, is part of the technical equipment that any society needs before it can successfully reach the next stage of eco-technological development. It is an absolute precondition for post-technocratic planning and change management.

This humanization of planning, moreover, must be reflected in our political structures as well. To connect the super-industrial social intelligence system with the decisional centers of society, we must institutionalize a concern for the quality of life. Thus Bertram Gross and others in the social indicators movement have proposed the creation of a Council of Social Advisers to the President. Such a Council, as they see it, would be modeled after the already existing Council of Economic Advisers and would perform parallel functions in the social field. The new agency would monitor key social indicators precisely the way the CEA keeps its eye on economic indices, and interpret changes to the President. It would issue an annual report on the quality of life, clearly spelling out our social progress (or lack of it) in terms of specified goals. This report would thus supplement and balance the annual economic report prepared by the CEA. By providing reliable, useful data about our social condition, the Council of Social Advisers would begin to influence planning generally, making it more sensitive to social costs and benefits, less coldly technocratic and econocentric.*

The establishment of such councils, not merely at the federal level but at state and municipal levels as well, would not solve all our problems; it would not eliminate conflict; it would not guarantee that social indicators are exploited properly. In brief, it would not eliminate politics from political life. But it would lend recognition—and political force—to the idea that the aims of progress reach beyond economics. The designation of agencies to watch over the indicators of change in the quality of life would carry us a long way toward that humanization of the planner which is the essential first stage of the strategy of social futurism.

* Proponents differ as to whether the Council of Social Advisers ought to be organizationally independent or become a part of a larger Council of Economic *and* Social Advisers. All sides agree, however, on the need for integrating economic and social intelligence.

Time Horizons

Technocrats suffer from myopia. Their instinct is to think about immediate returns, immediate consequences. They are premature members of the now generation.

If a region needs electricity, they reach for a power plant. The fact that such a plant might sharply alter labor patterns, that within a decade it might throw men out of work, force large-scale retraining of workers, and swell the social welfare costs of a nearby city—such considerations are too remote in time to concern them. The fact that the plant could trigger devastating ecological consequences a generation later simply does not register in their time frame.

In a world of accelerant change, next year is nearer to us than next month was in a more leisurely era. This radically altered fact of life must be internalized by decision-makers in industry, government and elsewhere. Their time horizons must be extended.

To plan for a more distant future does not mean to tie oneself to dogmatic programs. Plans can be tentative, fluid, subject to continual revision. Yet flexibility need not mean shortsightedness. To transcend technocracy, our social time horizons must reach decades, even generations, into the future. This requires more than a lengthening of our formal plans. It means an infusion of the entire society, from top to bottom, with a new socially aware future-consciousness.

One of the healthiest phenomena of recent years has been the sudden proliferation of organizations devoted to the study of the future. This recent development is, in itself, a homeostatic response of the society to the speed-up of change. Within a few years we have seen the creation of future-oriented think tanks like the Institute for the Future; the formation of academic study groups like the Commission on the Year 2000 and the Harvard Program on Technology and Society; the appearance of futurist journals in England, France, Italy, Germany and the United States; the spread of university courses in forecasting and related subjects; the convocation of international futurist meetings in Oslo, Berlin and Kyoto; the coalescence of groups like Futuribles, Europe 2000, Mankind 2000, the World Future Society.

Futurist centers are to be found in West Berlin, in Prague, in

London, in Moscow, Rome and Washington, in Caracas, even in the remote jungles of Brazil at Belém and Belo Horizonte. Unlike conventional technocratic planners whose horizons usually extend no further than a few years into tomorrow, these groups concern themselves with change fifteen, twenty-five, even fifty years in the future.

Every society faces not merely a succession of *probable* futures, but an array of *possible* futures, and a conflict over *preferable* futures. The management of change is the effort to convert certain possibilities into probables, in pursuit of agreed-on preferables. Determining the probable calls for a science of futurism. Delineating the possible calls for an art of futurism. Defining the preferable calls for a politics of futurism.

The worldwide futurist movement today does not yet differentiate clearly among these functions. Its heavy emphasis is on the assessment of probabilities. Thus in many of these centers, economists, sociologists, mathematicians, biologists, physicists, operations researchers and others invent and apply methods for forecasting future probabilities. At what date could aquaculture feed half the world's population? What are the odds that electric cars will supplant gas-driven automobiles in the next fifteen years? How likely is a Sino-Soviet détente by 1980? What changes are most probable in leisure patterns, urban government, race relations?

Stressing the interconnectedness of disparate events and trends, scientific futurists are also devoting increasing attention to the social consequences of technology. The Institute for the Future is, among other things, investigating the probable social and cultural effects of advanced communications technology. The group at Harvard is concerned with social problems likely to arise from bio-medical advances. Futurists in Brazil examine the probable outcomes of various economic development policies.

The rationale for studying probable futures is compelling. It is impossible for an individual to live through a single working day without making thousands of assumptions about the probable future. The commuter who calls to say, "I'll be home at six" bases his prediction on assumptions about the probability that the train will run on time. When mother sends Johnny to school, she tacitly assumes the school will be there when he arrives. Just as a pilot cannot steer a ship without projecting its course, we cannot steer our personal lives without continually making such assumptions, consciously or otherwise.

Societies, too, construct an architecture of premises about tomorrow. Decision-makers in industry, government, politics, and other sectors of society could not function without them. In periods of turbulent change, however, these socially-shaped images of the probable future become less accurate. The breakdown of control in society today is directly linked to our inadequate images of probable futures.

Of course, no one can "know" the future in any absolute sense. We can only systematize and deepen our assumptions and attempt to assign probabilities to them. Even this is difficult. Attempts to forecast the future inevitably alter it. Similarly, once a forecast is disseminated, the act of dissemination (as distinct from investigation) also produces a perturbation. Forecasts tend to become self-fulfilling or self-defeating. As the time horizon is extended into the more distant future, we are forced to rely on informed hunch and guesswork. Moreover, certain unique events—assassinations, for example—are, for all intents and purposes, unpredictable at present (although we can forecast classes of such events).

Despite all this, it is time to erase, once and for all, the popular myth that the future is "unknowable." The difficulties ought to chasten and challenge, not paralyze. William F. Ogburn, one of the world's great students of social change, once wrote: "We should admit into our thinking the idea of approximations, that is, that there are varying degrees of accuracy and inaccuracy of estimate." A rough idea of what lies ahead is better than none, he went on, and for many purposes extreme accuracy is wholly unnecessary.

We are not, therefore, as helpless in dealing with future probabilities as most people assume. The British social scientist Donald G. MacRae correctly asserts that "modern sociologists can in fact make a large number of comparatively short term and limited predictions with a good deal of assurance." Apart from the standard methods of social science, however, we are experimenting with potentially powerful new tools for probing the future. These range from complex ways of extrapolating existing trends, to the construction of highly intricate models, games and simulations, the preparation of detailed speculative scenarios, the systematic study of history for relevant analogies, morphological research, relevance analysis, contextual mapping and the like. In a comprehensive investigation of technological forecasting, Dr. Erich Jantsch, formerly a consultant to the OECD and a research associate at MIT, has identified scores of distinct new techniques either in use or in the experimental stage.

The Institute for the Future in Middletown, Connecticut, a prototype of the futurist think tank, is a leader in the design of new forecasting tools. One of these is Delphi—a method largely developed by Dr. Olaf Helmer, the mathematician-philosopher who is one of the founders of the IFF. Delphi attempts to deal with very distant futures by making systematic use of the "intuitive" guesstimates of large numbers of experts. The work on Delphi has led to a further innovation which has special importance in the attempt to prevent future shock by regulating the pace of change. Pioneered by Theodore J. Gordon of the IFF, and called Cross Impact Matrix Analysis, it traces the effect of one innovation on another, making possible, for the first time, anticipatory analysis of complex chains of social, technological and other occurrences—and the rates at which they are likely to occur.

We are, in short, witnessing a perfectly extraordinary thrust toward more scientific appraisal of future probabilities, a ferment likely, in itself, to have a powerful impact on the future. It would be foolish to oversell the ability of science, as yet, to forecast complex events accurately. Yet the danger today is not that we will overestimate our ability; the real danger is that we will under-utilize it. For even when our still-primitive attempts at scientific forecasting turn out to be grossly in error, the very effort helps us identify key variables in change, it helps clarify goals, and it forces more careful evaluation of policy alternatives. In these ways, if no others, probing the future pays off in the present.

Anticipating *probable* futures, however, is only part of what needs doing if we are to shift the planner's time horizon and infuse the entire society with a greater sense of tomorrow. For we must also vastly widen our conception of possible futures. To the rigorous discipline of science, we must add the flaming imagination of art.

Today as never before we need a multiplicity of visions, dreams and prophecies—images of potential tomorrows. Before we can rationally decide which alternative pathways to choose, which cultural styles to pursue, we must first ascertain which are possible. Conjecture, speculation and the visionary view thus become as coldly practical a necessity as feet-on-the-floor "realism" was in an earlier time.

This is why some of the world's biggest and most tough-minded corporations, once the living embodiment of presentism, today hire intuitive futurists, science fiction writers and visionaries as consultants. A gigantic European chemical company employs a futurist who combines a scientific background with training as a theologian. An American communications empire engages a future-minded social critic. A glass manufacturer searches for a science fiction writer to imagine the possible corporate forms of the future. Companies turn to these "blue-skyers" and "wild birds" not for scientific forecasts of probabilities, but for mind-stretching speculation about possibilities.

Corporations must not remain the only agencies with access to such services. Local government, schools, voluntary associations and others also need to examine their potential futures imaginatively. One way to help them do so would be to establish in each community "imaginetic centers" devoted to technically assisted brainstorming. These would be places where people noted for creative imagination, rather than technical expertise, are brought together to examine present crises, to anticipate future crises, and to speculate freely, even playfully, about possible futures.

What, for example, are the possible futures of urban transportation? Traffic is a problem involving space. How might the city of tomorrow cope with the movement of men and objects through space? To speculate about this question, an imaginetic center might enlist artists, sculptors, dancers, furniture designers, parking lot attendants, and a variety of other people who, in one way or another, manipulate space imaginatively. Such people, assembled under the right circumstances, would inevitably come up with ideas of which the technocratic city planners, the highway engineers and transit authorities have never dreamed.

Musicians, people who live near airports, jack-hammer men and subway conductors might well imagine new ways to organize, mask or suppress noise. Groups of young people might be invited to ransack their minds for previously unexamined approaches to urban sanitation, crowding, ethnic conflict, care of the aged, or a thousand other present and future problems.

In any such effort, the overwhelming majority of ideas put forward will, of course, be absurd, funny or technically impossible. Yet the essence of creativity is a willingness to play the fool, to toy with the absurd, only later submitting the stream of ideas to harsh critical judgment. The application of the imagination to the future thus requires an environment in which it is safe to err, in which novel juxtapositions of ideas can be freely expressed before being critically sifted. We need sanctuaries for social imagination.

While all sorts of creative people ought to participate in conjecture about possible futures, they should have immediate access —in person or via telecommunications—to technical specialists, from acoustical engineers to zoologists, who could indicate when a suggestion is technically impossible (bearing in mind that even impossibility is often temporary).

Scientific expertise, however, might also play a generative, rather than merely a damping role in the imaginetic process. Skilled specialists can construct models to help imagineers examine all possible permutations of a given set of relationships. Such models are representations of real life conditions. In the words of Christoph Bertram of the Institute for Strategic Studies in London, their purpose is "not so much to predict the future, but, by examining alternative futures, to show the choices open."

An appropriate model, for example, could help a group of imagineers visualize the impact on a city if its educational expenditures were to fluctuate—how this would affect, let us say, the transport system, the theaters, the occupational structure and health of the community. Conversely, it could show how changes in these other factors might affect education.

The rushing stream of wild, unorthodox, eccentric or merely colorful ideas generated in these sanctuaries of social imagination must, after they have been expressed, be subjected to merciless screening. Only a tiny fraction of them will survive this filtering process. These few, however, could be of the utmost importance in calling attention to new possibilities that might otherwise escape notice. As we move from poverty toward affluence, politics changes from what mathematicians call a zero sum game into a non-zero sum game. In the first, if one player wins another must lose. In the second, all players can win. Finding non-zero sum solutions to our social problems requires all the imagination we can muster. A system for generating imaginative policy ideas could help us take maximum advantage of the non-zero opportunities ahead.

While imaginetic centers concentrate on partial images of tomorrow, defining possible futures for a single industry, an organization, a city or its sub-systems, however, we also need sweeping, visionary ideas about the society as a whole. Multiplying our images of possible futures is important; but these images need to be organized, crystallized into structured form. In the past, utopian literature did this for us. It played a practical, crucial role in ordering men's dreams about alternative futures. Today we suffer for lack of utopian ideas around which to organize competing images of possible futures.

Most traditional utopias picture simple and static societies—i.e., societies that have nothing in common with super-industrialism. B. F. Skinner's *Walden Two*, the model for several existing experimental communes, depicts a pre-industrial way of life—small, close to the earth, built on farming and handcraft. Even those two brilliant anti-utopias, *Brave New World* and *1984,* now seem oversimple. Both describe societies based on high technology and low complexity: the machines are sophisticated but the social and cultural relationships are fixed and deliberately simplified.

Today we need powerful new utopian and anti-utopian concepts that look forward to super-industrialism, rather than backward to simpler societies. These concepts, however, can no longer be produced in the old way. First, no book, by itself, is adequate to describe a super-industrial future in emotionally compelling terms. Each conception of a super-industrial utopia or anti-utopia needs to be embodied in many forms—films, plays, novels and works of art—rather than a single work of fiction. Second, it may now be too difficult for any individual writer, no matter how gifted, to describe a convincingly complex future. We need, therefore, a revolution in the production of utopias: collaborative utopianism. We need to construct "utopia factories."

One way might be to assemble a small group of top social scientists—an economist, a sociologist, an anthropologist, and so on—asking them to work together, even live together, long enough to hammer out among themselves a set of well-defined values on which they believe a truly super-industrial utopian society might be based.

Each member of the team might then attempt to describe in nonfiction form a sector of an imagined society built on these values. What would its family structure be like? Its economy, laws, religion, sexual practices, youth culture, music, art, its sense of time, its degree of differentiation, its psychological problems? By working together and ironing out inconsistencies, where possible, a comprehensive and adequately complex picture might be drawn of a seamless, temporary form of super-industrialism.

At this point, with the completion of detailed analysis, the project would move to the fiction stage. Novelists, film-makers, science fiction writers and others, working closely with psychologists, could prepare creative works about the lives of individual characters in the imagined society.

Meanwhile, other groups could be at work on counter-utopias. While Utopia A might stress materialist, success-oriented values, Utopia B might base itself on sensual, hedonistic values, C on the primacy of aesthetic values, D on individualism, E on collectivism, and so forth. Ultimately, a stream of books, plays, films and television programs would flow from this collaboration between art, social science and futurism, thereby educating large numbers of people about the costs and benefits of the various proposed utopias.

Finally, if social imagination is in short supply, we are even more lacking in people willing to subject utopian ideas to systematic test. More and more young people, in their dissatisfaction with industrialism, are experimenting with their own lives, forming utopian communities, trying new social arrangements, from group marriage to living-learning communes. Today, as in the past, the weight of established society comes down hard on the visionary who attempts to practice, as well as merely preach. Rather than ostracizing utopians, we should take advantage of their willingness to experiment, encouraging them with money and tolerance, if not respect.

Most of today's "intentional communities" or utopian colonies, however, reveal a powerful preference for the past. These may be of value to the individuals in them, but the society as a whole would be better served by utopian experiments based on super- rather than pre-industrial forms. Instead of a communal farm, why not a computer software company whose program writers live and work communally? Why not an education technology company whose members pool their money and merge their families? Instead of raising radishes or crafting sandals, why not an oceanographic research installation organized along utopian lines? Why not a group medical practice that takes advantage of the latest medical technology but whose members accent modest pay and pool their profits to run a completely new-style medical school? Why not recruit living groups to try out the proposals of the utopia factories?

In short, we can use utopianism as a tool rather than an escape, if we base our experiments on the technology and society of tomorrow rather than that of the past. And once done, why not the most rigorous, scientific analysis of the results? The findings could be priceless, were they to save us from mistakes or lead us toward more workable organizational forms for industry, education, family life or politics.

Such imaginative explorations of possible futures would deepen and enrich our scientific study of probable futures. They would lay a basis for the radical forward extension of the society's time horizon. They would help us apply social imagination to the future of futurism itself.

Indeed, with these as a background, we must consciously begin to multiply the scientific future-sensing organs of society. Scientific futurist institutes must be spotted like nodes in a loose network throughout the entire governmental structure in the techno-societies, so that in every department, local or national, some staff devotes itself systematically to scanning the probable long-term future in its assigned field. Futurists should be attached to every political party, university, corporation, professional association, trade union and student organization.

We need to train thousands of young people in the perspectives and techniques of scientific futurism, inviting them to share in the exciting venture of mapping probable futures. We also need national agencies to provide technical assistance to local communities in creating their own futurist groups. And we need a similar center, perhaps jointly funded by American and European foundations, to help incipient futurist centers in Asia, Africa, and Latin America.

We are in a race between rising levels of uncertainty produced by the acceleration of change, and the need for reasonably accurate images of what at any instant is the most probable future. The generation of reliable images of the most probable future thus becomes a matter of the highest national, indeed, international urgency.

As the globe is itself dotted with future-sensors, we might consider creating a great international institute, a world futures data bank. Such an institute, staffed with top caliber men and women from all the sciences and social sciences, would take as its purpose the collection and systematic integration of predictive reports generated by scholars and imaginative thinkers in all the intellectual disciplines all over the world.

Of course, those working in such an institute would know that they could never create a single, static diagram of the future. Instead, the product of their effort would be a constantly changing geography of the future, a continually re-created overarching image based on the best predictive work available. The men and women engaged in this work would know that nothing is certain; they would know that they must work with inadequate data; they would appreciate the difficulties inherent in exploring the uncharted territories of tomorrow. But man already knows more about the future than he has ever tried to formulate and integrate in any systematic and scientific way. Attempts to bring this knowledge together would constitute one of the crowning intellectual efforts in history—and one of the most worthwhile.

Only when decision-makers are armed with better forecasts of future events, when by successive approximation we increase the accuracy of forecast, will our attempts to manage change improve perceptibly. For reasonably accurate assumptions about the future are a precondition for understanding the potential consequences of our own actions. And without such understanding, the management of change is impossible.

If the humanization of the planner is the first stage in the strategy of social futurism, therefore, the forward extension of our time horizon is the second. To transcend technocracy, we need not only to reach beyond our economic philistinism, but to open our minds to more distant futures, both probable and possible.

Anticipatory Democracy

In the end, however, social futurism must cut even deeper. For technocrats suffer from more than econo-think and myopia; they suffer, too, from the virus of elitism. To capture control of change, we shall, therefore, require a final, even more radical breakaway from technocratic tradition: we shall need a revolution in the very way we formulate our social goals.

Rising novelty renders irrelevant the traditional goals of our chief institutions—state, church, corporation, army and university. Acceleration produces a faster turnover of goals, a greater transience of purpose. Diversity or fragmentation leads to a relentless multiplication of goals. Caught in this churning, goal-cluttered environment, we stagger, future shocked, from crisis to crisis, pursuing a welter of conflicting and self-cancelling purposes.

Nowhere is this more starkly evident than in our pathetic attempts to govern our cities. New Yorkers, within a short span, have suffered a nightmarish succession of near disasters: a water shortage, a subway strike, racial violence in the schools, a student insurrection at Columbia University, a garbage strike, a housing shortage, a fuel oil strike, a breakdown of telephone service, a teacher walkout, a power blackout, to name just a few. In its City Hall, as in a thousand city halls over the high-technology nations, technocrats dash, firebucket in fist, from one conflagration to another without the least semblance of a coherent plan or policy for the urban future.

This is not to say no one is planning. On the contrary; in this seething social brew, technocratic plans, sub-plans and counterplans pour forth. They call for new highways, new roads, new power plants, new schools. They promise better hospitals, housing, mental health centers, welfare programs. But the plans cancel, contradict and reinforce one another by accident. Few are logically related to one another, and none to any overall image of the preferred city of the future. No vision—utopian or otherwise—energizes our efforts. No rationally integrated goals bring order to the chaos. And at the national and international levels, the absence of coherent policy is equally marked and doubly dangerous.

It is not simply that we do not know which goals to pursue, as a city or as a nation. The trouble lies deeper. For accelerating change has made obsolete the methods by which we arrive at social goals. The technocrats do not yet understand this, and, reacting to the goals crisis in knee-jerk fashion, they reach for the tried and true methods of the past.

Thus, intermittently, a change-dazed government will try to define its goals publicly. Instinctively, it establishes a commission. In 1960 President Eisenhower pressed into service, among others, a general, a judge, a couple of industrialists, a few college presidents, and a labor leader to "develop a broad outline of coordinated national policies and programs" and to "set up a series of goals in various areas of national activity." In due course, a red-white-and-blue paperback appeared with the commission's report, *Goals for Americans.* Neither the commission nor its goals had the slightest impact on the public or on policy. The juggernaut of change continued to roll through America untouched, as it were, by managerial intelligence.

A far more significant effort to tidy up governmental priorities was initiated by President Johnson, with his attempt to apply PPBS (Planning-Programming-Budgeting-System) throughout the federal establishment. PPBS is a method for tying programs much more closely and rationally to organizational goals. Thus, for example, by applying it, the Department of Health, Education and Welfare can assess the costs and benefits of alternative programs to accomplish specified goals. But who specifies these larger, more important goals? The introduction of PPBS and the systems approach is a major governmental achievement. It is of paramount importance in managing large organizational efforts. But it leaves entirely untouched the profoundly political question of how the overall goals of a government or a society are to be chosen in the first place.

President Nixon, still snarled in the goals crisis, tried a third tack. "It is time," he declared, "we addressed ourselves, consciously and systematically, to the question of what kind of a nation we want to be . . ." He thereupon put his finger on the quintessential question. But once more the method chosen for answering it proved to be inadequate. "I have today ordered the establishment, within the White House, of a National Goals Research Staff," the President announced. "This will be a small, highly technical staff, made up of experts in the collection . . . and processing of data relating to social needs, and in the projection of social trends."

Such a staff, located within shouting distance of the Presidency, could be extremely useful in compiling goal proposals, in reconciling (at least on paper) conflicts between agencies, in suggesting new priorities. Staffed with excellent social scientists and futurists, it could earn its keep if it did nothing but force high officials to question their primary goals.

Yet even this step, like the two before it, bears the unmistakable imprint of the technocratic mentality. For it, too, evades the politically charged core of the issue. How are preferable futures to be defined? And by whom? Who is to set goals for the future?

Behind all such efforts runs the notion that national (and, by extension, local) goals for the future of society ought to be formulated at the top. This technocratic premise perfectly mirrors the old bureaucratic forms of organization in which line and staff were separated, in which rigid, undemocratic hierarchies distinguished leader from led, manager from managed, planner from plannee.

Yet the real, as distinct from the glibly verbalized, goals of any society on the path to super-industrialism are already too complex, too transient and too dependent for their achievement upon the willing participation of the governed, to be perceived and defined so easily. We cannot hope to harness the runaway forces of change by assembling a kaffee klatsch of elders to set goals for us or by turning the task over to a "highly technical staff." A revolutionary new approach to goal-setting is needed.

Nor is this approach likely to come from those who play-act at revolution. One radical group, seeing all problems as a manifestation of the "maximization of profits" displays, in all innocence, an econocentricism as narrow as that of the technocrats. Another hopes to plunge us willy-nilly back into the pre-industrial past. Still another sees revolution exclusively in subjective and psychological terms. None of these groups is capable of advancing us toward post-technocratic forms of change management.

By calling attention to the growing ineptitudes of the technocrats and by explicitly challenging not merely the means, but the very goals of industrial society, today's young radicals do us all a great service. But they no more know how to cope with the goals crisis than the technocrats they scorn. Exactly like Messrs. Eisenhower, Johnson and Nixon, they have been noticeably unable to present any positive image of a future worth fighting for.

Thus Todd Gitlin, a young American radical and former president of the Students for a Democratic Society, notes that while "an orientation toward the future has been the hallmark of every revolutionary—and, for that matter, liberal—movement of the last century and a half," the New Left suffers from "a disbelief in the future." After citing all the ostensible reasons why it has so far not put forward a coherent vision of the future, he succinctly confesses: "We find ourselves incapable of formulating the future."

Other New Left theorists fuzz over the problem, urging their followers to incorporate the future in the present by, in effect, living the life styles of tomorrow today. So far, this has led to a pathetic charade—"free societies," cooperatives, pre-industrial communes, few of which have anything to do with the future, and most of which reveal, instead, only a passionate penchant for the past.

The irony is compounded when we consider that some (though hardly all) of today's young radicals also share with the technocrats a streak of virulent elitism. While decrying bureaucracy and demanding "participatory democracy" they, themselves, frequently attempt to manipulate the very groups of workers, blacks or students on whose behalf they demand participation.

The working masses in the high-technology societies are totally indifferent to calls for a political revolution aimed at exchanging one form of property ownership for another. For most people, the rise in affluence has meant a better, not a worse, existence, and they look upon their much despised "suburban middle class lives" as fulfillment rather than deprivation.

Faced with this stubborn reality, undemocratic elements in the New Left leap to the Marcusian conclusion that the masses are too bourgeoisified, too corrupted and addled by Madison Avenue to know what is good for them. And so, a revolutionary elite must establish a more humane and democratic future even if it means stuffing it down the throats of those who are too stupid to know their own interests. In short, the goals of society have to be set by an elite. Technocrat and anti-technocrat often turn out to be elitist brothers under the skin.

Yet systems of goal formulation based on elitist premises are simply no longer "efficient." In the struggle to capture control of the forces of change, they are increasingly counter-productive. For under super-industrialism, democracy becomes not a political luxury, but a primal necessity.

Democratic political forms arose in the West not because a few geniuses willed them into being or because man showed an "unquenchable instinct for freedom." They arose because the historical pressure toward social differentiation and toward faster paced systems demanded sensitive social feedback. In complex, differentiated societies, vast amounts of information must flow at ever faster speeds between the formal organizations and subcultures that make up the whole, and between the layers and sub-structures within these.

Political democracy, by incorporating larger and larger numbers in social decision-making, facilitates feedback. And it is precisely this feedback that is essential to control. To assume control over accelerant change, we shall need still more advanced—and more democratic—feedback mechanisms.

The technocrat, however, still thinking in top-down terms, frequently makes plans without arranging for adequate and instantaneous feedback from the field, so that he seldom knows how well his plans are working. When he does arrange for feedback, what he usually asks for and gets is heavily economic, inadequately social, psychological or cultural. Worse yet, he makes these plans without sufficiently taking into account the fast-changing needs and wishes of those whose participation is needed to make them a success. He assumes the right to set social goals by himself or he accepts them blindly from some higher authority.

He fails to recognize that the faster pace of change demands—and creates—a new kind of information system in society: a loop, rather than a ladder. Information must pulse through this loop at accelerating speeds, with the output of one group becoming the input for many others, so that no group, however politically potent it may seem, can independently set goals for the whole.

As the number of social components multiplies, and change jolts and destabilizes the entire system, the power of subgroups to wreak havoc on the whole is tremendously amplified. There is, in the words of W. Ross Ashby, a brilliant cyberneticist, a mathematically provable law to the effect that "when a whole system is composed of a number of subsystems, the one that tends to dominate is the one that is *least* stable."

Another way of stating this is that, as the number of social components grows and change makes the whole system less stable, it becomes less and less possible to ignore the demands of political minorities—hippies, blacks, lower-middle-class Wallacites, school teachers, or the proverbial little old ladies in tennis shoes. In a slower-moving, industrial context, America could turn its back on the needs of its black minority; in the new, fast-paced cybernetic society, this minority can, by sabotage, strike, or a thousand other means, disrupt the entire system. As interdependency grows, smaller and smaller groups within society achieve greater and greater power for critical disruption. Moreover, as the rate of change speeds up, the length of time in which they can be ignored shrinks to near nothingness. Hence: "Freedom now!"

This suggests that the best way to deal with angry or recalcitrant minorities is to open the system further, bringing them into it as full partners, permitting them to participate in social goal-setting, rather than attempting to ostracize or isolate them. A Red China locked out of the United Nations and the larger international community, is far more likely to destabilize the world than one laced into the system. Young people forced into prolonged adolescence and deprived of the right to partake in social decision-making will grow more and more unstable until they threaten the overall system. In short, in politics, in industry, in education, goals set without the participation of those affected will be increasingly hard to execute. The continuation of top-down technocratic goal-setting procedures will lead to greater and greater social instability, less and less control over the forces of change; an ever greater danger of cataclysmic, man-destroying upheaval.

To master change, we shall therefore need both a clarification of important long-range social goals *and* a democratization of the way in which we arrive at them. And this means nothing less than the next political revolution in the techno-societies—a breath-taking affirmation of popular democracy.

The time has come for a dramatic reassessment of the directions of change, a reassessment made not by the politicians or the sociologists or the clergy or the elitist revolutionaries, not by technicians or college presidents, but by the people themselves. We need, quite literally, to "go to the people" with a question that is almost never asked of them: "What kind of a world do you want ten, twenty, or thirty years from now?" We need to initiate, in short, a continuing plebiscite on the future.

The moment is right for the formation in each of the high-technology nations of a movement for total self-review, a public self-examination aimed at broadening and defining in social, as well as merely economic, terms, the goals of "progress." On the edge of a new millennium, on the brink of a new stage of human development, we are racing blindly into the future. But where do we *want* to go?

What would happen if we actually tried to answer this question?

Imagine the historic drama, the power and evolutionary impact, if each of the high-technology nations literally set aside the next five years as a period of intense national self-appraisal; if at the end of five years it were to come forward with its own tentative agenda for the future, a program embracing not merely economic targets but, equally important, broad sets of social goals—if each nation, in effect, stated to the world what it wished to accomplish for its people and mankind in general during the remaining quarter century of the millennium.

Let us convene in each nation, in each city, in each neighborhood, democratic constituent assemblies charged with social stocktaking, charged with defining and assigning priorities to specific social goals for the remainder of the century.

Such "social future assemblies" might represent not merely geographical localities, but social units—industry, labor, the churches, the intellectual community, the arts, women, ethnic and religious groups, students, with organized representation for the unorganized as well. There are no sure-fire techniques for guaranteeing equal representation for all, or for eliciting the wishes of the poor, the inarticulate or the isolated. Yet once we recognize the need to include them, we shall find the ways. Indeed, the problem of participating in the definition of the future is not merely a problem of the poor, the inarticulate and the isolated. Highly paid executives, wealthy professionals, extremely articulate intellectuals and students—all at one time or another feel cut off from the power to influence the directions and pace of change. Wiring them into the system, making them a part of the guidance machinery of the society, is the most critical political task of the coming generation. Imagine the effect if at one level or another a place were provided where all those who will live in the future might voice their wishes about it. Imagine, in short, a massive, global exercise in anticipatory democracy.

Social future assemblies need not—and, given the rate of transience—cannot be anchored, permanent institutions. Instead, they might take the form of ad hoc groupings, perhaps called into being at regular intervals with different representatives participating each time. Today citizens are expected to serve on juries when needed. They give a few days or a few weeks of their time for this service, recognizing that the jury system is one of the guarantees of democracy, that, even though service may be inconvenient, someone must do the job. Social future assemblies could be organized along similar lines, with a constant stream of new participants brought together for short periods to serve as society's "consultants on the future."

Such grass roots organisms for expressing the will of large numbers of hitherto unconsulted people could become, in effect, the town halls of the future, in which millions help shape their own distant destinies.

To some, this appeal for a form of neo-populism will no doubt seem naive. Yet nothing is more naive than the notion that we can continue politically to run the society the way we do at present. To some, it will appear impractical. Yet nothing is more impractical than the attempt to impose a human future from above. What was naive under industrialism may be realistic under super-industrialism; what was practical may be absurd.

The encouraging fact is that we now have the potential for achieving tremendous breakthroughs in democratic decision-making if we make imaginative use of the new technologies, both "hard" and "soft," that bear on the problem. Thus, advanced telecommunications mean that participants in a social future assembly need not literally meet in a single room, but might simply be hooked into a communications net that straddles the globe. A meeting of scientists to discuss research goals for the future, or goals for environmental quality, could draw participants from many countries at once. An assembly of steelworkers, unionists and executives, convened to discuss goals for automation and for the improvement of work, itself, could link up participants from many mills, offices and warehouses, no matter how scattered or remote.

A meeting of the cultural community in New York or Paris— artists and gallery-goers, writers and readers, dramatists and audiences—to discuss appropriate long-range goals for the cultural development of the city could be shown, through the use of video recordings and other techniques, actual samples of the kinds of artistic production under discussion, architectural designs for new facilities, samples of new artistic media made available by technological advance, etc. What kind of cultural life should a great city of the future enjoy? What resources would be needed to realize a given set of goals?

All social future assemblies, in order to answer such questions, could and should be backed with technical staff to provide data on the social and economic costs of various goals, and to show the costs and benefits of proposed trade-offs, so that participants would be in a position to make reasonably informed choices, as it were, among alternative futures. In this way, each assembly might arrive, in the end, not merely in vaguely expressed, disjointed hopes, but at coherent statements of priorities for tomorrow— posed in terms that could be compared with the goal statements of other groups.

Nor need these social future assemblies be glorified "talkfests." We are fast developing games and simulation exercises whose chief beauty is that they help players clarify their own values. At the University of Illinois, in Project Plato, Charles Osgood is experimenting with computers and teaching machines that would involve large sectors of the public in planning imaginary, preferable futures through gaming.

At Cornell University, José Villegas, a professor in the Department of Design and Environmental Analysis, has begun constructing with the aid of black and white students, a variety of "ghetto games" which reveal to the players the consequences of various proposed courses of action and thus help them clarify goals. *Ghetto 1984* showed what would happen if the recommendations made by the Kerner riot commission—the U. S. National Advisory Commission on Civil Disorder—were actually to be adopted. It showed how the sequence in which these recommendations were enacted would affect their ultimate impact on the ghetto. It helped players, both black and white, to identify their shared goals as well as their unresolved conflicts. In games like *Peru 2000* and *Squatter City 2000*, players design communities for the future.

In *Lower East Side,* a game Villegas hopes actually to play in the Manhattan community that bears that name, players would not be students, but real-life residents of the community—poverty workers, middle-class whites, Puerto Rican small businessmen or youth, unemployed blacks, police, landlords and city officials.

In the spring of 1969, 50,000 high school students in Boston, in Philadelphia and in Syracuse, New York, participated in a televised game involving a simulated war in the Congo in 1975. While televised teams simulated the cabinets of Russia, Red China, and the United States, and struggled with the problems of diplomacy and policy planning, students and teachers watched, discussed, and offered advice via telephone to the central players.

Similar games, involving not tens, but hundreds of thousands, even millions of people, could be devised to help us formulate goals for the future. While televised players act out the role of high government officials attempting to deal with a crisis—an ecological disaster, for example—meetings of trade unions, women's clubs, church groups, student organizations and other constituencies might be held at which large numbers could view the program, reach collective judgments about the choices to be made, and forward those judgments to the primary players. Special switchboards and computers could pick up the advice or tabulate the yes-no votes and pass them on to the "decision-makers." Vast numbers of people could also participate from their own homes, thus opening the process to unorganized, otherwise non-participating millions. By imaginatively constructing such games, it becomes not only possible but practical to elicit futural goals from previously unconsulted masses.

Such techniques, still primitive today, will become fantastically more sophisticated in the years immediately ahead, providing us with a systematic way to collect and reconcile conflicting images of the preferable future, even from people unskilled in academic debate or parliamentary procedure.

It would be pollyanna-like to expect such town halls of the future to be tidy or harmonious affairs, or that they would be organized in the same way everywhere. In some places, social future assemblies might be called into being by community organizations, planning councils or government agencies. Elsewhere, they might be sponsored by trade unions, youth groups, or individual, future-oriented political leaders. In other places, churches, foundations or voluntary organizations might initiate the call. And in still other places, they might arise not from a formal convention call, but as a spontaneous response to crisis.

It would similarly be a mistake to think of the goals drawn up by these assemblies as constituting permanent, Platonic ideals, floating somewhere in a metaphysical never-never land. Rather, they must be seen as temporary direction-indicators, broad objectives good for a limited time only, and intended as advisory to the elected political representatives of the community or nation.

Nevertheless, such future-oriented, future-forming events could have enormous political impact. Indeed, they could turn out to be the salvation of the entire system of representative politics—a system now in dire crisis.

The mass of voters today are so far removed from contact with their elected representatives, the issues dealt with are so technical, that even well educated middle-class citizens feel hopelessly excluded from the goal-setting process. Because of the generalized acceleration of life, so much happens so fast between elections, that the politician grows increasingly less accountable to "the folks back home." What's more, these folks back home keep changing. In theory, the voter unhappy with the performance of his representative can vote against him the next time around. In practice, millions find even this impossible. Mass mobility removes them from the district, sometimes disenfranchising them altogether. Newcomers flood into the district. More and more, the politician finds himself addressing new faces. He may never be called to account for his performance—or for promises made to the last set of constituents.

Still more damaging to democracy is the time-bias of politics. The politician's time horizon usually extends no further than the next election. Congresses, diets, parliaments, city councils—legislative bodies in general—lack the time, the resources, or the organizational forms needed to think seriously about the long-term future. As for the citizen, the last thing he is ever consulted about are the larger, more distant, goals of his community, state or nation.

The voter may be polled about specific issues, never about the general shape of the preferable future. Indeed, nowhere in politics is there an institution through which an ordinary man can express his ideas about what the distant future ought to look, feel or taste like. He is never asked to think about this, and on the rare occasions when he does, there is no organized way for him to feed his ideas into the arena of politics. Cut off from the future, he becomes a political eunuch.

We are, for these and other reasons, rushing toward a fateful breakdown of the entire system of political representation. If legislatures are to survive at all, they will need new links with their constituencies, new ties with tomorrow. Social future assemblies could provide the means for reconnecting the legislator with his mass base, the present with the future.

Conducted at frequent and regular intervals, such assemblies could provide a more sensitive measure of popular will than any now available to us. The very act of calling such assemblies would attract into the flow of political life millions who now ignore it. By confronting men and women with the future, by asking them to think deeply about their own private destinies as well as our accelerating public trajectories, it would pose profound ethical issues.

Simply putting such questions to people would, by itself, prove liberating. The very process of social assessment would brace and cleanse a population weary to death of technical discussions of how to get someplace it is not sure it wants to go. Social future assemblies would help clarify the differences that increasingly divide us in our fast-fragmenting societies; they would, conversely, identify common social needs—potential grounds for temporary unities. In this way, they would bring various polities together in a fresh framework out of which new political mechanisms would inevitably spring.

Most important of all, however, social future assemblies would help shift the culture toward a more super-industrial time-bias. By focusing public attention for once on long-range goals rather than immediate programs alone, by asking people to choose a preferable future from among a range of alternative futures, these assemblies could dramatize the possibilities for humanizing the future—possibilities that all too many have already given up as lost. In so doing, social future assemblies could unleash powerful constructive forces—the forces of conscious evolution.

By now the accelerative thrust triggered by man has become the key to the entire evolutionary process on the planet. The rate and direction of the evolution of other species, their very survival, depends upon decisions made by man. Yet there is nothing inherent in the evolutionary process to guarantee man's own survival.

Throughout the past, as successive stages of social evolution unfolded, man's awareness followed rather than preceded the event. Because change was slow, he could adapt unconsciously, "organically." Today unconscious adaptation is no longer adequate. Faced with the power to alter the gene, to create new species, to populate the planets or depopulate the earth, man must now assume conscious control of evolution itself. Avoiding future shock as he rides the waves of change, he must master evolution, shaping tomorrow to human need. Instead of rising in revolt against it, he must, from this historic moment on, anticipate and design the future.

This, then, is the ultimate objective of social futurism, not merely the transcendence of technocracy and the substitution of more humane, more far-sighted, more democratic planning, but the subjection of the process of evolution itself to conscious human guidance. For this is the supreme instant, the turning point in history at which man either vanquishes the processes of change or vanishes, at which, from being the unconscious puppet of evolution he becomes either its victim or its master.

A challenge of such proportions demands of us a dramatically new, a more deeply rational response toward change. . . . In calling for the moderation and regulation of change, [I have] called for additional revolutionary changes. This is less paradoxical than it appears. Change is essential to man. . . . Change is life itself. But change rampant, change unguided and unrestrained, accelerated change overwhelming not only man's physical defenses but his decisional processes—such change is the enemy of life.

Our first and most pressing need, therefore, before we can begin to gently guide our evolutionary destiny, before we can build a humane future, is to halt the runaway acceleration that is subjecting multitudes to the threat of future shock while, at the very same moment, intensifying all the problems they must deal with—war, ecological incursions, racism, the obscene contrast between rich and poor, the revolt of the young, and the rise of a potentially deadly mass irrationalism.

*   *   *

These pages will have served their purpose if, in some measure, they help create the consciousness needed for man to undertake the control of change, the guidance of his evolution. For, by making imaginative use of change to channel change, we cannot only spare ourselves the trauma of future shock, we can reach out and humanize distant tomorrows.

Scientists

Scientists, according to C. P. Snow, "have the future in their bones." In some respects, they also have it in their hands. Here a group of science-trained or science-oriented writers and researchers tackles the problems and promise of forecasting. Diverse in national background, political ideology, and personal character, they are part of a transnational culture that views the world through certain shared lenses. At the outset, Arthur C. Clarke warns us to remember how terribly wrong even the most intelligent scientists can sometimes be. Other contributors tell us a bit about how forecasters work. Still others discuss the political and human implications of futurism.

Hazards of Prophecy

Arthur C. Clarke

Prophecy is always a risky business—a fact dramatically demonstrated in this selection. Arthur C. Clarke, the prolific author of novels, essays, and stories (one of which served as the basis for the movie *2001*), himself has made more than one mind-jogging forecast. In 1945, he predicted the use of satellites for radio and television communication. *Profiles of the Future,* from which this delightful piece is drawn, presents a series of startling assertions about our technological tomorrow.

The Failure of Nerve. Before one attempts to set up in business as a prophet, it is instructive to see what success others have made of this dangerous occupation—and it is even more instructive to see where they have failed.

With monotonous regularity, apparently competent men have laid down the law about what is technically possible or impossible—and have been proved utterly wrong, sometimes while the ink was scarcely dry from their pens. On careful analysis, it appears that these debacles fall into two classes, which I will call "failures of nerve" and "failures of imagination."

The failure of nerve seems to be the more common; it occurs when *even given all the relevant facts* the would-be prophet cannot see that they point to an inescapable conclusion. Some of these failures are so ludicrous as to be almost unbelievable, and would form an interesting subject for psychological analysis. "They said it couldn't be done" is a phrase that occurs throughout the history of invention; I do not know if anyone has ever looked into the reasons *why* "they" said so, often with quite unnecessary vehemence.

It is now impossible for us to recall the mental climate which existed when the first locomotives were being built, and critics gravely asserted that suffocation lay in wait for anyone who reached the awful speed of thirty miles an hour. It is equally difficult to believe that, only eighty years ago, the idea of the domestic electric light was pooh-poohed by all the "experts"— with the exception of a thirty-one-year-old American inventor named Thomas Alva Edison. When gas securities nose-dived in 1878 because Edison (already a formidable figure, with the phonograph and the carbon microphone to his credit) announced that he was working on the incandescent lamp, the British Parliament set up a committee to look into the matter. (Westminster can beat Washington hands down at this game.)

The distinguished witnesses reported, to the relief of the gas companies, that Edison's ideas were "good enough for our transatlantic friends . . . but unworthy of the attention of practical or scientific men." And Sir William Preece, engineer-in-chief of the British Post Office, roundly declared that "Subdivision of the electric light is an absolute *ignis fatuus.*" One feels that the fatuousness was not in the *ignis.*

The scientific absurdity being pilloried, be it noted, is not some wild-and-woolly dream like perpetual motion, but the humble little electric light bulb, which three generations of men have taken for granted, except when it burns out and leaves them in the dark. Yet although in this matter Edison saw far beyond his contemporaries, he too in later life was guilty of the same shortsightedness that afflicted Preece, for he opposed the introduction of alternating current.

The most famous, and perhaps the most instructive, failures of nerve have occurred in the fields of aero- and astronautics. At the beginning of the twentieth century, scientists were almost unanimous in declaring that heavier-than-air flight was impossible, and that anyone who attempted to build airplanes was a fool. The great American astronomer, Simon Newcomb, wrote a celebrated essay which concluded:

The demonstration that no possible combination of known substances, known forms of machinery and known forms of force, can be united in a practical machine by which man shall fly long distances through the air, seems to the writer as complete as it is possible for the demonstration of any physical fact to be.

Oddly enough, Newcomb was sufficiently broad-minded to admit that some wholly new discovery—he mentioned the neutralization of gravity—might make flight practical. One cannot, therefore, accuse him of lacking imagination; his error was in attempting to marshal the facts of aerodynamics when he did not understand that science. His failure of nerve lay in not realizing that the means of flight were already at hand.

For Newcomb's article received wide publicity at just about the time that the Wright brothers, not having a suitable antigravity device in their bicycle shop, were mounting a gasoline engine on wings. When news of their success reached the astronomer, he was only momentarily taken back. Flying machines *might* be a marginal possibility, he conceded—but they were certainly of no practical importance, for it was quite out of the question that they could carry the extra weight of a passenger as well as that of a pilot.

Such refusal to face facts which now seem obvious has continued throughout the history of aviation. Let me quote another astronomer, William H. Pickering, straightening out the uninformed public a few years *after* the first airplanes had started to fly.

The popular mind often pictures gigantic flying machines speeding across the Atlantic and carrying innumerable passengers in a way analogous to our modern steamships. . . . It seems safe to say that such ideas must be wholly visionary, and even if a machine could get across with one or two passengers the expense would be prohibitive to any but the capitalist who could own his own yacht.

Another popular fallacy is to expect enormous speed to be obtained. It must be remembered that the resistance of the air increases as the square of the speed and the work as the cube. . . . If with 30 h.p. we can now attain a speed of 40 m.p.h., then in order to reach a speed of 100 m.p.h. we must use a motor capable of 470 h.p. . . . it is clear that with our present devices there is no hope of competing for racing speed with either our locomotives or our automobiles.

It so happens that most of his fellow astronomers considered Pickering far *too imaginative;* he was prone to see vegetation—and even evidence for insect life—on the Moon. I am glad to say that by the time he died in 1938 at the ripe age of eighty, Professor Pickering had seen airplanes traveling at 400 m.p.h., and carrying considerably more than "one or two" passengers.

Closer to the present, the opening of the space age has produced a mass vindication (and refutation) of prophecies on a scale and at a speed never before witnessed. Having taken some part in this myself, and being no more immune than the next man to the pleasures of saying, "I told you so," I would like to recall a few of the statements about space flight that have been made by prominent scientists in the past. It is necessary for *someone* to do this, and to jog the remarkably selective memories of the pessimists. The speed with which those who once declaimed, "It's impossible" can switch to, "I said it could be done all the time" is really astounding.

As far as the general public is concerned, the idea of space flight as a serious possibility first appeared on the horizon in the 1920's, largely as a result of newspaper reports of the work of the American Robert Goddard and the Rumanian Hermann Oberth. (The much earlier studies of Tsiolkovsky in Russia then being almost unknown outside his own country.) When the ideas of Goddard and Oberth, usually distorted by the press, filtered through to the scientific world, they were received with hoots of derision. For a sample of the kind of criticism the pioneers of astronautics had to face, I present this masterpiece from a paper published by one

Professor A. W. Bickerton, in 1926. It should be read carefully, for as an example of the cocksure thinking of the time it would be very hard to beat.

This foolish idea of shooting at the moon is an example of the absurd length to which vicious specialisation will carry scientists working in thought-tight compartments. Let us critically examine the proposal. For a projectile entirely to escape the gravitation of the earth, it needs a velocity of 7 miles a second. The thermal energy of a gramme at this speed is 15,180 calories. . . . The energy of our most violent explosive—nitro-glycerine—is less than 1,500 calories per gramme. Consequently, even had the explosive nothing to carry, it has only one-tenth of the energy necessary to escape the earth. . . . Hence the proposition appears to be basically impossible. . . .

Indignant readers in the Colombo public library pointed angrily to the **Silence** notices when I discovered this little gem. It is worth examining it in some detail to see just where "vicious specialisation," if one may coin a phrase, led the professor so badly astray.

His first error lies in the sentence: "The energy of our most violent explosive—nitro-glycerine . . ." One would have thought it obvious that *energy,* not violence, is what we want from a rocket fuel; and as a matter of fact nitroglycerin and similar explosives contain much less energy, weight for weight, than such mixtures as kerosene and liquid oxygen. This had been carefully pointed out by Tsiolkovsky and Goddard years before.

Bickerton's second error is much more culpable. What of it, if nitroglycerin has only a tenth of the energy necessary to escape from the Earth? That merely means that you have to use at least ten pounds of nitroglycerin to launch a single pound of payload.[1]

For the fuel itself has not got to escape from Earth; it can all be burned quite close to our planet, and as long as it imparts its energy to the payload, this is all that matters. When Lunik II lifted thirty-three years after Professor Bickerton said it was impossible, most of its several hundred tons of kerosene and liquid oxygen never got very far from Russia—but the half-ton payload reached the Mare Imbrium.

As a comment on the above, I might add that Professor Bickerton, who was an active popularizer of science, numbered among his published books one with the title *Perils of a Pioneer.* Of the perils that all pioneers must face, few are more disheartening than the Bickertons.

Right through the 1930's and 1940's, eminent scientists continued to deride the rocket pioneers—when they bothered to notice them at all. Anyone who has access to a good college library can find, preserved for posterity in the dignified pages of the January 1941 *Philosophical Magazine,* an example that makes a worthy mate to the one I have just quoted.

It is a paper by the distinguished Canadian astronomer Professor J. W. Campbell, of the University of Alberta, entitled "Rocket Flight to the Moon." Opening with a quotation from a 1938 Edmonton paper to the effect that "rocket flight to the Moon now seems less remote than television appeared a hundred years ago," the professor then looks into the subject mathematically. After several pages of analysis, he arrives at the conclusion that it would require *a million tons* of take-off weight to carry *one pound* of payload on the round trip.

The correct figure, for today's primitive fuels and technologies, is very roughly one ton per pound—a depressing ratio, but hardly as bad as that calculated by the professor. Yet his mathematics was impeccable; so what went wrong?

Merely his initial assumptions, which were hopelessly unrealistic. He chose a path for the rocket which was fantastically extravagant in energy, and he assumed the use of an acceleration so low that most of the fuel would be wasted at low altitudes, fighting the Earth's gravitational field. It was as if he had calculated the performance of an automobile—when the brakes were on. No wonder that he concluded: "While it is always dangerous to make a negative prediction, it would appear that the statement that rocket flight to the moon does not seem so remote as television did less than one hundred years ago is over-optimistic." I am sure that when the *Philosophical Magazine* subscribers read those words, back in 1941, many of them thought, "Well, *that* should put those crazy rocket men in their place!"

Yet the correct results had been published by Tsiolkovsky, Oberth and Goddard years before; though the work of the first two would have been very hard to consult at the time, Goddard's paper "A Method of Reaching Extreme Altitudes" was already a classic and had been issued by that scarcely obscure body, the

Smithsonian Institution. If Professor Campbell had only consulted it (or indeed *any* competent writer on the subject—there were some, even in 1941) he would not have misled his readers and himself.

The lesson to be learned from these examples is one that can never be repeated too often, and is one that is seldom understood by laymen—who have an almost superstitious awe of mathematics. But mathematics is only a tool, though an immensely powerful one. No equations, however impressive and complex, can arrive at the truth if the initial assumptions are incorrect. It is really quite amazing by what margins competent but conservative scientists and engineers can miss the mark, when they start with the preconceived idea that what they are investigating is impossible. When this happens, the most well-informed men become blinded by their prejudices and are unable to see what lies directly ahead of them. What is even more incredible, they refuse to learn from experience and will continue to make the same mistake over and over again.

Some of my best friends are astronomers, and I am sorry to keep throwing stones at them—but they do seem to have an appalling record as prophets. If you still doubt this, let me tell a story so ironic that you might well accuse me of making it up. But I am not that much of a cynic; the facts are on file for anyone to check.

Back in the dark ages of 1935, the founder of the British Interplanetary Society, P. E. Cleator, was rash enough to write the first book on astronautics published in England. His *Rockets through Space* gave an (incidentally highly entertaining) account of the experiments that had been carried out by the German and American rocket pioneers, and their plans for such commonplaces of today as giant multi-stage boosters and satellites. Rather surprisingly, the staid scientific journal *Nature* reviewed the book in its issue for March 14, 1936, and summed up as follows:

It must be said at once that the whole procedure sketched in the present volume presents difficulties of so fundamental a nature that we are forced to dismiss the notion as essentially impracticable, in spite of the author's insistent appeal to put aside prejudice and to recollect the supposed impossibility of heavier-than-air flight before it was actually accomplished. An analogy such as this may be misleading, and we believe it to be so in this case. . . .

Well, the whole world now knows just how misleading this analogy was, though the reviewer, identified only by the unusual initials R.v.d.R.W. was of course fully entitled to his opinion.

Just twenty years later—*after* President Eisenhower had announced the United States satellite program—a new Astronomer Royal arrived in England to take up his appointment. The press asked him to give his views on space flight, and after two decades Dr. Richard van der Riet Woolley had seen no reason to change his mind. "Space travel," he snorted, "is utter bilge."

The newspapers did not allow him to forget this, when Sputnik I went up the very next year. And now—irony piled upon irony—Dr. Woolley is, by virtue of his position as Astronomer Royal, a leading member of the committee advising the British government on space research. The feelings of those who have been trying, for a generation, to get the United Kingdom interested in space can well be imagined.[2]

Even those who suggested that rockets might be used for more modest, though much more reprehensible, purposes were overruled by the scientific authorities—except in Germany and Russia.

When the existence of the 200-mile-range V-2 was disclosed to an astonished world, there was considerable speculation about intercontinental missiles. This was firmly squashed by Dr. Vannevar Bush, the civilian general of the United States scientific war effort, in evidence before a Senate committee on December 3, 1945. Listen:

There has been a great deal said about a 3,000 miles high-angle rocket. In my opinion such a thing is impossible for many years. The people who have been writing these things that annoy me, have been talking about a 3,000 mile high-angle rocket shot from one continent to another, carrying an atomic bomb and so directed as to be a precise weapon which would land exactly on a certain target, such as a city.

I say, technically, I don't think anyone in the world knows how to do such a thing, and I feel confident that it will not be done for a very long period of time to come. . . . I think we can leave that out of our thinking. I wish the American public would leave that out of their thinking.

A few months earlier (in May 1945) Prime Minister Churchill's scientific advisor Lord Cherwell had expressed similar views in a House of Lords debate. This was only to be expected, for Cherwell was an extremely conservative and opinionated scientist who had advised the government that the V-2 itself was only a propaganda rumor.[3]

In the May 1945 debate on defense, Lord Cherwell impressed his peers by a dazzling display of mental arithmetic from which he correctly concluded that a very long-range rocket must consist of more than 90 per cent fuel, and thus would have a negligible payload. The conclusion he let his listeners draw from this was that such a device would be wholly impracticable.

That was true enough in the spring of 1945, but it was no longer true in the summer. One astonishing feature of the House of Lords debate is the casual way in which much-too-well-informed peers used the words "atomic bomb," at a time when this was the best-kept secret of the war. (The Alamogordo test was still two months in the future!) Security must have been horrified, and Lord Cherwell—who of course knew all about the Manhattan Project—was quite justified in telling his inquisitive colleagues not to believe everything they heard, even though in this case it happened to be perfectly true.

When Dr. Bush spoke to the Senate committee in December of the same year, the only important secret about the atomic bomb was that it weighed five tons. Anyone could then work out in his head, as Lord Cherwell had done, that a rocket to deliver it across intercontinental ranges would have to weigh about 200 tons—as against the mere 14 tons of the then awe-inspiring V-2.

The outcome was the greatest failure of nerve in all history, which changed the future of the world—indeed, of many worlds. Faced with the same facts and the same calculations, American and Russian technology took two separate roads. The Pentagon—accountable to the taxpayer—virtually abandoned long-range rockets for almost half a decade, until the development of thermonuclear bombs made it possible to build warheads five times lighter yet several hundred times more powerful than the low-powered and now obsolete device that was dropped on Hiroshima.

The Russians had no such inhibitions. Faced with the need for a 200-ton rocket, they went right ahead and built it. By the time it was perfected, it was no longer required for military purposes, for Soviet physicists had bypassed the United States' billion-dollar tritium bomb cul-de-sac and gone straight to the far cheaper lithium bomb. Having backed the wrong horse in rocketry, the Russians then entered it for a much more important event—and won the race into space.

Of the many lessons to be drawn from this slice of recent history, the one that I wish to emphasize is this. Anything that is theoretically possible will be achieved in practice, no matter what the technical difficulties, if it is desired greatly enough. It is no argument against any project to say: "The idea's fantastic!" Most of the things that have happened in the last fifty years have been fantastic, and it is only by assuming that they will continue to be so that we have any hope of anticipating the future.

To do this—to avoid that failure of nerve for which history exacts so merciless a penalty—we must have the courage to follow all technical extrapolations to their logical conclusion. Yet even this is not enough, as I shall now demonstrate. To predict the future we need logic; but we also need faith and imagination which can sometimes defy logic itself.

The Failure of Imagination. [Until now I have] suggested that many of the negative statements about scientific possibilities, and the gross failures of past prophets to predict what lay immediately ahead of them, could be described as failures of nerve. All the basic facts of aeronautics were available—in the writings of Cayley, Stringfellow, Chanute, and others—when Simon Newcomb "proved" that flight was impossible. He simply lacked the courage to face those facts. All the fundamental equations and principles of space travel had been worked out by Tsiolkovsky, Goddard, and Oberth for years—often decades—when distinguished scientists were making fun of would-be astronauts. Here again, the failure to appreciate the facts was not so much intellectual as moral. The critics did not have the courage that their scientific convictions should have given them; they could not believe the truth even when it had been spelled out before their eyes, in their own language of mathematics. We all know this type of cowardice, because at some time or other we all exhibit it.

The second kind of prophetic failure is less blameworthy, and more interesting. It arises when all the available facts are appreciated *and* marshaled correctly—but when the really vital facts are still undiscovered, and the possibility of their existence is not admitted.

A famous example of this is provided by the philosopher Auguste Comte, who in his *Cours de Philosophie Positive* (1835) attempted to define the limits within which scientific knowledge must lie. In his chapter on astronomy (Book 2, Chapter 1) he wrote these words concerning the heavenly bodies:

We see how we may determine their forms, their distances, their bulk, their motions, but we can never know anything of their chemical or mineralogical structure; and much less, that of organised beings living on their surface. . . . We must keep carefully apart the idea of the solar system and that of the universe, and be always assured that our only true interest is in the former. Within this boundary alone is astronomy the supreme and positive science that we have determined it to be . . . the stars serve us scientifically only as providing positions with which we may compare the interior movements of our system.

In other words, Comte decided that the stars could never be more than celestial reference points, of no intrinsic concern to the astronomer. Only in the case of the planets could we hope for any definite knowledge, and even that knowledge would be limited to geometry and dynamics. Comte would probably have decided that such a science as "astrophysics" was *a priori* impossible.

Yet within half a century of his death, almost the whole of astronomy *was* astrophysics, and very few professional astronomers had much interest in the planets. Comte's assertion had been utterly refuted by the invention of the spectroscope, which not only revealed the "chemical structure" of the heavenly bodies but has now told us far more about the distant stars than we know of our planetary neighbors.

Comte cannot be blamed for not imagining the spectroscope; *no one* could have imagined it, or the still more sophisticated instruments that have now joined it in the astronomer's armory. But he provides a warning that should always be borne in mind; even things that are undoubtedly impossible with existing or foreseeable techniques may prove to be easy as a result of new scientific breakthroughs. From their very nature, these breakthroughs can never be anticipated; but they have enabled us to bypass so many insuperable obstacles in the past that no picture of the future can hope to be valid if it ignores them.

Another celebrated failure of imagination was that persisted in by Lord Rutherford, who more than any other man laid bare the internal structure of the atom. Rutherford frequently made fun of those sensation mongers who predicted that we would one day be able to harness the energy locked up in matter. Yet only five years after his death in 1937, the first chain reaction was started in Chicago. What Rutherford, for all his wonderful insight, had failed to take into account was that a nuclear reaction might be discovered that would release more energy than that required to start it. To liberate the energy of matter, what was wanted was a nuclear "fire" analogous to chemical combustion, and the fission of uranium provided this. Once that was discovered, the harnessing of atomic energy was inevitable, though without the pressures of war it might well have taken the better part of a century.

The example of Lord Rutherford demonstrates that it is not the man who knows most about a subject, and is the acknowledged master of his field, who can give the most reliable pointers to its future. Too great a burden of knowledge can clog the wheels of imagination; I have tried to embody this fact of observation in Clarke's Law, which may be formulated as follows:

When a distinguished but elderly scientist states that something is possible, he is almost certainly right. When he states that something is impossible, he is very probably wrong.

Perhaps the adjective "elderly" requires definition. In physics, mathematics, and astronautics it means over thirty; in the other disciplines, senile decay is sometimes postponed to the forties. There are, of course, glorious exceptions; but as every researcher just out of college knows, scientists of over fifty are good for nothing but board meetings, and should at all costs be kept out of the laboratory!

Too much imagination is much rarer than too little; when it occurs, it usually involves its unfortunate possessor in frustration and failure—unless he is sensible enough merely to write about his ideas, and not to attempt their realization. In the first category we find all the science-fiction authors, historians of the future, creators of utopias—and the two Bacons, Roger and Francis.

Friar Roger (c. 1214–1292) imagined optical instruments and mechanically propelled boats and flying machines—devices far beyond the existing or even foreseeable technology of his time. It is hard to believe that these words were written in the thirteenth century:

Instruments may be made by which the largest ships, with only one man guiding them, will be carried with greater velocity than if they were full of sailors. Chariots may be constructed that will move with incredible rapidity without the help of animals. Instruments of flying may be formed in which a man, sitting at his ease and meditating in any subject, may beat the air with his artificial wings after the manner of birds . . . as also machines which will enable men to walk at the bottom of the seas. . . .

This passage is a triumph of imagination over hard fact. Everything in it has come true, yet at the time it was written it was more an act of faith than of logic. It is probable that all long-range prediction, if it is to be accurate, must be of this nature. The real future is not *logically* foreseeable.

A splendid example of a man whose imagination ran ahead of his age was the English mathematician Charles Babbage (1792–1871). As long ago as 1819, Babbage had worked out the principles underlying automatic computing machines. He realized that all mathematical calculations could be broken down into a series of step-by-step operations that could, in theory, be carried out by a machine. With the aid of a government grant which eventually totaled £17,000—a very substantial sum of money in the 1820's—he started to build his "analytical engine."

Though he devoted the rest of his life, and much of his private fortune, to the project, Babbage was unable to complete the machine. What defeated him was the fact that precision engineering of the standard he needed to build his cogs and gears simply did not exist at the time. By his efforts he helped to create the machine-tool industry—so that in the long run the government got back very much more than its £17,000—and today it would be a perfectly straightforward matter to complete Babbage's computer, which now stands as one of the most fascinating exhibits in the London Science Museum. In his own lifetime, however, Babbage was only able to demonstrate the operation of a relatively small portion of the complete machine. A dozen years after his death, his biographer wrote: "This extraordinary monument of theoretical genius accordingly remains, and doubtless will forever remain, a theoretical possibility."

There is not much left of that "doubtless" today. At this moment there are thousands of computers working on the principles that Babbage clearly outlined more than a century ago—but with a range and a speed of which he could never have dreamed. For what makes the case of Charles Babbage so interesting, and so pathetic, is that he was not one but *two* technological revolutions ahead of his time. Had the precision-tool industry existed in 1820, he could have built his "analytical engine" and it would have worked, much faster than a human computer, but very slowly by the standards of today. For it would have been geared—literally— to the speed with which cogs and shafts and cams and ratchets can operate.

Automatic calculating machines could not come into their own until electronics made possible speeds of operation thousands and millions of times swifter than could be achieved with purely mechanical devices. This level of technology was reached in the 1940's, and Babbage was then promptly vindicated. His failure was not one of imagination: it lay in being born a hundred years too soon.

One can only prepare for the unpredictable by trying to keep an open and unprejudiced mind—a feat which is extremely difficult to achieve, even with the best will in the world. Indeed, a completely open mind would be an empty one, and freedom from all prejudices and preconceptions is an unattainable ideal. Yet there is one form of mental exercise that can provide good basic training for would-be prophets: Anyone who wishes to cope with the future should travel back in imagination a single lifetime—say to 1900—and ask himself just how much of today's technology would be, not merely incredible, but *incomprehensible* to the keenest scientific brains of that time.

1900 is a good round date to choose because it was just about then that all hell started to break loose in science. As James B. Conant has put it:

Somewhere about 1900 science took a *totally* unexpected turn. There had previously been several revolutionary theories and more than one epoch-making discovery in the history of science, but what occurred between 1900 and, say, 1930 was something different; it was a failure of a general prediction about what might be confidently expected from experimentation.

P. W. Bridgman has put it even more strongly:

The physicist has passed through an intellectual crisis forced by the discovery of experimental facts of a sort which he had not previously envisaged, and which he would not even have thought possible.

The collapse of "classical" science actually began with Roentgen's discovery of X-rays in 1895; here was the first clear indication, in a form that everyone could appreciate, that the common-sense picture of the universe was not sensible after all. X-rays —the very name reflects the bafflement of scientists and laymen alike—could travel through solid matter, like light through a sheet of glass. No one had ever imagined or predicted such a thing; that one would be able to peer into the interior of the human body—and thereby revolutionize medicine and surgery—was something that the most daring prophet had never suggested.

The discovery of X-rays was the first great breakthrough into the realms where no human mind had ever ventured before. Yet it gave scarcely a hint of still more astonishing developments to come —radioactivity, the internal structure of the atom, relativity, the quantum theory, the uncertainty principle. . . .

As a result of this, the inventions and technical devices of our modern world can be divided into two sharply defined classes. On the one hand there are those machines whose working would have been fully understood by any of the great thinkers of the past; on the other, there are those that would be utterly baffling to the finest minds of antiquity. And not merely of antiquity; there are devices now coming into use that might well have driven Edison or Marconi insane had they tried to fathom their operation.

Let me give some examples to emphasize this point. If you showed a modern diesel engine, an automobile, a steam turbine, or a helicopter to Benjamin Franklin, Galileo, Leonardo da Vinci, and Archimedes—a list spanning two thousand years of time—not one of them would have any difficulty in understanding how these machines worked. Leonardo, in fact, would recognize several from his notebooks. All four men would be astonished at the materials and the workmanship, which would have seemed magical in its precision, but once they had got over that surprise they would feel quite at home—as long as they did not delve too deeply into the auxiliary control and electrical systems.

But now suppose that they were confronted by a television set, an electronic computer, a nuclear reactor, a radar installation. Quite apart from the complexity of these devices, the individual elements of which they are composed would be incomprehensible to any man born before this century. Whatever his degree of education or intelligence, he would not possess the mental framework that could accommodate electron beams, transistors, atomic fission, wave guides and cathode-ray tubes.

The difficulty, let me repeat, is not one of complexity; some of the simplest modern devices would be the most difficult to explain. A particularly good example is given by the atomic bomb (at least, the early models). What could be simpler than banging two lumps of metal together? Yet how could one explain to Archimedes that the result could be more devastation than that produced by all the wars between the Trojans and the Greeks?

Suppose you went to any scientist up to the late nineteenth century and told him: "Here are two pieces of a substance called uranium 235. If you hold them apart, nothing will happen. But if you bring them together suddenly, you will liberate as much energy as you could obtain from burning ten thousand tons of coal." No matter how farsighted and imaginative he might be, your pre-twentieth century scientist would have said: "What utter nonsense! That's magic, not science. Such things can't happen in the real world." Around 1890, when the foundations of physics and thermodynamics had (it seemed) been securely laid, he could have told you exactly why it was nonsense.

"Energy cannot be created out of nowhere," he might have said. "It has to come from chemical reactions, electrical batteries, coiled springs, compressed gas, spinning flywheels, or some other clearly defined source. All such sources are ruled out in this case —and even if they were not, the energy output you mention is absurd. Why, it is more than a *million* times that available from the most powerful chemical reaction!"

The fascinating thing about this particular example is that, even when the existence of atomic energy was fully appreciated—say right up to 1940—almost all scientists would still have laughed at the idea of liberating it by bringing pieces of metal together. Those who believed that the energy of the nucleus ever could be released almost certainly pictured complicated electrical devices—"atom smashers" and so forth—doing the job. (In the long run, this will probably be the case; it seems that we will need such machines to fuse hydrogen nuclei on the industrial scale. But once again, who knows?)

The wholly unexpected discovery of uranium fission in 1939 made possible such absurdly simple (in principle, if not in practice) devices as the atomic bomb and the nuclear chain reactor. No scientist could ever have predicted them; if he had, all his colleagues would have laughed at him.

It is highly instructive, and stimulating to the imagination, to make a list of the inventions and discoveries that have been anticipated—and those that have not. Here is my attempt to do so.

All the items on the left have already been achieved or discovered, and all have an element of the unexpected or the downright astonishing about them. To the best of my knowledge, not one was foreseen very much in advance of the moment of revelation.

On the right, however, are concepts that have been around for hundreds or thousands of years. Some have been achieved; others will be achieved; others may be impossible. But which?

The Unexpected	The Expected
X-rays	automobiles
nuclear energy	flying machines
radio, TV	steam engines
electronics	submarines
photography	spaceships
sound recording	telephones
quantum mechanics	robots
relativity	death rays
transistors	transmutation
masers; lasers	artificial life
superconductors; superfluids	immortality
atomic clocks; Mössbauer effect	invisibility
determining composition of	levitation
celestial bodies	teleportation
dating the past (Carbon 14, etc.)	communication with dead
detecting invisible planets	observing the past, the future
the ionosphere; Van Allen Belts	telepathy

The right-hand list is deliberately provocative; it includes sheer fantasy as well as serious scientific speculation. But the only way of discovering the limits of the possible is to venture a little way past them into the impossible. . . . this is exactly what I hope to do; yet I am very much afraid that from time to time I too will exhibit failure of imagination if not failure of nerve. For as I glance down the left-hand column I am aware of a few items which, only ten years ago, I would have thought were impossible. . . .

Prospects of Technological Progress

Olaf Helmer

A mathematician-philosopher, Olaf Helmer is best known as the codeveloper (with Norman Dalkey) of the so-called "Delphi" method of forecasting. He also helped found, and is research director of, the Institute for the Future, one of the world's leading futurist "think tanks." Here, in nontechnical language, he makes a series of highly optimistic suggestions about the way things may turn out. Are they too optimistic?

Much has already been said about the prospects of technological progress during the remainder of this century, and I have little to add to these prognostications. I would like to use this opportunity, not primarily to make technological forecasts, but to discuss the role that the forecasting of technological developments plays in shaping the future of our society. In presenting some specific forecasts for the year 2000, I would like merely to provide a certain amount of substantive illustrative material for such a discussion.

The year 2000 . . . is only one third of a century away from us. But the pace of change in our time, due to scientific and technological advances, is greater than it used to be and is still accelerating. Consequently, the world of 2000 will be far less like our present world than our present world is like that of a third of a century ago. Thus a high degree of uncertainty has to attach to many things we may wish to say about the year 2000.

Nevertheless, quite a few statements can be made with some confidence about that world of the future. Let me give a few examples.

It is virtually certain that:

The world population will be over 5 billion.

The rate of population increase will have begun to decelerate, due to the widespread acceptance of cheap and effective means of fertility control.

Absolute food production will be substantially higher than it is today, aided primarily by large-scale desalination of sea water.

The world GNP will be more than 3 times and possibly 4 times what it is today, resulting probably in an approximate doubling and possibly in a tripling of per-capita GNP.

People will largely live in urban complexes, surrounded by numerous automata. In particular, there will be central data banks and libraries with fully automated access, a credit card economy in which cash transactions will be virtually eliminated, highly sophisticated teaching machines will be in wide use, portable video telephones will facilitate communication among persons everywhere, and this process will be further enhanced by the availability of automated translation from one language to another.

Personality-affecting drugs will be as widely used and accepted as alcohol beverages are today.

The life span of many people will be extended through the common practice of replacing worn or diseased organs by implanting artificial plastic and electronic organs.

A permanent colony will exist on the Moon, and men will almost certainly have landed on Mars.

Not quite so certain as the statements just made, but still very probable, are the following:

Controlled thermonuclear power will be economically competitive with other sources of power.

It will be possible to control the weather regionally to a large extent.

Ocean mining on a large scale will be in progress.

Artificial life will have been created in the test tube.

Immunization against all bacterial and viral diseases will be available.

Highly intelligent machines will exist that will act as effective collaborators of scientists and engineers.

Next let me list a few developments that are less probable but still have a good chance of being part of the world of 2000:

Large-scale ocean farming may be practiced.

Our highway transportation may be fully automated.

Cooperation between man and machine may have progressed to the point of actual symbiosis, in the sense of enabling man to extend his intelligence by direct electromechanical interaction between his brain and a computing machine.

We may have learned, through molecular engineering, to control hereditary defects in man, to control the aging process, and to induce the artificial growth of new limbs and organs. We may also have drugs available that raise a person's level of intelligence.

In space, we may be mining ores and manufacturing propellents on the Moon, we may have established a permanent Mars base, and we may have landed on Jupiter's moons.

This sample of forecasts, I think, will provide a sufficient substantive background for the following discussion, which will be focusing upon three considerations: (i) the changed role that forecasts play in our thinking about the future of our society, (ii) some of the specific tasks that lie ahead in organizing a systematic analysis of the future, and (iii) the prospects of accomplishing these tasks in the decades before us.

The purpose of long-range forecasts generally is not just to satisfy mankind's persistent curiosity about its future destiny, but

. . . to inform decision-makers in both the public and private sectors of a nation of potential future dangers that must be avoided and of potential future opportunities that must be seized.

This new, pragmatic, view of the value of forecasting is of relatively recent origin. It reflects a wholly new attitude toward the future among planners and researchers. The fatalistic view of the future as unforeseeable but unique and hence inevitable has been abandoned. We see instead a growing awareness that there is a whole spectrum of possible futures, with varying degrees of probability, and that through proper planning we may exert considerable influence over these probabilities. Although our control over the future, which we might thus aspire to exercise, is merely marginal, we have learned from the economists that small marginal adjustments in planning the domestic affairs of a nation can make all the difference between misery and contentedness for large segments of its people.

This newly acquired realization of our power to affect our own destiny through deliberate long-range planning brings with it a new social responsibility for the scientist and analyst. It falls upon him to provide the kind of comprehensive analysis of the future on which the political process of influencing the future must rest.

A responsible analysis of the future calls for a program with these three components:

1. *A survey of alternatives,* that is, a full exploration of potential future developments, together with estimates of their a priori probabilities; and a description of the major alternatives with regard to the future state of the world in terms of coherent conglomerations of such developments.
2. *An analysis of preferences,* that is, an explication of the extent to which the pursuit of any particular alternative state would serve the public interest. In this context, "the public interest" may well have to be viewed from several standpoints, namely, as seen by the executive branch of its government, and—in some sense—as seen by the world community. This analysis of differential preferences should in no way prejudge the issues. Rather, by analyzing the moral implications of professed attitudes and the degree to which the probable consequences of contemplated policies would comply with them, it should enhance the rationality of the democratic decision-making process.
3. *Constructive policy research:* Having aided the process of selecting the more desirable among the possible futures of the world, the final

and most demanding step is that of devising the means of attaining these futures, or at least of raising their probabilities of occurrence as much as possible through appropriate policies and programs.

These then, summed up briefly, are the obvious desiderata: To find out about the possible futures that lie ahead; to single out the more desirable ones among them; and to invent the instrumentalities for their deliberate pursuit.

An organized effort to enhance our capability, as analysts, to deal with these three tasks is prerequisite to putting the process of shaping the future of our society on a more rational foundation. It constitutes the basis for the application of social technology, that is, for the invention of social institutions and the design of social policies that promise to fulfill our reasonable aspirations. And it is on the prospects of socio-technological progress, in this sense, that I want to concentrate in the remainder of this paper.

The prospects of substantial socio-technological progress during the third third of this century, in my opinion, are very high. I base this optimism on four clearly recognizable trends.

One is the ongoing, explosively increasing, effort devoted to scientific research generally. Judging by the trend during the second third of the century and extrapolating very conservatively, the world's scientific manpower in the year 2000 is likely to be at least five times what it is today. In addition, because of the availability of more sophisticated instruments and, above all, of more powerful computing machines, the productivity of the individual researcher is apt to rise at the very least by a factor of two. Consequently we may expect the total rate of scientific productivity to grow at least tenfold by the end of the century. The increased understanding of the world we live in that is implied by this development is the first reason for my optimism regarding socio-technological progress.

The second reason, already partly implied by the first, is the second computer revolution, which is already well under way. It took just twenty years for the first computer revolution to be completed, from the mid-forties to the mid-sixties, during which time the computer grew up from being a bookkeeping device to becoming a highly versatile data processor and research tool.

During that period the size and the cost of electronic computer components have gone down by factors of 100 and 100,000 respectively, and their speed has gone up by a factor of 100,000.

While these trends will continue for some time and, together with long-distance time-sharing arrangements, will account during the next decade for a continued annual doubling of the amount of computer power in the world, the second computer revolution will add a significantly new flavor to this resource of ours. It will consist of the amalgamation of two separate trends, which in combination promise to have a powerful impact on planning processes generally. They are (i) the relative automation of the computer, in the sense of doing away with many of the cumbersome aspects of computer programming and thereby facilitating direct communication between the individual researcher and the computer; and (ii) the invention of numerous highly versatile display devices, coupled directly to the computer, that permit a designer to construct visual and, when necessary, moving images of his ideas as he develops them. These two trends, which are well under way, will constitute the beginning of a true symbiosis between man and machine, where in a very real sense man's intelligence will be enhanced through collaboration with a computer.

My third reason for taking a bright view of future progress in social technology is that there is yet another, subtle, revolution in the making, namely a reorientation among social scientists toward policy-related research. Instead of continuing the relatively futile endeavor to emulate the physical *sciences,* researchers in the social-science area are realizing that the time has come to emulate physical *technology.* They are beginning to do this by seeking an interdisciplinary systems approach to the solution of sociopolitical problems. They will accomplish this by transferring the methods of operations research from the area of physical technology to that of social technology.

The potential reward from this evolving reorientation of some of the effort in the social-science area toward social technology, employing operations-analytical techniques, is considerable; it may even equal or exceed in importance that of the achievements credited to the technologies arising out of the physical sciences.

Operations analysis was first brought into being through the exigencies of World War II; it has since continued to develop and become a widely accepted tool, not only in the peacetime management of military affairs, but throughout the operations of commerce and industry.

Among the principal operations research techniques that have proven themselves in these areas and that show great promise of being transferable to that of social technology are the construction of mathematical models, simulation procedures, and a systematic approach to the utilization of intuitive expert judgment. All of these techniques—it is almost needless to say—are greatly aided and continually refined through the availability of the computer, and the second computer revolution which I described may well add another order of magnitude to their potency. In particular, automated access to central data banks, in conjunction with appropriate socioeconomic models, will provide the soft sciences with the same kind of massive data processing and interpreting capability that, in the physical sciences, created the breakthrough which led to the understanding and management of atomic energy.

One of the results of the greater receptivity of social scientists to mathematical models and to an interdisciplinary systems approach may well be the development of a comprehensive theory of organizations; . . . by this term I mean the general discipline concerned with human interactions in decision-making situations. Taken in this sense, organization theory is a direct extension of the so-called theory of games—an extension which it is necessary to achieve before we can deal with social conflict situations that the present theory has been unable to resolve. Any form of social interaction, be it among persons or among business firms or among states, can be viewed as a game we are playing, or rather a continuing series of games, in which in some sense we strive to maximize our individual or corporate or national utilities. The next great breakthrough in the social sciences, comparable in significance to such physical breakthroughs as the creation of artificial life or the control of thermonuclear energy, may well be the construction of a theory of organizations that succeeds in dealing rationally with situations of interpersonal or international conflict. My expectation that this breakthrough will occur is my fourth reason for hope in this general area.

How, specifically, will all these developments lead to improvements in the analysis of the future? How, in de Jouvenel's phrase, will they advance the "art of conjecture"?

I described earlier the three parts of which an analysis of the future has to consist. Let us reexamine them briefly.

The survey of possible futures, with which any analysis of the future must begin, will continue to have to rely primarily on the intuitive judgment of experts. The process of obtaining a consensus among specialists will be enormously improved through the developments which I mentioned. Not only will the expected gigantic increase in scientific knowledge raise the quality of available expertise by an order or magnitude, but the day is not too far off when we can establish a world-wide network of specialists, each equipped with a console tied to one central computer and to electronic data banks, who will be able to interact with one another via the computer network and thus obtain a consensus among themselves through a process of which the present-day Delphi technique is a primitive precursor.

Aside from procedural refinements in this technique, one of the major improvements that will have to be introduced is that potential future developments will not be inquired into in isolation but that proper attention will be paid to cross-correlations among such developments. For instance, the occurrence of one development may raise the probability of occurrence of another either because it facilitates the other technologically or because it makes the other socially more desirable. A systematic treatment of such cross-influences will be a necessary ingredient of any future survey of possible futures.*

With regard to the analysis of preferences, which is the second component of an analysis of the future, I expect that the general reorientation of the social sciences toward policy-directed systems research will lead to considerable advances in the selection and measurement of social indicators. Organization theory, in particular, if it develops in the direction which I outlined, will permit us to view a nation as an organization of individuals, or the world as

---

* Since the writing of this paper by Dr. Helmer, significant research has been done on the question of correlations between future events. Some of this work is described in Theodore Gordon's paper, *The Current Methods of Futures Research*, under the heading of "Cross-Impact Matrix Methods." [Ed.]

an organization of nations, in which the members have partly conflicting goals. We may then be able to attack the problem of the welfare of such communities more rationally by dealing with it within the systematic framework of a theory of organizational preferences.

Finally, there is the third aspect of the art of conjecture, namely the matter of constructive policy research. Here we are in the area of what may be called the systematization of social inventiveness. *It* is apt to benefit most profoundly from the acceptance of operations-research techniques within the social sciences. Program-budgeting, especially, will come of age, by utilizing the conceptual framework of organizational utilities and preferences that we may expect organization theory to furnish. Comprehensive simulated planning by multidisciplinary groups of experts, aided by electronic computers and display devices as well as by sophisticated mathematical models, will result in alternative developmental scenarios. Judging by past experience, the stimulating effect of interacting within a simulated environment will be highly conducive to inventiveness and imagination among the participants, and we may well look forward to the emergence of a new breed of modern-day constructive utopians, who will invent not only better futures but the social instrumentalities of attaining them.

In summary then, in view of what may reasonably be expected, the potential progress of social technology that lies within the grasp of the next generation is tremendous. First these new methods will find their application within the societies of the advanced nations. But the pace of events is fast in this century, and before it is over I think there is hope that international relations will not remain unaffected by such progress, so that some of us may live to see the beginning of the era when the ample resources of the world will be equitably distributed among all nations, and war will be obsolescent.

The Use of Scenarios

Herman Kahn and Anthony J. Wiener

Among futurists, Herman Kahn and Anthony Wiener are best known for their skillful use of the forecasting method known as "scenario writing" and for their sometimes outrageous predictions. In this brief selection from their book, *The Year 2000,* they tell what they mean by a scenario, why it is useful, and how a trace of paranoia does (or does not) help the scenario writer.

"Transition scenarios" . . . are attempts to describe in some detail a hypothetical sequence of events that could lead plausibly to the situation envisaged. Some scenarios may explore and emphasize an element of a larger problem, such as a crisis or other event that could lead to war, the process of "escalation" of a small war or local violence into a larger war, the spread or contraction of a limited war, the fighting of a war, the termination of the war, or the subsequent peace. The focus of such a scenario can be military events and activities, the internal dynamics of various countries, bargaining among enemies or inter-ally relations, and so on. Other scenarios can be used to produce, perhaps in impressionistic tones, the future development of the world as a whole, a culture, a nation, or some group or class. The scenario is particularly suited to dealing with events taken together—integrating several aspects of a situation more or less simultaneously. By the use of a relatively extensive scenario, the analyst may be able to get a feeling for events and the branching points dependent upon critical choices. These branches can then be explored more or less systematically or the scenario itself can be used as a context for discussion or as a "named" possibility that can be referred to for various purposes.

Some of the advantages of the scenario as an aid to thinking are:

1. They serve to call attention, sometimes dramatically and persuasively, to the larger range of possibilities that must be considered in the analysis of the future. They are one of the most effective tools in lessening the "carry-over" thinking that is likely even when it is clear to all that 2000 cannot be the same as 1965 or even 1985. Scenarios are one way to force oneself and others to plunge into the unfamiliar and rapidly changing world of the present and the future: They dramatize and illustrate the possibilities they focus on in a very useful way. (They may do little or nothing for the possibilities they do not focus on.)
2. They force the analyst to deal with details and dynamics that he might easily avoid treating if he restricted himself to abstract considerations. Typically no particular set of the many possible sets of details and dynamics seems specially worth treating, so none are treated, even though a detailed investigation of even a few arbitrarily chosen cases can be most helpful.
3. They help to illuminate the interaction of psychological, social, economic, cultural, political, and military factors, including the influence of individual political personalities upon what otherwise might be abstract considerations, and they do so in a form that permits the comprehension of many such interacting elements at once.
4. They can illustrate forcefully, sometimes in oversimplified fashion, certain principles, issues or questions that might be ignored or lost if one insisted on taking examples only from the complex and controversial real world.
5. They may also be used to consider alternative possible outcomes of

certain real past and present events, such as Suez, Lebanon, Laos, or Berlin.

6. They can be used as artificial "case histories" and "historical anecdotes" to make up to some degree for the paucity of actual examples.

While the conscious use of scenarios has become widespread, it has also been criticized. One criticism is that only a "paranoid" personality, unjustifiably distrustful, suspicious, and preoccupied with hostility, could conceive of the kind of crises, provocations, aggressions, and plots that characterize many politico-military scenarios. Unfortunately this characterization seems to have more to do with the kinds of politico-military events the real world provides and planners must prepare for than with the psychodynamics of the planner. His responsibilities require him to be most interested in the many unpleasant ways in which things can go wrong; he should also be interested in what can go right, but the latter tends to be both more difficult and usually less useful to explore by means of scenarios. Of course, any particular scenario may in fact contain paranoid ideas, but this must be judged on the basis of the plausibility of the particular scenario—often a difficult judgment in a world of many surprises—and care must be taken to allow for a possibly realistic inclusion of a not-implausible degree of paranoia in one or more decision-makers who have roles in the scenario.

A second criticism is that scenarios may be so divorced from reality as not only to be useless but also misleading, and therefore dangerous. However, one must remember that the scenario is not used as a predictive device. The analyst is dealing with the unknown and to some degree unknowable future. In many specific cases it is hard to see how critics can be so certain there is a sure divorce from a reality that is not yet known and may present surprises. Imagination has always been one of the principal means for dealing in various ways with the future, and the scenario is simply one of many devices useful in stimulating and disciplining the imagination. To the extent that particular scenarios may be divorced from reality, the proper criticism would seem to be of particular scenarios rather than of the method. And of course unrealistic scenarios are often useful aids to discussion, if only to point out that the particular possibilities are unrealistic.

It is also worth noting that for some purposes mistakes in particulars may be of secondary importance. For example, many today are concerned about France as an increasingly important nuclear power with vague and uncertain motivations and a dynamism unsuspected fifteen years ago. By 1980 France may be weak and disunited. But similar problems may then be posed by Italy or Japan. Many of these specific problems as viewed by the United States would be much the same as though the new power were France. This does not mean all problems would be the same, only that those problems of the real Japan of 1980, which perhaps could have been predicted by a supremely competent planner of 1967, might not look very different—in the abstract—from those problems actually predicted for the hypothetical France of 1980. However, if a scenario is to seem plausible to analysts and/or policy-makers it must, of course, relate at the outset to some reasonable version of the present, and must correspond throughout to the way analysts and/or policy-makers are likely to believe decision-makers and others are likely to behave. Since plausibility is a great virtue in a scenario, one should, subject to other considerations, try to achieve it. But it is important not to limit oneself to the *most* plausible, conventional, or probable situations and behavior. History is likely to write scenarios that most observers would find implausible not only prospectively but sometimes, even, in retrospect. Many sequences of events seem plausible now only because they have actually occurred; a man who knew no history might not believe any. Future events may not be drawn from the restricted list of those we have learned are possible; we should expect to go on being surprised.

The Current Methods of Futures Research

Theodore J. Gordon

In the attempt to predict, men have employed everything from astrology to corpses, puffs of smoke, pebbles, and the entrails of animals. Today one group of futurists is working to put forecasting on a more systematic basis. In this simple, straightforward paper, Theodore J. Gordon, space engineer-turned-social analyst, describes several different ways to go about making a forecast. He begins with what he calls "genius forecasting."

INTRODUCTION

This is a paper about the methods of futures research. . . . Now in a dozen countries there are institutions designed to study the future. Their staffs are dedicated to the development of systematic methods for understanding how current actions might affect the course of man's future history. There are at least three journals which are devoted solely to this field, and many others publish occasional articles on the future. There have been international conferences and symposia devoted to the topic of futures, substantive and methodological. Universities in the United States and elsewhere are designing and offering courses on technological, environmental, and social forecasting, or the mesh between them.[1] The published literature in the field is now so extensive that no single person could follow it all. In short, it appears that futures research, ready or not, has assumed many of the attributes of a protodiscipline.

Following de Jouvenel, most people in this field view the future as composed of a large set of alternatives.[2] Policies steer us through the maze of interlocking possibilities. Futures research is a means of discovering and articulating the more important of the alternative futures and estimating the trajectory likely to be produced by contemplated policies. Thus, forecasting is perceived as an aid to decision-making in the present, and not as a means of producing a list of chromium-plated potential mousetraps.

Forecasts indicate what might be. They speak of a process of selection from among possible worlds. They indicate that man has at least some control over his destiny. The concept is antinihilistic, antideterministic. If the discipline develops, it may provide a new orientation to education, a new means of communication between age groups, individuals, and nations, and a new method of conflict resolution. But the protodiscipline stands in danger of raising aspirations for rationality that cannot be fulfilled; its techniques are provocative and suggestive, but unproven; its practitioners are learning as they go. The future is a new intellectual frontier; the rewards there may be real or yet prove a chimera.

There are some important caveats about forecasting the future that must be noted. First, there is no way to state what the future will be. Regardless of the sophistication of the methods, all rely on judgment, not fact.

Second, there will always be blind spots in forecasts. If we try to guess what will happen in the future, we are likely to omit events for which there are no existing paradigms (forecasts made in 1964 did not contain pulsars or quasars); events which seem trivial but through secondary or tertiary effects became important (the Gulf of Tonkin resolution); and events based on whim, chance, or unexpected coincidence (an assassination).

Finally, potential futures are posed to serve as a backdrop for policy-making. If enacted, policies may be expected to change the future. Therefore, the notion of accuracy involves some paradoxical considerations.

The methods of this protodiscipline, described in the following pages, are: genius forecasting, trend extrapolation, consensus methods, simulation methods, cross-impact methods, scenarios, decision trees, and input-output matrices. This taxonomy is personal, but most other practitioners of futures research would recognize similar divisions.

METHODS OF FORECASTING
GENIUS FORECASTING

The category of genius forecasting includes a myriad of intuitive methods which an individual uses to estimate, assess, or predict some aspect of the future. Since the methods are internal rather than explicit, the quality of his forecasts depends almost entirely on the "inspiration" processes of the forecaster. The method is thus embroiled in the psychology of insight; somehow an individual engaged in genius forecasting integrates possibilities which he considers important, draws from his relevant experience, and states what he thinks might be.

Until relatively recently, most forecasts were of this sort. A chronology of the history of forecasting might show genius forecasting beginning at about the time of the French Revolution (although earlier examples can be cited, such as the Grecian utopias and some of the writings of Francis Bacon). S. C. Gilfillan, a sociologist, technological forecaster, and historian of forecasting, mentions in particular: d'Argenson, who in the 1750s wrote of future political arrangements; Turgot, who at about the same time articulated principles of the accumulation of scientific knowledge, technological diffusion, the future state of items such as the phonograph, cross-breeding, the swivel chair, the future role of hospitals, and waste purification; and Condorcet, who wrote of census taking, meteorology, eugenics, and the political role of women.[3]

Genius forecasting, in fictional form, has also had its share of spectacular successes. Swift, Verne, Wells, Huxley, Orwell, and

Clarke are a few fiction authors who come to mind. Swift, in his satire, *A Voyage to Laputa,* published in 1726, told of the two satellites of Mars, with the uncommonly short orbital periods of 10 and 21.5 hours. Mars was not known to have satellites until 1877 when two were discovered; their orbital periods were 7.6 and 30.4 hours. Wells, of course, wrote about trips to the moon, biological warfare, the role of sex in society, and the possibility of self-annihilation of the race by warfare. As for Huxley, we are uncomfortably close to his "brave new world."

Genius forecasting has not been completely contained in science fiction. Researchers at the RAND Corporation, in 1946, forecasted with some accuracy the implications of the launching of an orbital satellite. Herman Kahn, one of the foremost practitioners, uses the method with consummate skill in *On Thermonuclear War* and *The Year 2000.*

But, as one might expect, the method fails more often that it succeeds and its failures have been spectacular. The Library of Congress has compiled a list of faulty forecasts through history which reminds one somehow of slapstick comedy or the vintage movies showing intrepid would-be pilots sitting amidst collapsed wings.[4]

In 1902, *Harper's Weekly* stated, "The actual building of roads devoted to motor cars is not for the near future, in spite of many rumors to that effect." Henry Ford said the Edison Company once offered him a job on the condition he would "give up my gas engine and devote myself to something really useful." . . . Terman, the great electrical engineer, said FM radio was "not particularly satisfactory for transmitting intelligence"; and Millikan, the famous physicist, said in 1930, "There is no appreciable energy available to man through atomic disintegration."

In the end, genius forecasting depends on more than the genius of the forecaster; it depends on luck and insight. There may be many geniuses whose forecasts are made with full measure of both, but it is nearly impossible to recognize them a priori, and this, of course, is the weakness of the method.

TREND EXTRAPOLATION

Forecasts of potential developments may be made by assuming that trends established in recent history will continue into the future. This extrapolative method assumes, implicitly, that the forces which were at work to shape the trend in the past will continue to work in the future. Thus, for example, if world population doubled in the last forty years, we might expect, as a first approximation at least, that population would double again in a similar period in the future.

.   .   .

Trend forecasting need not be confined to demographic or technological performance data. In a recent study conducted by the Institute for the Future, forecasts were to be made about the likelihood of government-sponsored social-welfare programs.[5] Data on past performance in rate of adoption of such programs by twenty-four countries throughout the world lead to the curve shown in Figure 1. The following generalizations could be made from such a curve:

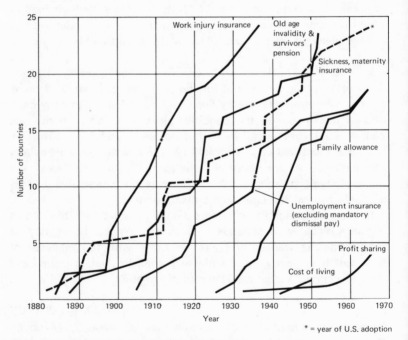

* = year of U.S. adoption

FIGURE 1. Historical Growth of Social Benefit Programs

1. The rate of spread of social-welfare programs among the countries studied has not varied much over the last 100 years.
2. The United States has never been an innovator in such programs.
3. Certain programs are now in existence in other countries in the group which the United States might expect to have within the next ten to twenty years.

Such a trend forecast exhibits the major weakness of this method: it assumes that forces which have been at work in the past will continue to be at work in the future. Such an assumption is probably warranted for the near term, but grows less satisfying the further the time horizon is stretched. Recognizing that this premise underlies all trend forecasting leads to the concept of "development inertia"; some systems are more easily changed as a result of external influences than others. Slow changes are symptomatic of high inertia systems. The wheeled automobile is imbedded in our economy and probably could not be replaced by another form of personal transportation (for example, hovercraft) very rapidly. On the other hand, there is little inertia to women's clothing styles.

Techniques for trend extrapolation have been devised which are somewhat more sophisticated than the "eyeball" extension of historical data. Curve-fitting methods, for example, allow more complex curves (curves with exponents of two, three, or above) to be matched to the available data points with least error. Factor analysis can be used to isolate parameters which correlate with one another, and the resulting curves provide a basis for trend forecasting. Some econometric modeling (through which future labor force and economic conditions may be forecasted) employs factor analysis and multiple correlation techniques to establish the basic regression equations.

But regardless of the sophistication of the application, trend forecasting assumes that the present is but a point on a continuum and that discontinuities in the flow of history are rare.

CONSENSUS METHODS

In areas of inquiry which are devoid of laws of causality, recourse to expert opinion is admissible.[6] An expert, after all, is defined as a person who is often correct in his judgment about the likely outcome of events in inexact fields.

If the services of more than a single expert are required (when several disciplines are involved, or when opinions of equally competent experts differ) methods of synthesizing opinion are required. One approach is to place the potential contributors in face-to-face confrontation and let them argue it out. This situation has several potential hazards: dominant individuals may carry the discussion by weight of their personality rather than force of argument; the psychology of the group may lead to consensus through "bandwagon" dynamics; or time may be lost in the establishment of intellectual "pecking orders." Nevertheless, as Norman Dalkey points out, given no other information, a group estimate is at least as reliable as that of a randomly chosen expert.[7] Furthermore, if the range of answers contributed by the individuals of the group contains the true answer, then the median of the group is a closer approximation to the true answer than are the answers provided by more than half the group.

The Delphi technique is a method of seeking a group consensus which avoids some of the problems of face-to-face confrontation. Generally a Delphi exercise engages experts in an anonymous debate, their opinions being exchanged through an intermediary. Anonymity exists at two levels; not only are participants unknown to each other, but the individual responses are never attributed to particular respondents. In the first round of a typical Delphi study, the participants might be asked when a future event might take place. Their answers would be collated by the experimenters and fed back to them in a second round. The second-round questionnaire would seek justification of extreme views expressed in round one. The responses would again be collated by the experimenters and furnished to the participants in a third (and usually final) round. This questionnaire would ask that the experts reassess their previous positions in view of those taken by the other participants.

Hundreds of studies using this general technique have been conducted in the past five years covering a diversity of subjects which included: scientific breakthroughs;[8] economic forecasts;[9] medical developments;[10] automation developments;[11] societal trends;[12] employee benefits;[13] physical and biomedical technologies;[14] education developments;[15] and corporate forecasting.[16]

The Delphi technique generally produces a narrowing of the initial spread of opinions and a shifting of the median as the questioning proceeds. If no consensus emerges, at least a crystallizing of the disparate positions usually becomes apparent.

Norman Dalkey at RAND recently performed a series of detailed experiments using the Delphi method. A relatively large number of UCLA students were given a questionnaire pertaining to issues with known answers against which the group consensus could be checked for accuracy.[17] Admittedly, questions of this sort differ from questions about the future, but they afforded an opportunity to observe some of the characteristics of group interactions and behavior under controlled conditions. The six major findings of the study were:

1. The spread of opinions narrows from the first to the second questionnaire and the median, more often than not, shifts toward the true answer.
2. Delphi interactions generally produce more accurate estimates than do face-to-face confrontations. If face-to-face discussions follow Delphi interactions, the results are generally degraded.
3. The error of the group is generally a function of the standard deviation.
4. Feeding back reasons for extreme opinions does not improve group accuracy.
5. Group self-appraised expertise is a powerful determinant of accuracy; if the group believes it is expert, it probably is.
6. Accuracy of the respondents improves when they are allowed one-half minute for answering; shorter or longer intervals (at least up to four minutes) lead to increased error.

Some of these results are surprising (for example, the extremely short time required for highest accuracy and the failure to improve accuracy with the feedback of reasons), but the overall findings of the study are encouraging.

Do these results reflect the performance of the Delphi method when the questions under study relate to the future? In Campbell's short-range forecasts of future economic conditions, made by Delphi and "normal" methods, the Delphi forecasts proved to be the more accurate.[18] Dalkey found that the responses obtained by Campbell followed the same kind of distribution as answers given to his encyclopedic questions. Martino has analyzed the data obtained in the responses to the study conducted by North and Pike of TRW, and found a similar distribution.[19]

TABLE 1.

Near Term Forecasts of 1964 RAND Report	50 percent occurrence probability			Has the development occurred?		
	LQ	median	UQ	yes	no	partly or uncertain
Scientific breakthroughs						
■ Economically useful desalination of sea water	1964	1970				•
■ Feasibility of effective large-scale fertility control by oral contraceptive or other simple and inexpensive means	1970	1970	1983	•		
Progress in space						
■ USSR orbital rendezvous	1964	1964	1966	•		
■ USA orbital rendezvous	1965	1967	1967	•		
■ Increased use of near-Earth satellites for weather prediction and control	1967	1967	1970	•		
■ Unmanned inspections and capability for destruction of satellites	1967	1967	1970		•	
■ USSR manned lunar fly-by	1967	1967	1970		•	
■ Establishment of global communications system	1967	1968	1970	•		
■ USA manned lunar fly-by	1967	1970	1970	•		
■ Manned lunar landing and return	1969	1969	1970	•		
■ Rescue of astronauts stranded in orbit	1968	1970	1975		•	
■ Operational readiness of laser for space communications	1968	1970	1975			•
■ Manned co-orbital inspection of satellites	1970	1970	1974		•	
■ Manned scientific orbital station—ten men	1970	1970	1975		•	

Future weapon systems

■ Tactical kiloton nuclear weapons for use by ground troops	1964	1965	1967	●
■ Extensive uses of devices that persuade without killing (water cannons, tear gas, etc.)	1968	1968	1970	●
■ Miniature improved sensors and transmitters for snooping, reconnaissance, arms control	1968	1968	1970	●
■ Rapid mobility of men and light weapons to any point on Earth for police action	1966	1969	1973	●
■ Incapacitating chemical (as opposed to biological) agents	1965	1970	1975	●
■ Use of lasers for radar-type sensors, illuminators, communications	1968	1970	1975	●
■ Incapacitating biological agents	1968	1970	1976	●
■ Lethal biological agents	1967	1970	1980	●

LQ and UQ = lower and upper quartile

Six years have passed since the 1964 long-range forecasts were made by the panels under Gordon and Helmer at RAND.[20] Ament at the Institute for the Future has compared these forecasts to actuality and has found that of the twenty-two events forecasted to have a probability of at least 50 percent to occur by 1970, fifteen have occurred, five have not, and two are uncertain.[21] His analysis is summarized in Table 1.

One of the interesting sidelights of Ament's review is the difficulty he encountered in determining whether or not an event had in fact actually occurred. For example, one original forecast was: "Direct link from stores to bank to check credit and to record transactions"; such links exist now but are not pervasive. In the end, Ament resorted to a brief opinion poll among the Institute staff to determine whether or not the events forecasted in 1964 had occurred yet. One reason for this difficulty is that many of the descriptions of events, in retrospect, were not specific enough, and defined trends rather than "happenings." Furthermore, the occurrence of highly specialized events is noted by specialists and may not be systematically recorded or generally accessible.

Delphi studies do not produce "truth" about the future; they yield, even under the best of circumstances, only consensus opinion about what might be. If the participants are experts, perhaps their opinion represents a possible future which deserves consideration in planning.

The Delphi technique has also been used to collect opinions about social changes. In one case the group was asked to forecast the likely impact on society of various technological changes and the desirability of those impacts. Figure 2 shows an example of the results of this inquiry.[22] In another study the panel was asked to provide its judgment on the likely course of social trends.[23] Some of the data produced in the portion of the study dealing with education are shown in Figure 3.

Social forecasting has proved to be much more difficult than scientific and technological forecasting. In a sense, scientific and technological forecasts have their roots in the research and development in progress in laboratories throughout the world; experts can base their forecasts on their knowledge of this work. But in the societal domain there is no analogous research in progress on

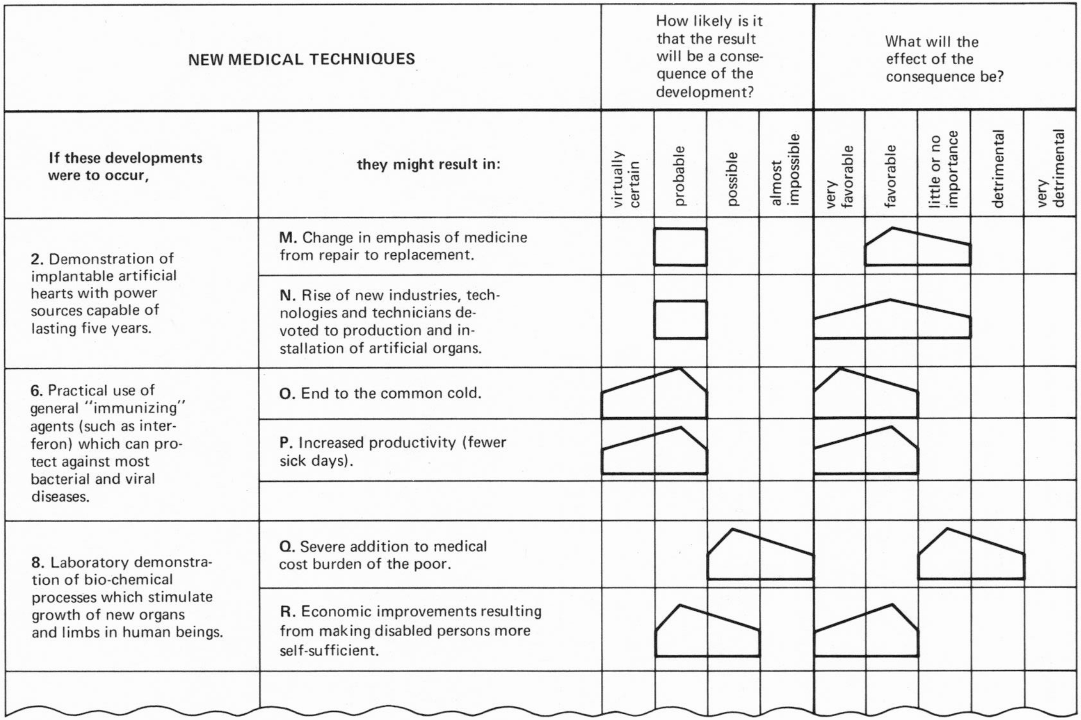

FIGURE 2. Display of Judgments of Consequences of Technology

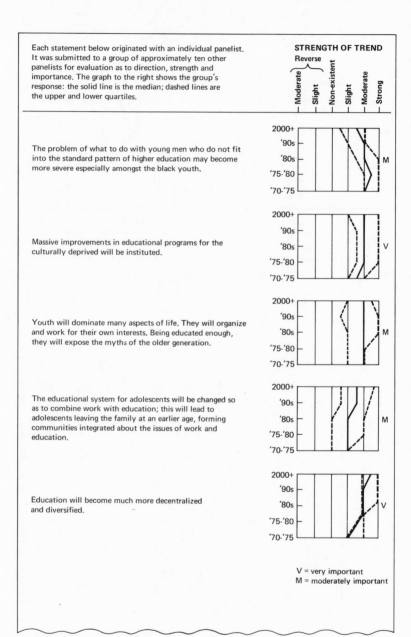

Each statement below originated with an individual panelist. It was submitted to a group of approximately ten other panelists for evaluation as to direction, strength and importance. The graph to the right shows the group's response: the solid line is the median; dashed lines are the upper and lower quartiles.

STRENGTH OF TREND

Reverse { Moderate, Slight } Non-existent, Slight, Moderate, Strong

The problem of what to do with young men who do not fit into the standard pattern of higher education may become more severe especially amongst the black youth.

Massive improvements in educational programs for the culturally deprived will be instituted.

Youth will dominate many aspects of life. They will organize and work for their own interests. Being educated enough, they will expose the myths of the older generation.

The educational system for adolescents will be changed so as to combine work with education; this will lead to adolescents leaving the family at an earlier age, forming communities integrated about the issues of work and education.

Education will become much more decentralized and diversified.

V = very important
M = moderately important

FIGURE 3. Display of Judgments of Trends in Education

which to base forecasts. As a result, there tends to be less agreement and less inclination to change opinion. Nevertheless, interesting results can be achieved which may also prove to be useful in planning.

.   .   .

The Institute for the Future has experimented with "mini-Delphi" interactions in which only a portion of the anonymity of Delphi interactions is preserved. Participants, in a face-to-face conference, are asked to write their opinions about the subject under discussion and give them to the moderator. These opinions are collated rapidly and fed back to the group. Reestimates are requested without divulging which members of the group held divergent views. This type of interaction has been found to produce the characteristic narrowing of opinions and median shifts found in the more elaborate studies.

SIMULATION METHODS

Simulation is the approximation of complex systems by dynamic models. These models may exist in several forms:

1. mechanical analogs (for example, a wind tunnel model of an SST)
2. mathematical analogs (a set of equations describing the economic situation of a country)
3. metaphorical analogs (the growth of a bacteria colony taken to depict human population growth)
4. game analogs (interactions between "players" taken to represent social interactions)

These models can change with time and are useful where experimentation with actual systems is too costly, is morally unacceptable, or involves the study of problems so complex that more precise analytic solution appears impractical. Mathematical and game analogs are of particular importance to futures research.

Mathematical models of physical systems have been used successfully in many applications. For example, computer simulations of the smog conditions in the Los Angeles basin have yielded insight into the relative contributions of automobiles and power stations to atmospheric pollution and the expected effect of varying either input. If the performance of a system can be approximated by an equation, then the mathematical relationship is a forecasting device which predicts the response of the system to anticipated external stimulation.

When one considers techno-social systems, the situation becomes enormously more complex. Attempts at modeling aspects of social behavior can be found in various economic and social-science publications. The economics literature, for example, now encompasses not only general economic theory relating to development growth in planning, but also models in the economics of health, education, poverty, crime, discrimination, and technological change. J. W. Forrester of M.I.T. has attempted in his recent book, *Urban Dynamics,* to model various aspects of the city and the people who use it. His model involves descriptions of the dynamic interactions between the availability of housing, employment levels, and certain demographic descriptors of the various socioeconomic classes that inhabit the city. The model design is similar to that employed in a control system, in that the behavior of various aspects of the model is described in terms of feedback loops, system gains, and so on. Forrester's model has produced some counter-intuitive results. For example, his work suggests that construction of low-cost housing within an urban area will cause conditions of the city to deteriorate even further.[24] The difficulty with such models is that they necessarily imply certain values and attitudes on the part of the society they describe. These values and attitudes are probably a complicated function of other social and technological changes. One approach to this difficulty is to substitute real people for mathematical constructions depicting their supposed behavior, that is, to use game analogies rather than mathematical analogies.

Simulation gaming involves the creation of an artificial game environment in which players (real people acting out assigned roles) are asked to interact. A simulation game generally has the following five elements:

1. Rules of play to govern the "moves" and interactions between players, and other variables of the game.
2. Objectives or goals; players may work cooperatively toward a joint goal or competitively toward goals which cannot be shared. (A single game may incorporate both modes, as in *Monopoly* when players decide to "gang up" on the "apartment house owner.")
3. A method of translating the moves of the players into indicators which

measure the degree of attainment of goals. This device may be a game board, a mathematical model, or another group of participants charged with responsibility of judging the effect of the players' moves.

4. A display system to illustrate the progress of the game.
5. A set of exogenous variables to introduce "outside events" into the play.

While simulation gaming has not yet demonstrated forecasting precision, it serves other ends. First, it can teach players and experimenters about the issue under study. A well-designed simulation game includes descriptive elements which acquaint the players with definitions of, and interrelationships among, some of the variables, at least as perceived by the experimenters. The experimenters, in designing the game, learn to define the parameters thought to be relevant to the issues being simulated and to describe their modes of interaction. Tolerance (or at least sensitivity) to various points of view is usually a part of the player's game experience.

Second, it can provide a framework for systematic review of the issue being studied. In constructing a game it is usually necessary to define the constituent elements of the issues being simulated and to consider how these elements are likely to interact. Because games generally require a structure of sorts, these considerations are usually orderly and may thus replace haphazard and sporadic probes into issues. The game structure often forces the role players to consider the issues surrounding the simulation from attitudes unfamiliar to them—usually in a systematic fashion.

Third, a simulation game can allow role players to exhibit emotions and make decisions normally excluded in real life but permitted in the game environment. In effect, the game may become a psychological device, a means of experimenting with and exerting power in circumstances not likely to be detrimental to society at large.

Finally, it can improve communications between players. The cooperation or competition engendered by the roles of a game may promote relationships between the players which last long after the game is over. By exposing concerns in the game environment, players may build new sensitivities to each other's personalities and behavior patterns in real life.

Simulation gaming has been used in diverse applications, includ-

ing the derivation and testing of military strategies and the teaching of certain aspects of political science. The method may
eventually be useful in resolving conflict between individuals,
groups, or even nations. With more experience and data, the tool
might also be developed into a more precise forecasting instrument.

CROSS-IMPACT MATRIX METHODS[25]
The various forecasting techniques already described often produce
lists of potential future events and their likely dates of occurrence. Yet potential relationships may exist between the forecasted events; that is, forecasted sets might well contain mutually
reinforcing or mutually inhibiting items. The cross-impact matrix
method is an experimental approach by which the probability of
each item in a forecasted set can be adjusted in view of judgments
relating to potential interactions of the forecasted items. Most
events and developments are in some way connected with other
events and developments. A single event, such as the production
of power from the first atomic reactor, was made possible by a
complex history of antecedent scientific, technological, political,
and economic "happenings." In its turn, the production of energy
from the first atomic reactor provided an intellectual conception
which influenced or shaped many of the events and developments
which followed. In a sense, history is a focusing of many apparently
diverse and unrelated occurrences which permit or cause singular
events and developments. From these flow ever-widening down-
stream effects which interact with other events and developments.
It is hard to imagine an event which had no predecessor making it
more or less likely or influencing its form—or one which, after
occurring, left no mark.

This interrelationship between events and developments is
called "cross-impact." The systematic description of all potential
modes of interaction and the assessment of the possible strength
of these interactions is vastly complex but methodologically important, since these descriptions and metrics may provide new
insight into historical analysis and permit greater accuracy and
precision in forecasting. A general theory of cross impact, which
is not yet available, would almost certainly permit the exploration
of the side-effects of decisions under consideration. It might also
be useful in illuminating less expensive means of attaining goals

through investment in high-payoff areas which initially seem to be unrelated or only weakly linked to the decision.

Although the computational techniques used in a cross-impact analysis are somewhat complicated, the basic concepts underlying the techniques are straightforward. Suppose that a set of developments had been forecasted to some year in the future, with varying levels of probability. If these developments are designated D_i ($i = 1, 2, \ldots, n$), with associated probabilities P_i, then the question can be posed: "If $P_m = 1$ (that is, if D_m happens) how do the other P_i change?" In other words, we speak of a cross-impact effect if the probability that one event occurs varies either positively or negatively with the occurrence or nonoccurrence of other events.

By way of illustration, suppose that the following developments and probabilities were forecasted for a given year.[26]

Development D_i	Probability P_i
1. One-month reliable weather forecasts	.4
2. Feasibility of limited weather control	.2
3. General biochemical immunization	.5
4. Elimination of crop damage from adverse weather	.5

These events might then be arranged in matrix form:

The upward arrows indicate an increase in probability. Thus if D_2 (the feasibility of limited weather control) were to occur, D_1 (one-month reliable weather forecast) and D_4 (elimination of crop damage from adverse weather) would become more probable as noted by the upward arrows.

This kind of array is called a "cross-impact matrix." Interactions between events are much more complex, of course, than those that can be indicated by an arrow. The arrow denotes only a linkage between events and the direction of the influence one event has on another. In addition, it is necessary to identify the linkage strength (how strongly the occurrence or nonoccurrence of one event influences the likelihood of another event).

Once the arrows have been replaced by the requisite numerical data and the relevant formulas have been developed for calculating the changes in probabilities, such a matrix can be analyzed on a computer. Briefly, the following seven steps are involved:

1. assessing the potential interactions (cross impacts) among individual events in a set of forecasts, in terms of:
   a. direction, or mode, of the interaction,
   b. strength of the interaction, and
   c. time delay of the effect of one event on another
2. selecting an event at random and "deciding" its occurrence or nonoccurrence on the basis of its assigned probability
3. adjusting the probability of the remaining events according to the interactions assessed as likely in Step 1
4. selecting another event from among those remaining and deciding it (using its new probability) as before
5. continuing this process until all events in the set have been decided
6. "playing" the matrix in this way many times so that the probabilities can be computed on the basis of the percentage of times that an event occurs during these plays; and
7. changing the initial probability of one or more events and repeating Steps 2 to 6.

By comparing the initial probabilities to those generated in Step 6, it is possible to determine how the initial probabilities might be modified to reflect the cross impacts of other events on the list. By comparing the results of Step 6 and Step 7, it is possible to determine how a change in the probability of occurrence of one or more events would, through the cross impacts, affect the probability of the other events.

The cross-impact method has been used experimentally in several situations. The first examples, which were completed in early 1968, related to the decision to deploy the Minuteman missile and the future of transportation services. Since then, numerous other cross-impact analyses have been completed, dealing with techno-social situations, corporate investment strategies, technological assessments, and political interactions. Otto Sulc has experimented with a similar method for relating forecasted technological and social changes.[27]

Of particular interest is the possibility of evaluating alternative policy decisions through cross-impact methods. An illustration of this policy-test capability is provided by a simple cross-impact analysis undertaken in connection with an Institute study of alternative future environments for education. Five specific future developments were postulated:

1. initiation of laws requiring negotiation between primary and secondary public school teachers and school boards in the United States;
2. most teachers belonging to negotiation unions;
3. most students in public secondary schools belonging to recognized unions;
4. increase in parent-teacher conflict (triple present levels); and
5. initiation of ethnic-studies programs in most secondary schools.

These developments were reviewed independently by several experts engaged in educational policy research, who assessed the probability of the developments' occurrence prior to the year 1985. The potential cross impacts among pairs of these developments were evaluated in terms of expected mode and strength of interaction.

The matrix was "played out" in accordance with techniques described earlier. The play suggested that several of the items were more probable than had been believed previously based on the judgments about the linkages between individual items.

Next, the initial probability of each item in turn was artificially increased and the estimated time of earliest occurrence reduced, in order to observe the effects of simulated policy action. For example, in the next set of 1000 runs the initial probability of "most students in public secondary schools belonging to recognized unions" was increased from 0.30 to 0.60, and the estimated time of its earliest occurrence changed from 1976 to 1972. The resulting probabilities of this set (after 1000 repetitions) were somewhat different from those obtained with the first set, Item 5 (ethnic programs) becoming significantly more likely. Thus, one might say that the subjective judgments about interactions contained in the cross-impact matrix led to the conclusion that policy action which increases the probability of "student unions" will also increase the probability of "ethnic-study programs."

This discussion illustrates the use of cross-impact matrices to test the expected effects of potential policy actions. Clearly, the results are an artifact of the judgments originally supplied when constructing the matrix cells. Nevertheless, the method permits systematic collation of judgment and makes explicit the sometimes hidden effect of multiple linkages between events under consideration in assessing potential outcomes of proposed action.

The cross-impact method raises a logical puzzle: if the initial probabilities are derived by a method which only loosely constrains the reasoning of the forecasters, then these initial probabilities themselves may already reflect some of the cross impacts described in the matrix. This would introduce a kind of "double accounting" that would be quite difficult to anticipate explicitly.

On the other hand, it might be assumed that the initial probability estimates are fully impacted, in the sense that the impact effect of the occurrence or nonoccurrence of other developments has been taken into account. This would mean that, ideally, the initial probabilities would coincide with the terminal probabilities resulting from the cross-impact analysis. If in fact they did not, the error would be the estimator's and stem from his inability to handle the complexity of the situation, which the cross-impact process helps to identify and to correct.

The discipline involved in the selection of items, and particularly the systematic questioning necessary to the establishment of cross impacts, are often enlightening. One is faced with deciding what events may be important and how they may affect one another. This confrontation often illustrates that issues once believed to be simple and independent are, in reality, interrelated. Just completing a matrix can force a level of introspection helpful in some planning situations. And of course, the mathematical play of the basic matrix using new initial conditions to simulate policies can show unexpected secondary and tertiary consequences of the potential actions.

OTHER METHODS

Scenarios. A "scenario," or "future history," is a narrative description of a potential course of developments which might lead to some future state of affairs. Such a scenario can be very powerful if constructed under the hand of an experienced and talented author, since it can carry the force of eloquent narrative prose. Herman Kahn, Anthony Wiener, and Paul Ehrlich are masters of the technique. Some brief excerpts from their work will serve to illustrate the methods.

In their book, *The Year 2000*, Kahn and Wiener wrote a scenario depicting social controls:

. . . Perhaps many (most) men would be kept in a permanently drugged state (pacified?) and adapted to the ecology to which they are assigned according to some computerized calculation. As always the central government would so likely be swamped by the problem of keeping the system functioning properly that it would be concerned only with marginal and immediate problems rather than with the increasing repulsiveness of the entire system or with other basic issues. In any event there may be no rational or moral (whatever these terms mean in the twenty-first century) feasible solution that does not reject the modern technology or condemn billions of surplus humans to death or deprivation.[28]

In *Ramparts*, Ehrlich described a future history of pollution:

The end of the ocean came late in the summer of 1979, and it came even more rapidly than the biologists had expected. There had been signs for more than a decade, commencing with the discovery in 1968 that DDT slows down photosynthesis in marine plant life. It was announced in a short paper in the technical journal, *Science,* but to ecologists it smacked of doomsday. They knew that all life in the sea depends on photosynthesis, the chemical process by which green plants bind the sun's energy and make it available to living things. And they knew that DDT and similar chlorinated hydrocarbons had polluted the entire surface of the earth, including the sea.[29]

Kahn and Wiener have attempted to categorize types of scenarios. They recognize "surprise-free" projections, which define a "standard world." They point out this world is highly unlikely since the future undoubtedly will contain surprises. "Canonical variations" can be derived from the surprise-free projections by asking, "What would happen to my surprise-free world if all things stayed as I expected except that. . . ."

The strength of the method is also its weakness. It is extremely dependent on the capability of the story-teller. It is easily dismissed as politically biased since it represents a single point of view. Nevertheless, it can be powerfully persuasive.

Decision trees. "Decision trees" are graphic devices which display the potential results of alternative approaches to crucial decisions. Figure 4 illustrates a portion of a very simplified decision tree which might describe some of the futures connected with establishing a base on Mars. There are sixteen future histories implicit in this diagram which range from: "No public, Presidential, or Congressional support" to "The establishment of a Mars base after the accomplishment of a scientifically interesting mission, supported enthusiastically by the public and the government." Of course, no path into the future is so clear-cut; every branch point has gradations of decisions, and decisions at one level might well feed back to decisions at other levels. These considerations lead to the construction of very complex maps. Such large trees can be contained on computers and various scenarios and future histories generated automatically. Subjective probabilities of the various paths also can be introduced so that the overall probability of following a particular path into the future may be computed.

Input-output analysis. "Input-output matrices" are used by economists to detail inter-industrial transactions. Typically, an input-output matrix is a kind of balance sheet; the row entries depict input sectors and the columns depict the sectors which utilize these inputs. The cells of the matrix contain coefficients which express conversion by which the products of the various listed input sectors are transformed into the various listed outputs. These coefficients are generally constructed from historical data, and of course any such matrix presents only a static picture at a particular point in time. Since time histories of the coefficients are computable, it is possible to forecast changing values of the coefficients through any of the methods mentioned earlier. Forecasting

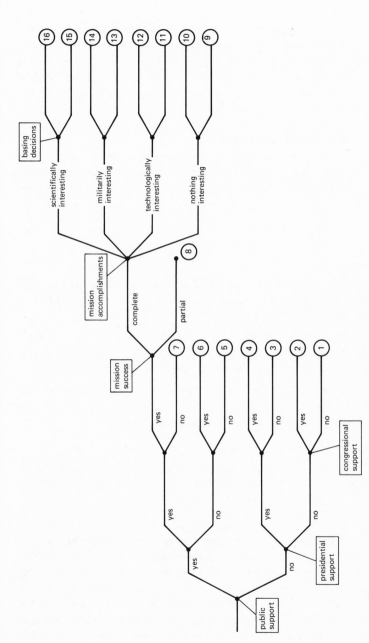

FIGURE 4. Decision Tree for the question, "Should we put a colony on Mars?"

187

of input-output coefficients under various projected economic circumstances has been attempted by researchers at Battelle Memorial Institute, Arthur D. Little, and Harvard. If such efforts prove successful, economists may be able to build projections of technological and social change into some of the models. Such a goal is well worth pursuing.

UNCERTAINTIES AND RESEARCH

As indicated in the Introduction to this paper, futures research is an embryonic discipline, a collection of techniques and estimates, with a partially unifying philosophy. Its research agenda is immense. Some of the questions currently facing futures researchers are:

To what extent will these techniques actually prove useful in decision-making?

Putting questions of accuracy aside, will the techniques lead to more effective teaching methods, approaches to conflict solution, or beneficial public attitudes?

Under what conditions will simulation accuracy be improved? How can good simulations and simulators be recognized?

How can a good forecaster be recognized? Can he be trained?

What kinds of events and developments are, by their nature, unanticipated?

How can potentially important events be recognized?

What are the attributes of plausibility (as opposed to probability)?

The systematic methods may sometimes lend more credibility to results than they may warrant. How can technique be subordinated to content?

Among the pressing problems facing the protodiscipline is that of value forecasting. Psychologists have not produced general models of value change, yet it is clear that values do change. They are shaped by pressures of technology (the effect of the automobile on sexual mores); advertising (the anticancer ads on TV); peer groups (long hair, short skirts, drugs); institutions (chauvinism); economic conditions (affluence permitting youth to look with disdain on the profit motive); and probably many other social interactions. Without some knowledge as to how values might change in the future, planners must work with the value set they have at hand, namely their own as of the moment of planning. Suppose a planner were to design a transportation system to provide economical and safe travel. Economy and safety are current values and his transportation system which might happen to cut through a mountain would satisfy those values. If, in some future society, the integrity of the countryside were more valued than cheap travel or safety, the planner would not only have been wrong, he would have been delinquent.

How can a planner anticipate what will be "good" and "right" and "proper" tomorrow? Even if we could, should we attempt to change the evolution of values so that our present values can prevail?

The implications for futures research are important, since forecasts raise value questions. Which future do we value the most or find in closest agreement with our own values? Planners answer this question implicitly by making choices among alternative plans.

But their values may be narrow. They are probably not values held by society as a whole. Perhaps worse, their values are today's values, not those which will be held by people in the future. This is a form of tyranny—the tyranny of the present.

If you make forecasts, be aware of this possibility.

Can We Transform into a Post-Industrial Society?

M. S. Iyengar

Must the less technologically developed nations follow in the footsteps of the industrial nations? For 100 years or more, men have assumed that the only path toward "development" in the poor nations was the path of industrialism. Here India's leading futurist argues the reverse. The developing nations could, he contends, move into the future directly, by-passing the whole stage of industrialism, and thereby leaving the rich and "advanced" nations behind.

[Recent scientific and technological developments could mean] that man, for the first time, will be freed from economic drudgery and will develop a society not based on want or necessity, but based on his own choice and free will. Society could be transformed from the "primary" or agricultural level to the "secondary" or industrial level to the "tertiary" level—that of a "learning society."

As technological change profoundly alters the nature and centrality of industrial activity as a major social institution, capital and heavy industrial enterprise will no longer be the key wealth-producing and innovative force in society. Increased knowledge, based on human resource capital, transferred into many forms of physical and social activities, becomes more directly the wealth generator.

The ways of earning a living, occupational status, economic and geographic location, and other categories will no longer be the constraining factors on the style of life. Occupation, location, environmental and social milieu may be changed many times in a lifetime. Lack of material attainment, decline of economic self-interest and possession, diversity of life style would be characteristic of post-industrial man.

Education, at present thought of as preparation for living, would be more pervasively viewed as an ongoing aspect of living itself. Research would be recast into a form that would encompass many types of individual and social explorations, of which specialized scientific research would be only one type.

Socio-ethical attitudes, which today are largely based on marginal and competitive survival because of the limited and unequally distributed resources, would completely change. Socio-ethical decisions regarding the human condition need no longer be phrased in terms of what we can do—but in terms of what we choose to do, both individually and collectively. Work would no longer be the central interest of life.

While the transformation of the advanced industrial countries like the USA to post-industrial societies is relatively easier, that of transforming a pre-industrial country like [India] to a post-industrial society, that is, the transformation of the "old" world to the "modern," is a gigantic one. How to modernize, which technological and industrialization patterns to choose, [and] what long-range consequences and implications do those have on the human environment [are the key questions].

We have the advantage of learning from the mistakes and maldevelopments of the West. We may be able to circumvent many of the dislocations, the physical and social environmental deterioration, which the "less self-conscious" process of Western modernization has occasioned. Through hindsight and our different value background, we have the opportunity of exploring innovative structures for socio-economic and technological developments, new models for institutional and individual relations to society.

Rather than retrace the traditional pattern of development followed by the advanced countries, we may "take off" higher on the technological scale with a much faster integration rate than the more established areas. We might even go from pre-industrial society forms to post-industrial in one transformative stage of development.

We have already with us some of the outer manifestations of post-industrial society. [The] majority of our people are unemployed or partially employed in the economic sense, and, to a good number of them, work is not the central life interest. The principle of rationality and efficiency and the notion of time as money, that is, as a scarce commodity and socially significant unit, do not exist. These are the very manifestations of a post-industrial society. Adaptation to similar conditions would be, therefore, much easier [here] than in Western society which, through industrialization, has already got conditioned to work as an economic force. We could, therefore, explore adopting the post-industrial pattern of production which would be largely automated or cybernated. Adoption of sophisticated technology and not "intermediate technology" might be the answer for quickly increasing production with minimum effort and time—as the following examples might illustrate.

A thermionic valve is more costly than a transistor, which is a generation ahead of the former. A transistor is more costly than the integrated circuit, which is again a generation ahead of the former. The integrated electronic component, being another generation ahead, would be still less costly. It is therefore prudent to adopt the integrated electronic component [rather] than begin with the thermionic valve.

The development of industrial bases in advanced countries has gone through three stages:

1. The localized growth of iron and steel.
2. Production of new steel and alloy steel by controlling the production

of materials like manganese, tungsten, nickel, cobalt, etc., and by . . . heavy dependence on coal and oil fuels as major energy sources.

3. Displacement of steel as the prime industrial material (for structural, machine, transport, and other uses) by other light metals, composite materials and plastics, and pairing of the light metals with electric power from hydro or nuclear sources, and . . . the increased use of metallic and non-metallic components and plastics with similar power resources.

Rather than invest in the production of conventional iron and steel the developing countries like [India] should switch over to the third phase directly.

The normal trend in industrialization in a conventional society has been towards urbanization with the city as a center. Yet we are now in the development phases of successive technological revolutions in which refined electronic means have displaced most of the present time, energy, and space relationships which were the guidelines of our thinking. Urbanization may be viewed as only one of a number of possible strategies for an overall pattern of living which goes on through the life cycle in many widely separated locations as in the predominantly rural areas of India.

We are attempting to transform what McLuhan calls an ear-oriented (tribal) society into a vision-oriented (modern) society when the advanced countries are again reverting back to an aural form of society! Today, new technologies—the telephone, the radio, the television, the computer—are causing an "implosion," forcing people back together in a tribal unity. This is in contradiction to the visual-sense dominated society based on print which causes an "explosion"—breaking society up into categories— "jobs," "prices," "departments," "specialties," "nations." We have to understand the compulsions of the "media" and the future technology and adopt a pattern of life which quickly transforms our society into a post-industrial society.

Bourgeois "Futurology" and the Future of Mankind

I. Bestuzhev-Lada

Despite official reservations about it, futurism has spread to the U.S.S.R., Czechoslovakia, Poland, Rumania, and other Communist countries. In this polemic, a Soviet futurist attacks his American and West European counterparts for serving the cause of imperialism—at the same time citing Marx, Lenin, and even Kosygin to establish the legitimacy of Marxist forecasting.

A New Term and Its Content. The term "futurology" (from the Latin *futurum,* or future, and the Greek *logos,* or science) appeared for the first time in 1943 in the articles of the German sociologist O. Flechtheim, who emigrated to the United States long before World War II. Commenting on the growing number of works containing social forecasts, he wrote about the emergence of a new science which, he claimed, was just coming into its own—the science of the future, or futurology. It must be added that futurology was unambiguously set in opposition to scientific communism, though it is common knowledge that it was Marxism which put the study of social concepts of the future on a scientific footing more than a century ago.

As they worked out the principles of scientific prognostication, Marx and Engels carried on an ideological struggle not only against utopianism but, first and foremost, against the agnostic approach to problems of the future common at the time among the leading bourgeois philosophers, who claimed that it was impossible to make scientific prognostications of social processes. Of great importance was also the Marxists' struggle against positivism with its empirical approach to cognition and its denial of the possibility of making scientific forecasts of qualitative changes in the future development of society.

Later on, Lenin developed the Marxist principles by analyzing the specific features of the epoch of imperialism and socialist revolutions. His tremendous contribution to the theory of scientific prognostication was related to the theory and practice of socialist planning in the Soviet Union. It may not be amiss to recall here that the question of the possibility, in principle, of forecasting and planning concrete social processes triggered a worldwide discussion at that time. To most bourgeois scientists the very idea of such a possibility seemed fantastic. Now that we are preparing to celebrate Lenin's centenary, it is particularly appropriate to stress that it was under the direct impact of his works that the study of problems of scientific prognostication of concrete social processes as the basis of national economic planning assumed extensive forms in the USSR at that time. This evoked a wide response abroad, stimulating public interest in the problem of mankind's future.

The term "futurology" swept back into use in the early sixties when the so-called prognosis boom set in in the West. This trend arose as a result of the development of relatively effective methods of forecasting social processes and the emergence of hundreds of large research establishments and departments specializing in prognostication in the development of science, technology, economics, social relations, the state and the law, domestic and foreign policies, international relations and further earth and space exploration.

The persistent tendency to look into the future, characteristic not only of a narrow group of scientists, bourgeois politicians and economic policy-makers, but of the broad public as well, was due to a complexity of causes. The development of the world socialist system, which pushed into the foreground the question of the trends and prospects of the contest between the two world social systems; the emergence of scores of new states and their search for ways of overcoming their economic and cultural backwardness; the appearance of nuclear missile weapons threatening humanity with total destruction; the technological revolution with its many-sided and contradictory influences on the economy and social relations; the continual growth of the productive forces and the resultant state-monopoly regulation of the economy; the population explosion and the prospects of food supplies for the world; finally, the accelerated pace of social development itself and the immense scale of the changes taking place in the world—all had the effect of sharply stimulating interest in the future and the demand for social prognostication.

Today the general term "futurology" denotes both a complex combination of specific social prognoses and prognostication proper, a new, gradually developing science of the laws, methods, and ways of prognostication. The sphere of prognostication has been substantially broadened to embrace not only economics but demography, the social implications of the technological revolution, politics, etc.

The technique of working out social prognoses (in the above-mentioned broad sense of the term) has made a great stride forward in the last five or ten years. Questionnaires, mathematical-statistical extrapolation, prognosis modeling and other methods borrowed from the arsenal of contemporary sociology, economy, mathematics and cybernetics help to make more durable, accurate and reliable prognoses. These are less and less often regarded as mere attempts to anticipate and foresee future events, although this too is an aspect of no small importance. The essence of social prognostication is increasingly determined by its special contribution to systematically raising the level of planning, programming, projecting, and control of social processes in general. This approach is extremely effective since it helps save money by optimizing plans, reduces the time spent on their development, increases the efficiency of technical-economic and military-political programs, and uses for the purposes of ideological struggle the keen interest of world public opinion in the problems of the future of the earth and of mankind.

In the present-day capitalist world futurology has a dual role to play: first, to participate in working out the economic and political strategy of imperialism; secondly, to supply new arguments in the ideological struggle against communism. A student of futurology must take this fact into account. A profound critical analysis of contemporary bourgeois concepts of the future and their exposure are as important as is a sober appraisal of its effectiveness and a careful and systematic study of its methods and machinery. It must also be remembered that prognostication is not just contemplation of the future but a formidable two-edged weapon. Superficial criticism which does not go beyond scathing epithets can do nothing but harm here. A few serious Marxist studies have recently appeared containing profound criticisms of separate aspects of bourgeois futurology. But much still remains to be done in this field.

Opposing bourgeois futurology is Marxist-Leninist social prognostication, which rests on the solid foundation of dialectical and historical materialism, on the theory of scientific communism, and is rooted materially in the socialist mode of production, thus opening up the broadest possibilities for planned development of the economy and society as a whole. Therein lies the basic advantage of Marxist-Leninist prognostication over bourgeois futurology. What is needed is to make better use of this advantage.

Some Contours of the Future. Studies in social prognostication during the past few years have brought out some important contours of the world of the next three decades.

Judging by population prognoses, the world population will nearly double by the year 2000 and amount to from 6 to 7 billion (6,129,-734,000 according to the mean version of the prognosis drawn up by UN experts), compared with 3.5 billion at the present time.

Scientific and technical prognoses suggest that mankind will then be consuming at least five times as much energy as today (26 to 30 billion tons of ideal fuel compared to 5.9 billion tons in 1965, according to the estimate made by some Soviet economists).

A powerful energy basis will make it possible to develop new raw material resources in new regions, including minerals to be found occurring in the deep layers of the earth's crust or on the world's ocean floor. Production of all kinds of natural and synthetic materials, probably even synthetic materials with predetermined properties, from the practically unlimited reserves of inorganic materials will grow in scope.

The further progress of automation in industry, building, agriculture, transport and communications, plus the new abundance of fuel, energy and raw material reserves, are capable in principle, as can be seen from the data of scientific-technical and socio-economic prognosis, of bringing about a sharp increase in the production of material goods as well as a further reduction in working hours. In any case, the number of automatic production lines, shops, factories, fully automated building enterprises, transport and communications systems, livestock and crop growing farms, must grow considerably over the next few decades. All these enterprises will be able to produce several times more than at present without expanding their physical space and with a considerably reduced work force.

Agriculture especially will be in a position to produce several times more foodstuffs than today. According to estimates by Soviet scientists, if the advanced agricultural techniques of today were applied to the areas cultivated throughout the world at present, it would be possible to provide food for about 10 billion people. Even as things stand, the level of production could be surpassed several times over with existing achievements of agricultural science and technology, as may be seen from the record yields already being secured. Besides, the tilled areas can be considerably expanded. Finally, the seas and oceans contain abundant food resources that are not yet fully utilized, not to mention the very real prospects held out by experiments already under way in the production of synthetic fodder and food.

On the whole, the gross per capita national product throughout the world will grow by at least 2.5 to 3 times by the year 2000.

Such are some of the conceivable contours of the world of tomorrow in the light of contemporary prognostication data. The details of these contours continue to serve as an object of scientific discussion. But on the whole the prospects described above have been more or less accepted by the majority of experts.*

The question arises, however, whether these prospects will be realized. This will depend on the concrete socioeconomic and political conditions in which the world will develop in the second half of the 20th century; in other words, it will depend on the trends and prospects of development of the general crisis of capitalism, the world revolutionary process, socialist and communist construction in the socialist countries, and the competition between two social systems in the world arena. Naturally, on this score the data of Marxist and bourgeois social prognosis are diametrically opposed to one another.

Basic Trends of Bourgeois Futurology. In analyzing bourgeois futurology, the idea must be rejected that it is homogeneous and all of a piece. In the first place there are differences, if one may put it so, in the genres of futurology. In this respect it divides into at least three groups of works that differ radically from one another.

One group comprises works on prognostication as such—that is, the methodology, methods, problems and other theoretical questions of prognostication. Actually these are not prognoses (though they may be used as illustrations) but works about prognosis— about those who make the forecasts (i.e., scientific establishments and their output), what they prognosticate (problems of social prognoses) and, most important of all, how prognoses are made (methods of prognostication). Among the most important works in the genre mention may be made of books by Bertrand de Jouvenel, Daniel Bell, Olaf Helmer, Erich Jantsch, and Fred L. Polak.

Another group includes books and articles which contain the ideas on the future of scientists and writers who are not necessarily prognostication experts. This group comprises the overwhelming majority of "futurological" works. Strictly speaking, they too are not prognoses in the most modern sense, but simply

---

* This is an optimistic judgment. Many futurists would challenge the estimate that advanced agriculture could feed a global population of 10 billion. They question whether the very attempt to do so might not produce dangerous ecological side effects. [Ed.]

attempts to anticipate and to foresee certain social phenomena of the future based either on the experience and intuition of the authors or on information obtained from scientific and popular science literature. But it would be a mistake to underestimate these men's work on such grounds: as a rule, it contains—although often in a raw embryonic form—scientific hypotheses which later make up the nucleus of concepts of the future in comprehensive up-to-date scientific forecasts.

Outstanding among the works of this type published in the nineteen-fifties and sixties are the world-famous works of N. Wiener, J. Thomson, F. Baade, A. Clarke, O. Flechtheim, J. Fourastie, D. Gabor, R. Jungk, K. Jaspers, C. von Weizsacker, and others. (We do not touch here upon the works of J. D. Bernal and other Western Marxist scientists, which merit special attention.)

Finally, the third group includes the contemporary social forecasts proper, i.e., the scientific output of specialized research establishments, which takes the form of individual, or more often collective, development of prognostic models of various social phenomena based on opinion polls taken among experts, questionnaires distributed among specific social groups, complex extrapolation of statistical information with the application of a number of theories of mathematics and cybernetics (the theory of probability, the theory of games, etc.), analyses of a mass of patent information and other documents, etc. As has already been said, prognoses of this kind are not an end in themselves but serve to substantiate plans, programs, projects, and general decisions pertaining to the control of social processes. They play a decisive role particularly in the system of "planning-programming-budgeting" widely practiced in the West in the attempts to control economic development under state-monopoly capitalism.

Most of the output of this sort is intended for a close circle of experts or is kept secret. Among the published works, the best-known forecasts are those prepared by groups of prominent Western experts on the development of the economies of the United States, Britain, France, and West Germany.

Of course, any attempt to outline the anatomy, as it were, of futurology—an attempt, to my mind, necessary for the understanding of the complicated and contradictory bourgeois concept of the future—is in a sense an abstraction. In reality, the situation is much more complex because "pure" forms of any of the genres are seldom met with. More often one and the same work contains prognoses, the author's speculation on the future, and resumes of forecasts that have already been made.

As regards the content of the concepts of the future, three main trends may be distinguished here too. Prevailing among them is the one which unreservedly supports the thesis that capitalism will not only survive the 20th century but will be capable of overcoming its inherent contradictions in the future as well—with the aid of the current scientific and technological revolution. The authors of these theories usually portray the future of the capitalist world (in which they simply "dissolve" the world socialist system) in bright, optimistic colors. A social utopia of eternal capitalism— such is the gist of the trend which for the sake of brevity may tentatively be called apologetic. As an illustration we may take any of the works enumerated in the last group (it is no secret that all of them carry a definite propaganda load and some, particularly the forecast, *Germany, 1975*, were written especially for propaganda purposes).

The representatives of another trend are aware that the preservation of capitalism is incompatible with the socioeconomic implications of the scientific and technological revolution, but see no way out of the critical impending situation. Their concepts are usually given in pessimistic, sometimes even apocalyptic tones. Specifically, this is manifest in their prophecies on the inevitable "decline of civilization" (the tradition is traced back to the notorious *Decline of The West* by Oswald Spengler, and kindred works of the nineteen-twenties). More and more often one hears talk about the inevitability of contemporary civilization being superseded by a machine civilization, with people becoming completely subordinated to the cybernetic organisms of their own creation. Sometimes a call is heard to "go back to nature," to the idyll of country life, etc. Actually, these are the peculiar neo-eschatological views of the ideologists of a social system that is already doomed. Views characteristic of this trend may be found among Western thinkers of the most diverse political persuasions, for example, in the works of K. Jaspers and A. Clarke, already mentioned above.

The representatives of the third trend also assume that the socioeconomic consequences of the scientific and technological revolution are incompatible with the preservation of capitalism in its present form. But they believe it possible to reform capitalism, to "adapt" it to the future at all costs, even to the point of complete "convergence" with socialism (with recognition of the need for a gradual strengthening of socialist principles). This trend is strong for its criticism of the vices of the bourgeois system. Quite a few progressively minded Western scientists, men like N. Wiener, F. Baade, A. Clarke and R. Jungk, belong to it.

It is noteworthy that in contrast to the authors of the official forecasts which bear the earmarks of propaganda, nearly every prominent thinker in the West speculating on the future as a rule shows little optimism in assessing the prospects of development of the capitalist world. Their statements are usually voiced in the spirit of either the second or the third trend (and sometimes of both at once). This is a very remarkable fact, vividly testifying to the crisis of contemporary bourgeois ideology.

Of course, it would be oversimplifying matters to pigeonhole all Western thinkers by fixed categories. Features characteristic of two, and sometimes even of all three, trends are contradictorily intertwined in many works. We can point out that the second and third trends are represented somewhat more conspicuously in Western Europe, whereas the first trend prevails in North America. All this creates additional difficulties by making it necessary to analyze every important work in the field of futurology separately, with a view to the specifics of the various genres and the often contradictory nature of the concept of the future outlined in each.

That is why it is not easy to make a thorough examination of bourgeois literature on the future, all the more so since futurology as a whole is only just becoming an object of special research. The diversity and inner contradictoriness of these concepts of the future is so significant that any attempt to "tell a little about everything" inevitably leads to vulgarization in the evaluation of one of the most complicated phenomena of contemporary social thought.

It seems more expedient to pick out the most significant works among the recent publications of the bourgeois specialists, those combining the typical features of contemporary Western futurology and giving a fairly full idea about the range of studies in this field. The most suitable work for this purpose, we think, is the monograph *The Year 2000,* by H. Kahn and A. Wiener.

We made this choice for several reasons. First, the work contains questions of forecasting methodology and speculations on the future belonging to recognized United States authorities on futurology, and also gives the results of studies in social prognostication carried out by one of the leading United States research establishments in the field (the book was written with the help of staff members of the Hudson Institute directed by H. Kahn). Secondly, the monograph is in all respects typical of the apologetic trend which prevails in contemporary bourgeois futurology. Finally, it may be considered the most significant, the "last word" in bourgeois futurology.*

Biased Extrapolation. Kahn and Wiener's book is largely devoted to a particular problem of social forecasting—the methodological principles on which forecasts of military-political situations are built. It is intended to stimulate broad and intensive investigations concerning military-political forecasting for the White House, the Pentagon, and the State Department. In accordance with this purpose the authors show the advantages of a systematic approach to long-range problems of foreign policy and international relations, demonstrating methods of working out models of further development of the system of international relations according to the chief versions as they see them, and constructing on this basis prognostic scripts of the possible course and outcome of the most probable conflicts in the world arena. They base these models and scripts on a comprehensive concept of the future socioeconomic development of society. It is this concept that is of prime interest to us.

On closer examination it appears that Kahn and Wiener's concept (like those of most of the other representatives of the apologetic trend) is based on the "theory of phased development" which has won wide acceptance in the West. It was most completely expounded in the works of W. W. Rostow, Raymond Aron, and J. Galbraith. This theory, as is known, treats the history of mankind not as a succession of socioeconomic formations but as a long series of stages of socioeconomic and political development according to the growth of the gross national product (GNP) in general and its per capita ratio in particular. This approach reduces the differences

* The Kahn–Wiener book was published in 1967, Bestuzhev-Lada's essay in 1969. [Ed.]

between the world capitalist and socialist systems to purely political motives of confrontation between hostile groups of powers.
Preeminence is given to the GNP value which is claimed completely to determine the position of any country, regardless of its
social system.

It is clear that this approach puts the United States, which has
the highest GNP, in the top "stage of development." Strung out
behind it—depending on their GNP level—are the developed capitalist countries, followed by the USSR and the European socialist countries, with the countries of Latin America, Asia and
Africa lagging far behind. From this standpoint, the sense of the
socioeconomic development of every country is to move up the
rungs of the "GNP ladder" and—in some more or less far-off future
—to reach the present-day level of the United States, which
appears as the pinnacle of creation—just as Hegel conceived the
Prussian monarchy of the middle of the last century.

Kahn and Wiener divide the countries of the world into five categories: "pre-industrial" (less than $200 of GNP per capita a year),
"traditional" ($200 to $600), "industrial" ($600 to $1,500), "highly
industrial" ($1,500 to $4,000), and "post-industrial" (more than
$4,000). They then estimate what they believe to be the most prob-
able rates of growth of the GNP in these countries. Finally they
calculate how many years it would take this or that country at its
given rate of progress to pass to the next category, and eventually
to reach the present-day level of the United States. The picture
they get is really impressive: even the "highly industrial" and
economically developed countries will require from 11 to 42 years,
whereas "pre-industrial" India will take no less than 117 years,
Nigeria 339 years, and Indonesia 593 years to achieve this.

However, a serious scientific examination of these figures shows
that the gap between the United States and other countries is several times less, and the anticipated rates of development of some
of the countries are much higher, so that the time required to close
the gap is much shorter. But the most objectionable point of principle is the concept of the future itself, which pictures the year
2000 as a greater or lesser approximation to the U.S. level in the
nineteen-fifties and sixties, and the United States as having rid
itself of its present-day troubles by passing into the "post-industrial"
stage. But the authors do not simply calculate the average per

capita income in dollars. Their theory implies that as one country after another approaches the U.S. level—irrespective of their social systems—they will come more and more to resemble the United States both economically and socially.

Any such theory is untenable inasmuch as it is a mistake to make a direct extrapolation of the data for the past few years (moreover, selected and calculated with a definite slant), and to ignore the possibility and even inevitability of serious qualitative changes. Prognostication experts know full well that any direct extrapolation into a remote future of any more or less important social process—be it growth of population, development of the economy or culture, etc.—inevitably leads to mistaken conclusions. This is so because we live in an age of scientific and technological revolution the socioeconomic implications of which, to judge by prognosis data, will far exceed even those considerable changes that are observable today. This important factor is discarded by the authors of the "theory of phased development" because it avowedly undermines their concept.

Is it really conceivable that in the year 2000—as contemporary social forecasts picture it, in a world of the successful struggle of progressive social forces, of a final transformation of science into a powerful productive force, in short, a world of the triumphant march of automation, of unprecedented productivity and, consequently, of real potential for the creation of an abundance (or at least a sufficiency) of the most important necessities—is it conceivable that in the year 2000 the countries of Asia, Africa and Latin America will still be lagging behind the U.S.A. by 100, 300, 500 years, with the U.S.A. becoming a kind of never-to-be-reached ideal for all the rest of the world?

This would be possible only if we presumed (which is wholly improbable) that the world capitalist system were by some miracle to get rid of its inherent contradictions and vices while the world socialist system were also, by some miracle, deprived of all the advantages of its socioeconomic development, which now permit it to count on an early victory in the competition with capitalism, and the developing countries were to continue meekly to bear the neocolonialist yoke, remaining in the vise of backwardness and poverty, suffering from hunger and epidemics, from shortages not only of qualified experts but of educated people in general. In other words, this could happen only if one assumed that the world socialist system were somehow to "dissolve" in the capitalist world, that the international working class movement were to abandon its ultimate revolutionary goals, and the national liberation movement were just to wither away.

What has been said above should by no means be taken as any underestimation of the economic factor in determining the prospects of development of one country or another, including such important indices of economic growth as the increase of the GNP in general and its per capita level in particular. It is well known that the prospects of the competition between the two world systems depend largely on socialism gradually gaining the upper hand precisely in respect to labor productivity and economic potential, in respect to the per capita GNP ratio. But how the GNP is produced and distributed is also of great importance. No less important are the place and role of the goods produced in the general system of social demands, which undergo serious changes in the course of the scientific and technological revolution.

The fact that the United States has reached a relatively high per capita GNP average does not overshadow the fact that tens of millions of people in that country are deprived of their rights by the capitalist system and live in poverty or on the brink of poverty. It is a fair forecast that the situation will hardly change by the year 2000, no matter how high the GNP may grow, if the capitalist mode of production and distribution of material benefits remains unchanged. Consequently the leading capitalist country will continue to be torn by acute social conflicts which weaken its capitalist foundations, by greater class battles which undermine the outdated mode of production. At the same time we can observe a growth of opposition sentiments among the intellectuals, a growing student movement—a selfless struggle of people not only for bread and shelter but also for such social values as genuine democracy, human dignity, life with a meaning, elementary social justice, confidence in the morrow, the right to education, creative work, decent living conditions, the right to effective social security in the broad sense of the word.

Will these tendencies disappear or on the contrary grow stronger under the impact of the struggle between the two world systems now taking place in conditions of the growing scientific and technological revolution? For the answer to be substantiated, let us examine some of the most important socioeconomic implications of this revolution.

Impact of the Scientific-Technological Revolution. It is known that the automation of all branches of social production and the swift growth of labor productivity sharply accelerate the process of redistribution of labor resources: the number of workers employed in the sphere of material production is decreasing, whereas the number of those employed in the services and cultural production is growing. Not so long ago the first of the above-mentioned spheres included up to nine-tenths of all workers, even in the economically developed countries. Now the ratio approaches 50:50, and in some cases even exceeds it. If this rate is maintained, by the year 2000 further significant changes may have taken place.

It is also known that automation and the growth of productivity call for a sharp change in the correlation and content of working and leisure time. The share and importance of mental labor are growing in all spheres of work without exception. The importance of cultural leisure for the intellectual and physical training of a full-fledged worker in modern social production is growing. Under the pressure of this objective demand of modern production and as a result of the persistent struggle of the workers for shorter working hours, the capitalist employers are being forced to make concessions and to reduce the share of working time and increase the share of leisure time. Not so long ago the working year consisted of 3,000 to 4,000 hours, and the work week was 60 to 70 hours long and longer. Now working time in many countries has been reduced by 30 to 50 per cent, and it is quite probable that it will drop as much again by the year 2000. There is already talk in some places about going over to a four-day working week. In view of this, leisure time is growing into one of the most pressing social problems.

Finally, it is known that the scientific and technological revolution, which accelerates the integration of science and production, at the same time intensifies the process of intellectualization of society. The sphere of mental labor is spreading far and wide and creating a strong demand for highly qualified workers. Here too a revolution is under way. Not long ago skilled men with even a secondary education did not exceed 10 per cent of all the workers in many developed countries. In the United States on the eve of World War I, only 4 per cent of youths aged from 16 to 21 years went to college, while the remaining 96 per cent were at best only able to read, write, and do simple arithmetic. Now the share of college students in that country has topped 40 per cent and keeps growing from year to year. The socialist countries are one after another going over to universal secondary education, and correspondingly increasing the enrollment at their higher educational establishments. The results of this process for the year 2000 can easily be expressed in simple prognostic models.

Is it conceivable, then, that the social requirements of mankind in 2000—mankind as it is developing before our very eyes under the impact of the struggle between socialism and capitalism in conditions of the scientific and technological revolution—will be reduced to the simple ambition to reach the United States level of fifty years earlier? Is it not more logical to suppose that the development of the sphere of spiritual production, the increase in leisure time, the intellectualization of society, will all prove to be mighty allies of the world socialist system, of the international working class and the national liberation movements, in their struggle against the ulcers and vices of today's moribund social system? For the socioeconomic effects of the scientific and technological revolution as they appear in the light of modern forecasting data are in irreconcilable contradiction with the further existence of the capitalist mode of production. It may be said in this connection that the principal result of the scientific and technological revolution of our time is the objective formation of the material prerequisites of the communist mode of production everywhere.

The world's Communist parties carefully keep and augment the Marxist-Leninist traditions of a determined offensive against the positions of the bourgeois ideologists along this front. It must be admitted, however, that in the ideological struggle against capitalism, the problems of the future do not always receive due attention.

The Marxist View. Let us recall how passionately Lenin urged us to use every opportunity actively to oppose the manifold bourgeois concepts of the future with Marxist views. He emphasized that Marxist theory posed questions "not in the sense of explaining the past but also in the sense of a bold forecast of the future and of equally bold practical action for its achievement."[1] On all sides, at every step, one comes across problems which man is quite capable of solving immediately—but capitalism stands in the way. It has amassed enormous wealth—and has made men the slaves of this wealth. It has solved the most complicated technical problems—and has blocked the application of technical improvements because of the poverty and ignorance of the millions, because of the stupid avarice of a handful of millionaires.[2] Thus Lenin wrote about one purely "futurological" problem, the project of a tunnel to be built under the English Channel. This was how he utilized for purposes of communist propaganda one of the sensational problems concerning the future.

The importance of forecasting has also grown in the practical activities of the Communist parties. The successful solution of the complex tasks of socialist and communist construction in the Soviet Union and the fraternal countries, of the economic, scientific and technological competition with the world capitalist system, and of the struggle against the aggressive policies of imperialism, calls for the improvement of scientific Marxist-Leninist prognostication of the long-range prospects of development of the modern world. The effectiveness of the long-range economic programs and the political strategy of the socialist countries depends on how complex and reliable these forecasts can be.

In recent years the problems of social prognostication have become an object of special study in the USSR, the German Democratic Republic, Poland, Czechoslovakia, and some other socialist states. The Soviet Communist Party and the Soviet government attach great importance to the expansion of research in the field of scientific, technological and socioeconomic prognostication as a scientific basis for national economic planning. "The discussion of scientific prognoses must precede the working out of plans of development of national economic branches," said A. N. Kosygin at a session of the USSR State Planning Committee in March, 1965. "We must have at our disposal scientific forecasts for the development of each branch of industry, so as to give, in due time, the green light to everything advanced and progressive, and we must know the direction in which the plan should be worked out." The resolution of the Communist Party-Soviet Union Central Committee and the USSR Council of Ministers "On Measures for Raising the Efficiency of Scientific Organizations and Accelerating the Application in the National Economy of Scientific and Technical Achievements" (October, 1968) emphasized that "long-term scientific and technological forecasts (for 10, 15, and more years) should be drawn up in future in relation to the key problems of development of the national economy." These instructions call upon Soviet scientists to carry on the investigation and to intensify research work in this field.

For a Science of Man

Erich Jantsch
Interviewed by
G. R. Urban

Originally an astronomer, Erich Jantsch in the mid-sixties conducted the most comprehensive survey of forecasting techniques up to that time. Since then he has become passionately critical of those who believe that forecasting—or science, itself—can be neutral or value-free. In this thought-provoking interview, he voices fear for our ecological future along with sympathy for the young rebels who are forcing a reevaluation of the role of science in the future. G. R. Urban of the University of Southern California is a specialist in East-West relations.

Urban: Communist parties in the Soviet Union and Eastern Europe have been planning their economies and societies from the day they came to power. In Western Europe and especially in the

United States we are now being warned that unless we too heed the voices of the long-range planners, we might find ourselves in deep trouble as creators and consumers of the social product, as consumers of the world's energy resources, as men with a stake in the cultural heritage and educational resources of our civilisation. Have we just discovered what the Communist parties have known all along?

Jantsch: I don't think so. The philosophy underlying the development of all future-oriented thinking in the West is entirely different both from the Communist type of planning and from its first cousin: industrial product planning which has been employed by Western enterprises for a long time. This old type of planning—whereby you determine the likely consumption of soap-powder in New Jersey if the average man continues to buy five shirts a year, or the number of university places France will need when the results of the post-war baby boom reach the university admission offices—this type of planning is a purely mechanistic affair. Communist planning (I always have to add: "as practised in Eastern Europe") operates on almost identical lines. It is mechanistic because it assumes that the framework in which the planning has to be done is already given. Marxist planners presume that there is an objective law running through the lives of societies, that there is an objective framework of values and norms, and the question they have to ask themselves is simply: how do we attain our ends most efficiently within that framework? It is, therefore, a religious framework in all essentials, for the sort of questioning it permits does not extend beyond the mere operation of the system. The system itself—the hypothesis that there is in our time only one correct ideology for man to live by, and one natural state towards which society has to develop—is not called in question. So while the general framework of Communist planning is basically a religious affair, its execution shares a method with the linear product-planning ways of our more old-fashioned industries. In fact, it combines the worst of both worlds.

Urban: So both Marxist planning and the product-planning process in Western industries have a teleological principle running through them. They know their ends and the future will be bent to those ends.

Jantsch: They do. I should make it clear, though, that at a low level of planning, at what we call the operational level of planning, this rather elementary approach is valid. If you take industrial product planning, there is a time when you have to freeze in some of your options so that you can devote your resources to products which have a higher priority in your planning. It is then that a mechanistic model comes in handy.

Urban: You said a moment ago that the ideas governing future-oriented thinking in the West are entirely different from the kind of planning we have in the Soviet type of societies. What are the differences?

Jantsch: My answer to that, at its simplest, is that we try to develop a "human-action" model, which is our way of saying that it is man himself who takes the responsibility for designing his future and of finding ways of making that future just and liveable.

Urban: He is not governed by historic necessity or any goal which would pre-determine his actions?

Jantsch: No, he is not. Mankind is now pushing against limitations which are global in character. We are encountering the fact that the planet Earth has limited resources to feed us and house us and keep us warm. We are running up against boundaries when we talk about the world's population or the balance between nature and the man-made world. We are discovering that it is not only the normally peaceable chimpanzees that start fighting and then dying off of disease if they are forced to live in an over-crowded cage, but that overpopulation can, and already does, have the same effect on human beings. These are vast and pressing problems and we cannot hope to do justice to them with the old methods, Communist or Western. Man and his surroundings have to be conceived as one single whole, a system, in fact, in which changes in one part have an impact on all other parts, directly or indirectly. The picture we should have of our state on this globe is one of interdependence as between nations and regions, and also between man and the natural world which sustains him. We are all our brother's keepers.

Urban: How would you spell out the moral, cultural and aesthetic consequences which follow from perceiving man's situation in this way?

Jantsch: Before we can talk about the ethics of our situation we must have a clear picture of what is wrong with the direction we have taken so far. For it is clear that in many important respects the technological engine has landed us in a blind alley. Take our attitude to growth. We never question the proposition that economic growth, the growth of the material standard of living and the resulting competition between individuals, companies and nations are good things and ought to be encouraged. This is surely a prescription for disaster. We are already straining against the limits of growth: economies cannot go on growing much further, consumption and the exploitation of the earth's resources cannot increase indefinitely. So what we have to do is to sit down and think again. It is then that the need for fresh values and a new orientation impresses itself on us with very great urgency. We'll have to ask ourselves whether, for instance, the ethos of competition and growth should not be replaced by an ethos of responsibility, whether the scramble for squeezing the last inches of usable land out of the earth's surface and the last drops of unpoisoned water should not give way to some view which pays due attention to the overall ecological balance between man, society, technology and nature.

Urban: But aren't we then talking about a complete and almost revolutionary transformation of our values, our business mentality, the collective goals of society, the norms that guide us in our dealings with foreign races and so on?

Jantsch: Indeed, I'm talking about the need for a complete cultural, I might almost say anthropological, transformation. And this goes for the Eastern countries no less than for the West because the Communist growth-ethic is a replica of our own, pursued even more fiercely but perhaps less efficiently. And the tragedy is that the more highly developed the technology, the more intricate the inter-actions and the more difficult to undo the damage. So you can launch an ecologically misconceived production method in Japan and the results will be felt five years later in Europe and they may well be irreversible.

Urban: All this would militate for a fully international type of cooperation between governments, planners, data-collectors and digesters. How can this be done without world government or, at the very least, a voluntary but binding kind of international cooperation?

Jantsch: I have no ready-made solutions to these problems but I can indicate some ways that seem to me feasible. One need not go the whole hog and demand world government. It would not be realistic at the present time. There are enough problems that can be dealt with internationally on a delegated basis for us to make a start without wanting to write off nation-states at this stage. Some of these problems will demand the creation of new institutions, others can be farmed out to existing ones. I'm not saying that we'll have an orgy of nation-states voluntarily relinquishing their sovereign rights. National governments don't normally behave like philanthropic institutions, but they can be made to yield if public opinion is sufficiently roused and the consequences of the collision course on which we are now set are made clear to the passengers. It is not enough to tell the driver.

Urban: The Communist governments have been pioneers in trying to map out the future for their societies. Are they responsive to this highly dynamic, non-class approach to man's life on the planet Earth?

Jantsch: I have visited some of the Communist countries and spent time in Moscow on an official invitation. Certainly the Soviet Government is much concerned with the future. They argue from the fact that they have made considerable progress in giving their population a higher standard of living and made spectacular progress in some fields of technology. They don't want to see those achievements endangered. They are much more conscious than most West European governments that national interests may be defeated if global interests are not taken care of.

Urban: If the Soviet Government, and perhaps some of the other Communist governments, are aware of these problems, the peoples of Eastern Europe are certainly not. In Poland or Hungary one knows from personal experience that the man in the street wants more pollution rather than less, more technology rather than less provided that he can get the car he is dreaming of buying, or the refrigerator, or the weekend cottage. His standard of comparison is the Austrian worker who has many of these things, and he will dismiss all talk about unclean rivers and impure air as typical concerns of the rich. He would be most unresponsive to any suggestion that the Gross National Product ought to be tested against the Gross National Pollution, or the Affluent Society against the Effluent Society.

Jantsch: This may well be so, but I should hasten to add that what the little man feels in Russia, Poland or Hungary is shared by what little men feel about this problem in most developing countries. I have heard the argument in countless places in Asia and Africa, and it is very much in evidence at the United Nations.

Even in Japan one hears the kind of view you have just quoted. I remember a phrase used by the Director of the Japanese Economic Research Institute at a recent conference: "Harmony and progress: harmony for the developed countries, progress for the developing world." In other words, the developing countries want economic development irrespective of what systemic interactions it may cause; once the development has reached a certain level, they will, they say, take care of the harmony.

I, for one, don't believe this is a viable philosophy. The rapid progress of technology in the advanced countries has already brought us to the crossroads. It is, in terms of a global ecology, impossible to bring the living standards of the developing world anywhere near the standards enjoyed by the Western nations. Reflect for a moment on American statistics. The population of the United States is six per cent of the world's population. Yet it consumes forty per cent of the world's resources. If everybody in the world consumed on the scale of the United States, the world's consumption of resources would increase sevenfold and that would mean instant disaster.

Where do we go from here? The conclusion I draw, and I think it is the only possible conclusion, is that we shall have to get the Western countries not only to prevent their economies from growing, but that the West will have to take several steps backward, lowering the material standard of living of the population, cutting back on consumption and taking a share in a more equitable distribution of the world's resources. This is going to be very hard on the Western governments and even harder on the people.

Urban: It runs counter to the rising expectations of the Western countries all of which, with the possible exception of the United States, have themselves just escaped from centuries of grinding poverty.

What worries me more in what you are saying are the long-range prospects of growing populations fighting each other for practically static or diminishing resources of food, minerals, water, etc. Does this not spell the spectre of class-war on a global scale —have-not Asians ravaging the cities of well-fed Europeans and Americans? It is a horrifying thought, but if it is true that the world cannot satisfy *both* the Swiss *and* the Bolivians, then the larger part of the world's population would seem to be doomed to eternal and probably growing relative poverty, and we know that sooner or later such inequalities lead to violent eruptions. You are, in a sense, confirming what Maoists like Lin Piao tell us: the world's hungry countryside encircling and destroying the world's cities— the developed and bourgeois West.

Jantsch: I fear you may be right. The gap between rich and poor is growing throughout the world and I can readily believe that in ten years' time we will not be able to visit the developing countries for they will have accumulated an explosive hatred for us. It isn't that we can keep them in ignorance of our welfare. We have given them radio and television, and they can see for themselves that even though they may be slightly better off than they were five years ago, they are, compared to the American Express traveller, much worse off than they were five years ago. All our aid to these countries—Western or Eastern—hasn't had any real impact. It hasn't been given fast enough and the methods used were ineffective. In the UN Development Decade the advanced countries increased their *per capita* income by more than three hundred dollars per annum, whereas per capita incomes in the developing countries were stagnant. I can see no hope that a second UN Development Decade would do any better, unless it started with a completely fresh philosophy and a vastly increased programme of financial and technical aid. At the moment we are offering less than one per cent of our GNP.

Urban: So we are talking about the need for a fundamental reappraisal of our moral and cultural attitudes both as individuals and as nations. The individual would have to lower his sights, consume less and find a new balance between himself and his surroundings. The rich nations would have to make similar sacrifices on a collective scale. These are daunting prospects which neither individuals nor nations would readily adopt unless their very lives were endangered.

Jantsch: They *are* daunting prospects, but what are our options? We could muddle along as we have done so far, postponing the day of reckoning. However, it isn't that we have to start from scratch. We can draw on the economic experiences of the wealthy countries both in their own development and the experiences they have gained in the developing world, and we can go on using them for a few more years.

But I would regard it as more important to inculcate a different spirit, not only in the donor nations but also in those that are at the receiving end. I'm thinking, for instance, of the lessons we may draw from examples such as the Asian cultures offer. They are very different from the life-ethos we have deduced from Christianity. Christians talk of a beginning and an end of the world and the span between the two has to be filled in with productive achievement. The Christian ethic, especially the Protestant ethic, concentrates on concrete activity on this side of eternity, and the usual concomitant of that work is to create something out of nothing and, as the next step, to make things grow: it may be the growth of a man's wealth, the status of his family, his clan, his city or his nation. The strictly Catholic equivalent of this ethic is perhaps less clearly programmatic, but even there the rewards of thrift, good husbandry and wise planning—i.e., growth and achievement—are well recognised.

Now all this is different in some of the Asian cultures. There man is believed to be destined to have more than one sojourn on earth and therefore he is in no particular hurry to fill his life with feverish activity. He disdains competition, he cannot see much point in a multiplication of his tools or possessions. Rather, he values the unspectacular virtues of learning and contemplation which would seem to me to be much more in tune with the ecological requirements of the coming centuries than our growth-mania.

Urban: I would agree with you and go a step further. After all, man's exploitation of his natural environment is sanctioned by the Bible. In the first chapter of *Genesis* God says to man, "Be fruitful, multiply, and replenish the earth and subdue it: and have dominion over the fish of the sea, over the fowl of the air, and over every living thing that moveth upon the earth." Here we have a faultless Judeo-Christian prescription for the population explosion, for the pollution of the water and the air and for ecological disaster. True, one hears theologians argue that this picture is greatly modified by Christ's attitude to nature in the New Testament, and also by the dire warnings we are given of the impending environmental nemesis in the *Revelations* of St. John the Divine ("Hurt not the earth, neither the sea, nor the trees . . . And the third part of the waters became wormwood; and many men died of the waters, because they were made bitter . . . and the day shone not for a third part of it, and the night likewise . . . and the sun and the air were darkened by reason of the smoke of the pit" and so forth). Yet, in the most highly developed, industrialised countries it was the Protestant view of the world that set the public ethic, and that meant relying on *Genesis* more than on any other Biblical source. So, until quite recently, nature was looked upon as something to be overcome and suppressed. Taming the wilderness, cutting down trees, harnessing rivers were thought to be not only lucrative activities for man, but also attuned to God's purpose with man.

Jantsch: I agree with you, and when one remembers how Max Weber deduced the growth of capitalism from the Protestant ethic one has yet another reason for thinking that we may do well to look for cultural stimulants to India and China if we want to find a life-philosophy that would help us to do justice to our ecological problem. I'm reminded of Professor Chomsky's recent experiences in North Vietnam. As you know, Noam Chomsky is one of the most brilliant dissenters in the United States, an eloquent and influential opponent of American policies in Vietnam. Recently he was invited to North Vietnam, and in the course of his visit he asked the North Vietnamese Communist authorities what sort of technical help, what sort of engineering help they would need after the war has ended. To his surprise he was told that they didn't want engineers but rather the type of person who is well up in modern thinking in more general ways—scientists, philosophers, even artists. My guess would be that the North Vietnamese, with their tradition of sturdy independence, may not want to repeat the pattern of large-scale industrialisation which the Soviet Union and the East European countries have taken over from the West. They may want to try another alternative. That would mean not entering the race for increasing your GNP; it would mean the first conscious effort on the part of a developing nation not to join the suicide club.

And this takes me back to the spirit of cybernetic planning which we have already briefly discussed. The spirit of this modern planning does not set man apart from nature. There is no question of man subduing the earth or slaughtering the fish of the seas. On the contrary, it is realised that the man who subdues nature also subdues the human species. This is perhaps the easiest part of cybernetics to understand. But cybernetic planning applies the same philosophy to man-made systems and to the interplay between the man-made world and the natural environment. Its fundamental tenet is that systems—social systems, cities, industrial conglomerations and so on—are in permanent interaction with each other, with the earth, the air, the world's energy resources, and have to be continuously redesigned to protect the ecological balance and, through it, man's freedom. Quite obviously, this freedom presupposes the loss of *some* of our freedoms. An unbridled, competitive economic activity is clearly incompatible with that freedom for the simple reason that, within a very short time indeed, it would lead to quite crippling restrictions and worse. I can't do better than quote to you the opening paragraph of Gordon Rattray Taylor's new *Doomsday Book:*

Put bacteria in a test-tube, with food and oxygen, and they will grow explosively, doubling in number every twenty minutes or so, until they form a solid, visible mass. But finally multiplication will cease as they become poisoned by their own waste products. In the centre of the mass will be a core of dead and dying bacteria, cut off from the food and oxygen of their environment by the solid barrier of their neighbours. The number of living bacteria will fall almost to zero, unless the waste products are washed away.

Mankind today is in a similar position.

Here we have it all summed up in a few sentences.

Urban: You are saying that if men want to be free in the long run, or at any rate free within the possibilities of what our planet can afford to give us in terms of food, air, water, shelter and other resources, we must relinquish some of our freedoms in the short term, such as the freedom of untrammelled competition in the economic sphere, the pursuit of selfish national and individual interests and the like.

This, it would seem to me, is the sort of problem that exercises the rebellious young a great deal, but I perceive in their attitude a profound paradox. On the one hand the young are against anything that smacks of organisation. On the other hand, however, they are for the sort of freedom from environmental troubles which, according to what you have told us, only a proper understanding of the interactions between man, his technology and nature can secure, and that, you are arguing, imposes strict limits on our freedom. So even if the young managed to free the world of every trace of government and authority, they would still have to put up with, indeed they would have to create, agencies to curtail the freedoms they want.

Jantsch: Yes, I would say the romanticism and anarchism of the young is best understood as one manifestation of the spirit of competition and growth of which a free-enterprise economy is another. Now the paradox you mention is perhaps real but it gives me no cause for worry. One principle which is gradually emerging from the philosophy of future-oriented studies simply underlines the impossibility of solving certain problems with any finality and the necessity of learning to live with them. Our intellectual heritage is a great bind for us here, for, using the physical sciences and technology as our models, we have got used to the idea that conflicts are open to resolution even if they occur in complex systems. But this is not so. The paradoxes are numerous: the system I attempted to describe is weighted in some of its aspects against individual liberty, yet its whole purpose is to safeguard liberty. As Sir Geoffrey Vickers recently put it in *Freedom in a Rocking Boat:* "all human liberties are social artefacts, created, preserved and guaranteed by special social and political orders." In other words, liberty is created, not given; and it is as well to remember that freedom should not be confused with a situation free from all strains and pressures. There is also the dichotomy between instinct and rationality. Here again one has to realise that we can't hope to create the kind of consciousness that our ecological situation demands unless, like every good artist, we combine the two. By living these paradoxes rather than resolving them we may be approaching a kind of *modus vivendi.* This is no prescription for an easy life. It assumes that men, ordinary men, can be taught to live in a state of creative tension and perhaps taught to like it. This is the spirit of the ancient Greek tragedy, revived through ecological necessity, but of course enacted on a very different stage. It is the story of man rebelling against the system yet realising all the time that there are systemic boundaries to his actions. We understand that we are a part of nature yet we possess free will to contest the frontiers of our liberty. This may be a creative and constructive act or it may be mechanical and end in tragedy.

Now this may strike you as being slightly far-fetched but I believe that our dilemma is, basically at least, similar to those of the Greek tragedians.

Urban: I think this is a most stimulating analogy. It reminds me of one of Max Weber's books, *Wissenschaft als Beruf,* and a rejoinder written to it by Erich von Kahler, *Beruf der Wissenschaft.* Kahler was passionately arguing that science—he was thinking of both the hard and the soft sciences—is not, cannot be and shouldn't be, a morally neutral activity. Scientific work, he was saying, is value-laden. It should adapt its method to man and his emotional needs. Objective truths are irrelevant to its purpose. It should work in "homologies," not analogies. If my understanding of what you have said about man interacting with his social and natural environment is correct, then you should be agreeing with Kahler's point of view.

Jantsch: Yes, this type of thinking is entirely in line with what the new, future-oriented philosophy would seem to demand. The traditional view, as expounded by numberless scientists, has been that science is value-free, that technology is neutral and that only the use to which technology and science are put is loaded with moral issues. This is a false distinction. Science is a creation of man. It is not given in raw nature. In one way or another, every scientific activity creates anthropomorphic paradigms. Knowledge may be understood as a way of doing things, a mode of questioning, an approach to nature which implies, precisely because it asks certain questions, also the rejection of others. In other words it is a selective activity and therefore deeply influenced by the tastes, predilections and interests of the men who do the selecting.

I am not praising or condemning the subjective element in science, but it is as well for us to know that it is there because from it we may develop a quite unashamedly anthropomorphic kind of science which may become a culturally creative factor in the civilisation of the future. It will counteract the, to my mind, damaging influence of behaviourism and empiricism in the social sciences. It will have only the most tenuous links with practicability and will reaffirm our identity as men and not, as Professor Skinner would have it, as rats who happen to be bipeds endowed with an outsize cranium.

Urban: This is a very elevated view of scientific activity and I hope you will not think that I am disrespectful when I say that I am not sure that it is practicable.

Jantsch: Well, I happen to believe that defining and understanding the boundary conditions of science is a highly necessary practical activity. The system we want to design embraces every form of life and every type of society, and its purpose is to make it possible for man to continue living on this planet without destroying it, and with it, himself. So we have to shape an anthropomorphic system. But here is the snag: what is anthropomorphic? We have an elementary knowledge of what man is about: he needs to breathe air, if possible clean air. He needs food and he needs clean food. But over and above these simple facts our knowledge of human nature is very imperfect. Man can shape the environment. Is this a natural or an unnatural activity? And when the artificial environment he has created reacts back on him—is that so removed from the nature of man who has created it that we can say that it is alien to him and damaging to his nature? Let me quote another example. In the last hundred years we have adapted to vastly changing environments, and of course before that we have adapted to environmental change for thousands of years at a much slower pace. But we haven't the ability to adapt indefinitely. Some geneticists believe that eighty-five per cent of our genetic heritage is constantly in reserve to make it possible for us to adapt to new environments. Only fifteen per cent of it is actively engaged at one time. The mutations are extremely slow and man is in all essentials the same as he was in the stone age, three hundred generations ago. But we don't know how far we can go in adapting to artificial environments; we only know that there is a limit.

Futuristic speculations don't pay enough attention to such factors. We are told that in fifty years' time we shall all be living in vast, push-button glass and concrete environments, but we have no notion how that will affect us. There is, as René Dubos insists, a new science to be founded to study this kind of problem—the science of humanity. It will be a study of man as he encounters himself in an increasingly man-made world.

Urban: What kind of values would underlie the new civilisation you envisage?

Jantsch: Well, bringing new values into play is a difficult question and it is at the very core of this new planning philosophy. By going into a highly technological world we have given up the possibility of acting on instinct alone. Instinct gives you certain unerring certainties. Bees know precisely what they have to do to survive comfortably. We have lost that. We are now searching for something to give us a tolerably reliable yardstick, and that yardstick, that method is rationality. The great modern bet is that rational understanding can tell us what the world is about and, what is more important, that men will heed rational advice.

Urban: One would like to believe that man is a rational animal but there is little in history to confirm that he is. When the chips are down, when action has to be taken on essential issues, whether it be on the national or family level, the irrational element usually takes precedence over rational considerations. Khrushchev, as we know from his memoirs, ran the awful risk of a nuclear war with the United States for highly irrational reasons—he was out to humiliate the Americans and to teach them a lesson. American presidents have repeatedly stated that they won't be the first to lose America a war. That supposedly most rational of planning exercises, planning in the Communist countries, shows a pattern of irrationality and arbitrary tergiversations, compared to which the market economies of the Western countries are models of economic rationality. One could go on. My suspicion is that the colossal transformation we need is not likely to come about before we are reminded that it *must* come about by some huge ecological disaster or a nuclear war.

Jantsch: I'm afraid I have to agree with you. What disturbs me most is our lack of foresight. When man fell from Paradise he appears to have been endowed with a surprising lightheartedness about the consequences of his actions. He was taught to live in the present. This protective wrapping has now become a liability. Today we can foretell the consequences of our actions in many cases with unfailing certainty. We *know* that so many more cars will simply poison the inhabitants of London by the year 2050; we *know* that at the present rate of consumption the world's easily recoverable oil resources will dry up in so many years. Yet we are so poor in rationality, or, if you like, we are so heavily protected from seeing the results of our follies, that we refuse to see what really stares us in the face. We still hope, quite irrationally, that we'll muddle through.

Urban: But hasn't this protective mechanism served us extremely well? If a child were capable of being made *fully* conscious that he was heading for death from the moment he was born, could he bear to live a normal life in the first place? If every soldier who was killed in the First and Second World Wars had taken to heart the statistical forecasts, wouldn't the world's armies have disintegrated, or turned into psychiatric wards the day the war broke out? In 1939 everyone knew perfectly well that if the war were to last three or four years, a very large proportion of the young men drafted into the forces would not survive. And they didn't. But every soldier had this protective wrapping around him believing that *he* would be spared. This is surely something we ought to be thankful for.

Jantsch: I don't doubt for a moment that throughout the ages this protective shield has served us admirably, but our situation is essentially different from all earlier situations.

Urban: Hasn't this uniqueness been the cry of every age? Every new civilisation, like every young man in his teens, believes that he is unique. But on closer examination the neophyliacs turn out to be old hats.

Jantsch: The uniqueness of our situation is quite easy to explain: the time-scale on which we work has undergone a sea-change. In earlier times we had time to react to slow changes in our environment. It took thousands of years for man the hunter to become an agricultural worker, and for the latter to become an engineer in electronics. Today we have such a dangerously short time-factor at play that we have to act in anticipation. To spread the word around about this is going to make some of us highly unpopular. I have already said that the full satisfaction of short-range demands will almost automatically involve us in long-range disaster. So, to protect ourselves against long-range trouble, we ought to take restrictive steps right away, which people will not like. They will appeal to their protective shield ("hope" if you like) and shove the really important problems under the carpet. Alas, these problems will not go away.

Urban: This brings us back to an idea we have already touched on and which I would now formulate in slightly different language, namely that collective myopia is the original sin of mankind. The changes your new civilisation would demand in our consciousness seem so large that it is difficult to believe that they can be accomplished not in one but perhaps even a hundred generations. Why should we have any hope on this score when we cannot solve the simplest of techno-social problems, such as shifting freight transportation from our overcrowded roads to the railways which are running empty and at a great financial loss to the tax-payer? What could be more reasonable, economically sound, technologically feasible and more likely to save lives? We *all* want it (private road haulers excepted), and yet no country has managed to do anything about it.

A book recently published in Hungary makes great play with the phrase "cosmic alienation." The author, Imre Magyar, is an eminent physician, and his message is that while we can now go to the moon, we can't get our telephone system working, or our trains to run on time, or taps installed that don't flood our bathrooms, or organise the smooth distribution of even the simplest commodities. So, he says, man is cosmically alienated: he possesses "big science," which is of absolutely no use to him, but sitting in his prefabricated apartment he isn't really better off than was his grandfather on the farm. In fact he is worse off, because television tells him he lives in the space age, but his five senses tell him he is just beginning to drag himself into the 20th Century. Now I realise that this "alienation" is a European, especially an East European (and Third World), phenomenon, and that it applies much less to the United States, and I'm quoting these examples simply to stress the point that closing the gap in our consciousness between *knowing* about some long-distance contingency and getting this knowledge into our *bones*, is immense. Perhaps you are more hopeful.

Jantsch: The alienation you mention is part of the mismanagement of the global system. The little man feels that moonshots are a spectacular waste and dangerous distractions from our real problems, and I can't blame him for his cosmic alienation. But remember that there is also a perennial trait in man's ambition, his perfectionism, which urges him from time to time to do a superlative thing that has no real bearing on his daily life. Landing a human being on the moon was a faultless, one-shot operation. It required superb technology and organisation, well within the control of a small number of scientists. The result was a stunning demonstration of what men can achieve under optimal conditions.

The trouble is that this sense of the perfect operates only within very small dimensions. Your example of the road–rail controversy is a good one: the number of interests to be consulted, the number of ingrained habits to overcome is too large for effective action, and the end-result promises to have nothing perfect, nothing uplifting about it. So the malaise is allowed to continue. We would, thus, have to add to the dichotomy we have already discussed—that between rationality and instinct—another and perhaps equally important, namely the duality between man's urge for the inspiring, finite, perfect whole, and his need to go on tinkering, mending and improvising in his daily work. But this again simply gives added urgency to my view that an entirely new outlook is needed to establish the balance we need before a point of no return is reached in our mismanagement of ourselves and of our resources.

Urban: Are there any signs that this change in our consciousness is on its way?

Jantsch: Well, there are some signs. The whole young generation in Europe and America lives in a state of intense unease. They feel that our values have to change although they are less certain what our future values should be. Now some of this feeling can and should be funnelled into constructive channels.

One such channel, an essential one to my mind, is to combine a decentralisation of initiative with a concern for the impact of that initiative on society as a whole. It implies a two-way traffic. My model would be a large industrial corporation in which every employee is, or ought to be, aware of what his contribution (or the lack of it) may mean for the overall objectives of the enterprise, while on the other hand the objectives of the corporation are conceived with the employee's social needs, his health requirements and his cultural ambitions in mind. It would require an efficient feed-back mechanism and a fine sense of balance between initiative and responsibility.

Urban: Wasn't there a similar idea behind Soviet Man whose existence has been heavily called in question by Klaus Mehnert? Soviet Man was also supposed to be a serious and upright kind of gentleman who would curtail his material interests to serve the state which is his, in theory. He would not strike, for the factory is his, so why damage your own property, and so on.

Jantsch: Ah, but I can't allow you to put an equation mark between the two. Soviet Man has never been given a chance to show any real initiative. In fact, he has been the victim of a tight, mechanistic kind of planning which made a mockery not only of his initiative but of his humanity too. I believe it is possible to create a spirit of responsibility in man if you put the right challenge to him. Once his basic creature comforts have been satisfied, he will not be content with the challenge to "get rich," or "get yourself a perfect technology." We can see from the rebellion of the well-to-do young in America, France and Germany that affluence, like Dante's Paradiso, is a dull condition. But it is possible to go beyond it by being aware of the problems that surround us and doing something about them. Of course, one cannot redesign a system, or the individual's consciousness, by a stroke of the ecologist's wand. We cannot hope to motivate people for noble and responsible action by preaching at them.

But it is my profound belief that men will listen to reason provided that the challenge is put to them in a way which they understand. Take the matter of pollution. It was a non-problem and a non-subject ten, even five years ago. Not that the problem didn't exist before, but people simply hadn't been educated to recognize it. Within the last three years the world has brought forth ecologists and environmental scientists of all kinds, and ministries to employ them. There is intense concern with what the motor-car and the oil refinery are doing to the air we breathe, with the pollution of the rivers which supply our drinking water and so forth. There has been legislation in many countries, and the public, at least the opinion-making sections of the public, have been mobilised. This is a vast and very encouraging change for the better, the more important because it has succeeded in the teeth of opposition from very powerful interests such as some of the world's greatest industrial polluters. True, this is just scratching the surface of one of many problems, but if we have woken up to this one, I can't see why we should not tackle others.

Surely we can make a similar impact when it comes to explaining the consequences of the growth of the world's population. To feed the growing number of mouths each year, we are pushing agriculture to invest more in certain high-yield crops. Crops have been developed which yield three and four times the amount of the earlier species. But what we are developing here harbours very great dangers for the world's ecological balance. Chemical fertilisers and pesticides have poisonous ingredients. At the moment only the United States and Europe use them on an extensive scale. But supposing the rest of the world—and that is where the real food shortage is—started using similar techniques: the ecological equilibrium of the world would be very seriously affected. In other words, the land can bear only a limited amount of disequilibrium

before it starts reacting against its exploiters. All this sets a definite limit to the amount of food we can ever hope to extract from
agriculture, and this amount will be roughly enough to feed us up to
about 1990, possibly the year 2000, if the population goes on growing at the rate we envisage.

After that time we will have to go short, which means in plain
language that some of us will go on living as we do now, while
others will starve in very much greater numbers than they are
already doing. And this is where future-oriented research comes
in. We know that there are ways of checking the growth of the
world's population but we are already too late with our measures
if we want to have any practical impact by the year 2000. We also
know that there are alternative sources of food production which
are non-agricultural. But if we want to make use of them in thirty
years' time, we must make a start now. What we do not know at
the moment is how to restrict the growth of the population and
at the same time do away with the most effective pressure which
restricts population growth, namely food shortage. A little later
the same problem may present itself in a different form: how to
prevent the population from growing to the level of food production. The question is: how do you bring this view home to the
politicians and the public and how do you get them to fight off the
vested interests—commercial, military and plain psychological—
which constitute the fatal myopia you have mentioned? But, as I
say, we have done it with pollution and I'm fairly confident we
may do it with other issues.

Urban: In bringing the message home to the governments and the
public, do you expect to encounter different sorts of difficulties in
the Western and Communist societies?

Jantsch: When I talk about large-scale planning for the future, I
become unpopular both with the Communist planners and the
leaders of commerce and industry in the West. People on the
ideological Left tell me that I'm ignoring the most important point,
the class struggle. From the ideological Right I'm accused of
pushing Socialism. Well, if socialism means a concern for the
future of society, by all means let's call it Socialism. However,
the Western attitude to the systemic change I advocate is very
different from what one gets in Eastern Europe, and induces more

optimism. In the West we can engage the individual. We can do something about decentralisation. Also, we have the people, a great many people, who are burning to make a contribution. We have the ability to shift our attention and our methods from the corporations to the whole body of society—from product-design to social planning. Also, we are, at our universities, preparing the ground for a systematic study of macro-planning. These are considerable assets, so I would say we are in a more favourable position than the East European countries where, for decades, democratic centralism and the centralisation of planning have killed all initiative. It is only in the last two to three years that Hungary and Czechoslovakia have tried to escape from the straitjacket. Alas, their escape aims at imitating some of the features of the Western economy, so they'll probably have to go through our troubles before they can hope to pull their weight in extricating mankind from the quagmire in which we have landed ourselves through our rapacity, lack of foresight and sheer inertia.

Urban: Are you implying that the East European economies, even when they try to reform themselves, are consistently a step behind contemporary thinking?

Jantsch: You are being too kind: some of them are a generation behind. A certain amount of industrialisation and technological proficiency is, of course, essential in poorly developed countries (of which Russia was one), for technology is the only means given to man with which he can get a grip on nature. The Asian and African peoples are, by and large, still in a state where they cannot begin to live like human beings unless they have more technology. The danger comes with the next phase of development—the industrial take-off—and it is here that the East European reforms are not convincing.

Man's proper concern is with the quality of life. The United States has twice the GNP of Western Europe but, judging by what my American friends tell me and what I can see for myself, it does not at all follow that the quality of life in America is twice as good as it is in Europe. It is probably the other way around. There is a level of development where quantitative goals do not lead to better quality, where more money does not mean more wealth.

None of us can eat more than three square meals a day or wear more than one pair of shoes at a time.

To sum up: the West has to settle for falling expectations; in the developing world we may do well to go on supporting growing expectations up to the point where the development threatens to become counter-productive. And when the balance is reached, we may, with some luck, congratulate ourselves on having averted disaster. But until then we have a hard row to hoe.

Philosophers
and Planners

Poetry, economics, and religion are
all reflected in this collection of
provocative insights into the role of
tomorrow today. United not by a point
of view or an ideology, the writers in
this section, like those in the rest of
this book, are drawn together, despite
their vast differences, by a common
stance toward time itself—a belief in
the need for future-consciousness.

The Economics of the Coming Spaceship Earth

Kenneth E. Boulding

The cowboy and the spaceman confront each other
in this much-quoted essay by Kenneth E. Boulding,
philosopher of the social sciences and intellectual
prodder *extraordinaire.* Do we live on a limitless
plain with endless resources, or in an enclosed
space capsule in which we recycle—or die?

We are now in the middle of a long process of transition in the
nature of the image which man has of himself and his environment. Primitive men, and to a large extent also men of the early
civilizations, imagined themselves to be living on a virtually
illimitable plane. There was almost always somewhere beyond
the known limits of human habitation, and over a very large part
of the time that man has been on earth, there has been something
like a frontier. That is, there was always some place else to go

when things got too difficult, either by reason of the deterioration of the natural environment or a deterioration of the social structure in places where people happened to live. The image of the frontier is probably one of the oldest images of mankind, and it is not surprising that we find it hard to get rid of.

Gradually, however, man has been accustoming himself to the notion of the spherical earth and a closed sphere of human activity. A few unusual spirits among the ancient Greeks perceived that the earth was a sphere. It was only with the circumnavigations and the geographical explorations of the fifteenth and sixteenth centuries, however, that the fact that the earth was a sphere became at all widely known and accepted. Even in the nineteenth century, the commonest map was Mercator's projection, which visualizes the earth as an illimitable cylinder, essentially a plane wrapped around the globe, and it was not until the Second World War and the development of the air age that the global nature of the planet really entered the popular imagination. Even now we are very far from having made the moral, political, and psychological adjustments which are implied in this transition from the illimitable plane to the closed sphere.

Economists in particular, for the most part, have failed to come to grips with the ultimate consequences of the transition from the open to the closed earth. . . .

. . .

The closed earth of the future requires economic principles which are somewhat different from those of the open earth of the past. For the sake of picturesqueness, I am tempted to call the open economy the "cowboy economy," the cowboy being symbolic of the illimitable plains and also associated with reckless, exploitative, romantic, and violent behavior, which is characteristic of open societies. The closed economy of the future might similarly be called the "spaceman" economy, in which the earth has become a single spaceship, without unlimited reservoirs of anything, either for extraction or for pollution, and in which, therefore, man must find his place in a cyclical ecological system which is capable of continuous reproduction of material form even though it cannot escape having inputs of energy. The difference between the two types of economy becomes most apparent in the attitude towards consumption. In the cowboy economy, consumption is regarded as a good thing and production likewise; and the success of the economy is measured by the amount of the throughput from the "factors of production," a part of which, at any rate, is extracted from the reservoirs of raw materials and noneconomic objects, and another part of which is output into the reservoirs of pollution. If there are infinite reservoirs from which material can be obtained and into which effluvia can be deposited, then the throughput is at least a plausible measure of the success of the economy. The gross national product is a rough measure of this total throughput. It should be possible, however, to distinguish that part of the GNP which is derived from exhaustible and that which is derived from reproducible resources, as well as that part of consumption which represents effluvia and that which represents input into the productive system again. Nobody, as far as I know, has ever attempted to break down the GNP in this way, although it would be an interesting and extremely important exercise, which is unfortunately beyond the scope of this paper.

By contrast, in the spaceman economy, throughput is by no means a desideratum, and is indeed to be regarded as something to be minimized rather than maximized. The essential measure of the success of the economy is not production and consumption at all, but the nature, extent, quality, and complexity of the total capital stock, including in this the state of human bodies and minds included in the system. In the spaceman economy, what we are primarily concerned with is stock maintenance, and any technological change which results in the maintenance of a given total stock with a lessened throughput (that is, less production and consumption) is clearly a gain. This idea that both production and consumption are bad things rather than good things is very strange to economists, who have been obsessed with the income-flow concepts to the exclusion, almost, of capital-stock concepts.

There are actually some very tricky and unsolved problems involved in the questions as to whether human welfare or well-being is to be regarded as a stock or a flow. Something of both these elements seems actually to be involved in it, and as far as I know there have been practically no studies directed towards identifying these two dimensions of human satisfaction. Is it, for instance, eating that is a good thing, or is it being well fed? Does economic welfare involve having nice clothes, fine houses, good equipment, and so on, or is it to be measured by the depreciation and the wearing out of these things? I am inclined myself to regard the stock concept as most fundamental, that is, to think of being well fed as more important than eating, and to think even of so-called services as essentially involving the restoration of a depleting psychic capital. Thus I have argued that we go to a concert in order to restore a psychic condition which might be called "just having gone to a concert," which, once established, tends to depreciate. When it depreciates beyond a certain point, we go to another concert in order to restore it. If it depreciates rapidly, we go to a lot of concerts; if it depreciates slowly, we go to few. On this view, similarly, we eat primarily to restore bodily homeostasis, that is, to maintain a condition of being well fed, and so on. On this view, there is nothing desirable in consumption at all. The less consumption we can maintain a given state with, the better off we are. If we had clothes that did not wear out, houses that did not depreciate, and even if we could maintain our bodily condition without eating, we would clearly be much better off.

It is this last consideration, perhaps, which makes one pause. Would we, for instance, really want an operation that would enable us to restore all our bodily tissues by intravenous feeding while we slept? Is there not, that is to say, a certain virtue in throughput itself, in activity itself, in production and consumption itself, in raising food and in eating it? It would certainly be rash to exclude this possibility. Further interesting problems are raised by the demand for variety. We certainly do not want a constant state to be maintained; we want fluctuations in the state. Otherwise there would be no demand for variety in food, for variety in scene, as in travel, for variety in social contact, and so on. The demand for variety can, of course, be costly, and sometimes it seems to be too costly to be tolerated or at least legitimated, as in the case of marital partners, where the maintenance of a homeostatic state in the family is usually regarded as much more desirable than the variety and excessive throughput of the libertine. There are problems here which the economics profession has neglected with astonishing singlemindedness. My own attempts to call attention to some of them, for instance, in two articles,[1] as far as I can judge, produced no response whatever; and economists continue to think and act as if production, consumption, throughput, and the GNP were the sufficient and adequate measure of economic success.

It may be said, of course, why worry about all this when the spaceman economy is still a good way off (at least beyond the lifetimes of any now living), so let us eat, drink, spend, extract and pollute, and be as merry as we can, and let posterity worry about the spaceship earth. It is always a little hard to find a convincing answer to the man who says, "What has posterity ever done for me?" and the conservationist has always had to fall back on rather vague ethical principles postulating identity of the individual with some human community or society which extends not only back into the past but forward into the future. Unless the individual identifies with some community of this kind, conservation is obviously "irrational." Why should we not maximize the welfare of this generation at the cost of posterity? *"Après nous, le déluge"* has been the motto of not insignificant numbers of human societies. The only answer to this, as far as I can see, is to point out that the welfare of the individual depends on the extent to which he can identify himself with others, and that the most satisfactory individual identity is that which identifies not only with a community in space but also with a community extending over time from the past into the future. If this kind of identity is recognized as desirable, then posterity has a voice, even if it does not have a vote; and in a sense, if its voice can influence votes, it has votes too. This whole problem is linked up with the much larger one of the determinants of the morale, legitimacy, and "nerve" of a society, and there is a great deal of historical evidence to suggest that a society which loses its identity with posterity and which loses its positive image of the future loses also its capacity to deal with present problems, and soon falls apart.[2]

Even if we concede that posterity is relevant to our present problems, we still face the question of time-discounting and the closely related question of uncertainty-discounting. It is a well-known phenomenon that individuals discount the future, even in their own lives. The very existence of a positive rate of interest may be taken as at least strong supporting evidence of this hypothesis. If we discount our own future, it is certainly not unreasonable to discount posterity's future even more, even if we do give posterity a vote. If we discount this at 5 percent per annum, posterity's vote or dollar halves every fourteen years as we look into the future, and after a mere hundred years it is pretty small—only about 1½ cents on the dollar. If we add another 5 percent for uncertainty, even the vote of our grandchildren reduces almost to insignificance. We can argue, of course, that the ethical thing to do is not to discount the future at all, that time-discounting is mainly the result of myopia and perspective, and hence is an illusion which the moral man should not tolerate. It is a very popular illusion, however, and one that must certainly be taken into consideration in the formulation of policies. It explains, perhaps, why conservationist policies almost have to be sold under some other excuse which seems more urgent, and why, indeed, necessities which are visualized as urgent, such as defense, always seem to hold priority over those which involve the future.

All these considerations add some credence to the point of view which says that we should not worry about the spaceman economy at all, and that we should just go on increasing the GNP and indeed the gross world product, or GWP, in the expectation that the problems of the future can be left to the future, that when scarcities arise, whether this is of raw materials or of pollutable reservoirs, the needs of the then present will determine the solutions of the then present, and there is no use giving ourselves ulcers by worrying about problems that we really do not have to solve. There is even high ethical authority for this point of view in the New Testament, which advocates that we should take no thought for tomorrow and let the dead bury their dead. There has always been something rather refreshing in the view that we should live like the birds, and perhaps posterity is for the birds in more senses than one; so perhaps we should all call it a day and go out and pollute something cheerfully. As an old taker of thought for the morrow, however, I cannot quite accept this solution; and I would argue, furthermore, that tomorrow is not only very close, but in many respects it is already here. The shadow of the future spaceship, indeed, is already falling over our spendthrift merriment. Oddly enough, it seems to be in pollution rather than in exhaustion that the problem is first becoming salient. Los Angeles has run out of air, Lake Erie has become a cesspool, the oceans are getting full of lead and DDT, and the atmosphere may become man's major problem in another generation, at the rate at which we are filling it up with gunk. It is, of course, true that at least on a microscale, things have been worse at times in the past. The cities of today, with all their foul air and polluted waterways, are probably not as bad as the filthy cities of the pretechnical age. Nevertheless, that fouling of the nest which has been typical of man's activity in the past on a local scale now seems to be extending to the whole world society; and one certainly cannot view with equanimity the present rate of pollution of any of the natural reservoirs, whether the atmosphere, the lakes, or even the oceans.

I would argue strongly also that our obsession with production and consumption to the exclusion of the "state" aspects of human welfare distorts the process of technological change in a most undesirable way. We are all familiar, of course, with the wastes involved in planned obsolescence, in competitive advertising, and in poor quality of consumer goods. These problems may not be so important as the "view with alarm" school indicates, and indeed the evidence at many points is conflicting. New materials especially seem to edge towards the side of improved durability, such as, for instance, neolite soles for footwear, nylon socks, wash and wear shirts, and so on. The case of household equipment and automobiles is a little less clear. Housing and building construction generally almost certainly has declined in durability since the Middle Ages, but this decline also reflects a change in tastes towards flexibility and fashion and a need for novelty, so that it is not easy to assess. What is clear is that no serious attempt has been made to assess the impact over the whole of economic life of changes in durability, that is, in the ratio of capital in the widest possible sense to income. I suspect that we have underestimated, even in our spendthrift society, the gains from increased durability, and that this might very well be one of the places where the price system needs correction through government-sponsored research and development. The problems which the spaceship earth is going to present, therefore, are not all in the future by any means, and a strong case can be made for paying much more attention to them in the present than we now do.

It may be complained that the considerations I have been putting forth relate only to the very long run, and they do not much concern our immediate problems. There may be some justice in this criticism, and my main excuse is that other writers have dealt adequately with the more immediate problems of deterioration in the quality of the environment. It is true, for instance, that many of the immediate problems of pollution of the atmosphere or of bodies of water arise because of the failure of the price system, and many of them could be solved by corrective taxation. If people had to pay the losses due to the nuisances which they create, a good deal more resources would go into the prevention of nuisances. These arguments involving external economies and diseconomies are familiar to economists, and there is no need to recapitulate them. The law of torts is quite inadequate to provide for the correction of the price system which is required, simply because where damages are widespread and their incidence on any particular person is small, the ordinary remedies of the civil law are quite inadequate and inappropriate. There needs, therefore, to be special legislation to cover these cases, and though such legislation seems hard to get in practice, mainly because of the widespread and small personal incidence of the injuries, the technical problems involved are not insuperable. If we were to adopt in principle a law for tax penalties for social damages, with an apparatus for making assessments under it, a very large proportion of current pollution and deterioration of the environment would be prevented. There are tricky problems of equity involved, particularly where old established nuisances create a kind of "right by purchase" to perpetuate themselves, but these are problems again which a few rather arbitrary decisions can bring to some kind of solution.

The problems which I have been raising in this paper are of larger scale and perhaps much harder to solve than the more practical and immediate problems of the above paragraph. Our success in dealing with the larger problems, however, is not unrelated to the development of skill in the solution of the more immediate and perhaps less difficult problems. One can hope, therefore, that as a succession of mounting crises, especially in pollution, arouse public opinion and mobilize support for the solution of the immediate problems, a learning process will be set in motion which will eventually lead to an appreciation of and perhaps solutions for the larger ones. My neglect of the immediate problems, therefore, is in no way intended to deny their importance, for unless we at least make a beginning on a process for solving the immediate problems we will not have much chance of solving the larger ones. On the other hand, it may also be true that a long-run vision, as it were, of the deep crisis which faces mankind may predispose people to taking more interest in the immediate problems and to devote more effort for their solution. This may sound like a rather modest optimism, but perhaps a modest optimism is better than no optimism at all.

The Information-Centered Society

Yujiro Hayashi

We are being bombarded by more and more information. Will this torrent of new data, ideas, images, and values sharpen our differences? Or will it draw us together? Here a leading Japanese planner argues that the new information-centered society will create a transnational consciousness.

The Industrial Revolution that originated in England in the eighteenth century had enormous repercussions in the course of world development in subsequent years. It turned an agrarian into an industrial society. The emergence of manufacturing enterprises to a position of leadership in industry brought about far-reaching changes both nationally and internationally. Developing nations overtook and displaced the previously developed nations, creating changes that certainly merit the description "revolutionary."

Japan was certainly handicapped in this regard, as it was not until a century after England's Industrial Revolution, or toward the close of the nineteenth century, that the country finally made a slow start toward full industrialization. In subsequent years, however, Japan demonstrated tremendous vigor in its relentless efforts to catch up with the industrialized countries of the West, and the end result has been spectacular success.

One hundred years have elapsed since the Meiji Restoration, and twice as many years since the Industrial Revolution, and the world is again witnessing a new social metamorphosis in its early stage. As the Industrial Revolution signaled a transformation of preindustrial society into industrial society, we are now on the verge of accomplishing a new transformation of great historical significance: the transformation of industrial into postindustrial society. The social changes produced by this transformation will far exceed in magnitude changes experienced at the time of the Industrial Revolution, for what is implied is a complete overhaul of society's basic values.

Historically speaking, there is no denying that new values were recognized following evolution from an agrarian to an industrial society, but in both agricultural and industrial eras, values created by tangible commodities were commonly shared and esteemed. In the current stage of evolution, however, it appears that new values are being derived from intangible goods, in particular from information. The word "information" here needs to be defined in the interest of clarity.

Information is commonly defined as "a communication concerning a particular matter," but this definition is insufficient. Real information is a communication that serves its beneficiary in the process of decision making. It may be well to recall a Japanese proverb, "Buddhist invocations chanted into a horse's ear," meaning something quite worthless, like a cacophony. It is not information. Theoretically, information should be defined as "knowledge communicated indicating a particular choice of possibilities." The mere act of informing falls short of real information. In the narrower sense of the word, information may be interpreted as "the act of designating a particular grouping from among numerous possible groupings of elements of information." According to this definition, the smallest piece of information is the designation of one out of two possibilities, and, as is well known, this is called a "bit."

Employing the above definition, elements of information may be broken down into letters, languages, and numbers as one group, and designs, patterns, and colors as another. The second group of elements is extremely important, as it creates the strong motivational force that causes a prospective buyer to make a certain choice of goods.

A commodity has two kinds of value: physical and informational. Physical value may more appropriately be called *use value*, and informational value *esteem value*. These values are inseparably linked with two kinds of human needs: primary wants, or wants based on human instinct, and secondary wants, or wants based on human sensibility. Consider, for example, a piece of glassware. It is a product processed from a small chunk of glass, and obviously certain value is gained as a result of this processing. The glassware has use value in that it serves as a container for water. One's wish to drink water is basically an instinctive or primary desire, and the glassware, in order to satisfy this primary need, should function as a receptacle for water. Glassware with a crack or without a bottom, therefore, has no use value. Often, the glass is designed in different shapes and engraved with patterns that have little to do with its basic function of satisfying human thirst. Extraneous as this ornamentation is to the primary need, the product that receives extra processing has higher production costs, and these extraneous factors, such as designs and patterns, often prove to be highly essential to the product's sale value. Frequently, people are strongly motivated by good design and pattern in their selection of a product. This fact attests to the importance of taste or sensibility in determining man's secondary need, aside from his primary need which is merely to drink water. Additional processing is often required to fill the secondary want, irrelevant as it may be to the primary function of the product. This is clear testimony to the existence of informational value as against physical value, or esteem value as against use value.

The esteem value exists for no other reason than the admitted importance of catering to the secondary human need. In society, secondary desires appear more pronounced in proportion to the progress of civilization. In other words, the intensity of secondary desires serves as a common denominator of civilization.

Thus, a commodity is a combination of two things, esteem value and use value, each having a different weight relative to the other. The two values are inherent in all commodities. For example, a sales transaction in a raw material like coal or iron ore seems to be made solely on the basis of its use value, but actually its brand name plays an important role in the transaction, indicating that the esteem value in this case is considerable. Obviously, in the information industry, as the term suggests, the value of the commodities involved is predominantly informational and use value appears only marginal. Very few people, for example, ever bother to buy a newspaper just because they need paper. This is not to deny the use value of the paper, however, because even though it is primarily the news printed on paper, and not the paper itself, that is bought and sold, there is no doubt about the indispensable value of the paper that carries news. The use value of an information product is not zero; the paper has commodity value as a carrier of news. The value characteristics of commodities found in society may be diagramed as follows:

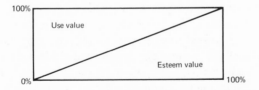

Obviously, the closer it is to the left axis of the diagram, the more the product assumes the characteristics of a durable good, and, the closer it gets to the right side, the more the product assumes the characteristics of a consumer good; farthest to the right, the product assumes the characteristics of information goods, like a newspaper. By applying this concept of value relationship, it may be possible to provide a whole new definition of capital goods and consumer goods. This, however, is not the purpose of my discussion here.

A comparison of primary and secondary wants reveals the existence of shape differences between them. In the first place, many people feel primary wants in the same way; they can be expressed quantitatively and communicated in universally specific terms. Secondary wants, on the other hand, vary in substance from one individual to another, and their quantitative expression and communication in specific terms are in many instances very difficult.

In a community where people view their secondary wants as being relatively unimportant, the need for information is equally small. Problems like the determination of the necessary amount of food, drinking water, clothing, and housing can be worked out with relative ease if, for instance, each resident of a community of, say, a hundred people has only primary wants. But in a community where secondary wants, compounded by diverse personal tastes, exist, people's demand for necessary information vastly increases. Inasmuch as sensory wants are hard to describe concretely, a person is normally inclined to make his wants known by selecting out of the wealth of available information that which most satisfies his taste and desires. In this situation, several times the amount of information actually needed should be available to each person. Thus it is evident that the amount of information required in connection with secondary wants is several times greater than that required in the case of primary wants.

Rapid accumulation of information at such a high rate creates the need for information processing, causing the information enterprise gradually to assume leadership over all industries and causing the popular trend toward computerization to accelerate at hurricane velocity. The more democratic the world gets, the greater the need for information processing will be. In feudal society, centuries ago, when man's mode of living was strictly regimented under a firmly established caste system, according to his predetermined station in that society, society itself took care of the need for social information processing in a manner perpetuated through time-honored traditions and customs. It was held to be immoral for a *samurai* warrior to live a life unfitting to his rank in the caste system, and it was considered insolent for a merchant to imitate the way of life of the *samurai* class. Secondary wants in feudal society were narrowly prescribed. This was somewhat true also of prewar Japanese society, in which social conventions and customs held strong rein over the individual citizen's life. Then, during the wartime period of national emergency, secondary wants came to be branded as evil since people were prohibited by the authoritarian government from expressing them. A strong tendency developed during the war to confine a man's wants to only primary wants, against his will. This trend, having accelerated to a considerable degree, facilitated the enforcement of tight controls on the economy, as evidenced by the strict enforcement of food rationing. Secondary wants, if any persisted, were invariably subjected to a collective selection by society, and, since society itself took care of the need for information processing, other ways of information and data processing were simply ignored.

Now that a wartime state of emergency and a caste system no longer exist, secondary human wants have suddenly come into full blossom in many countries. To the extent that secondary wants have been freed from collective selection by society, the quantity of necessary information has increased to tremendous proportions, and the need for information processing has greatly intensified. A pressing need now exists for technological innovation to be applied to data processing, and the electronic computer, an example of such innovation, symbolizes the advent of a new era.

Two mutually contradicting factors of importance should be noted in this connection: (1) secondary wants are highly sensory and difficult to describe quantitatively, and they tend to increase sharply the amount of information necessary; (2) a computer produced to meet social requirements of data processing can, because of its innate attributes, perceive things only quantitatively. To reconcile these two factors, certain means were devised by which unquantifiable information is replaced by quantifiable information that can be fed into a computer for perception. This method, however, has given rise to two significant problems:

1. The problem of ascertaining and ensuring the adequacy of replacement of the unquantifiable by the quantifiable.
2. The problem of improving the sensitivity of the computer to cover matters difficult to indicate numerically.

The first problem implies the utilization of social-technical innovation centering on the computer, and the second problem the generalization of pattern recognition by the computer. Development and research in both of these areas have only started but can be expected to bear final fruit in the twenty-first century. The key to materialization of a super-technical society in the twenty-first century lies in finding solutions to these problems.

At this point a study of the proliferation effect of information is in order. Information, by virtue of its inherent nature, proliferates, but this characteristic is not yet fully apparent. That is to say, although the information enterprise is flourishing at present, in this age of information, the flow of information in society actually remains a one-way traffic. In the maelstrom of unilaterally disgorged information, all that man can do on the receiving end is to express his own will on the basis of particular information that he chooses. This may of course be only a transitory phenomenon emanating from the basic proliferating characteristic of information. If the trend toward creation of an information-centered society is caused by free expression of secondary human wants, the proliferation of information should begin with the individual person, the source of the secondary want. Yet, the fact is that information always gravitates from a giant information industry or from a governmental organization, while little of it is feedback from the general mass of consumers. Not until the ever-increasing flow of information is established in genuine two-way traffic patterns can society change basically from what it is now, nor can a true image of the information-centered society be firmly drawn. Much of our current image of an information-centered society is based on extrapolation of the process of "informationalization" currently in progress, which is characterized by the one-way flow of information. Thus our current views must be completely reexamined, with special attention directed toward various revolutionary changes already taking place as a result of information proliferation.

First of all, the human faculty of perception is about to undergo thorough alteration. In pretelevision days, before the war, the manner in which news and information were brought to the people was one-dimensional, but in the postwar years, with a new generation practically brought up on television, it has become multidimensional. This alteration of the manner of receiving information is gradually changing the human faculty of perception and creating a deepening philosophical gap between generations, which contributes to creation of serious social problems. What are the main differences between the single- and the multidimensional ways of getting information?

One-dimensional describes the process in which information is received item by item, in sequence. Before television came into home life, information got around by word of mouth—including radio—or by reading, one-dimensional ways of transmitting and receiving information. Information received in fragments is interconnected by logic, and when it is finally integrated into a cause-effect relationship, new knowledge is born and settled in man's memory. No matter how plentiful the information supply may be, information cannot be converted into knowledge unless it is linked by a chain of logic. Information supplied pell-mell may be fragmentarily retained in memory, but, more often than not, it will be entirely forgotten. Such information is hardly an asset to enhancement of human knowledge. The important thing is the establishment of a chain of logic, linking one item of information with another. This is why logic was the most important weapon of the prewar generation.

The postwar popularization of television marked the beginning of a certain revolution. A person born in the television age practically grew up with a television receiver, to which he was exposed even when too young to understand language. There were motion pictures before the war, but, unlike the television, movies did not come into the home for daily performances; and, of course, when too young to appreciate movies, a child had very little chance of seeing them. So motion pictures, for all practical purposes, did not contribute to the development of human perception. On the other hand, the postwar generation, subjected to intensive exposure to the television screen even before attaining the age of discretion, has over the years acquired the ability to absorb unselectively new information from the television medium. To this generation, information via television is not imparted on a piecemeal basis but is relayed collectively as a pattern. Multidimensional perception has thus become possible. In this instance, logic as a medium of converting information into knowledge is not required, but, in its place, sensibility becomes important as a conversion medium. As such, sensibility is to the postwar generation what logic was to the prewar generation. Fundamental changes have been made in the method of comprehension, which is an element of knowledge. The new age of sensibility has thus dawned, replacing the age of logic; but this also means the beginning of an intergeneration gap.

As an example of the dissimilarity between logic and sensibility, let us examine the international concept held by industrial and information-centered societies. To begin with the conclusion, while internationalism and nationalism in the industrial society contain certain conflicting elements, no such tension is found in the information-centered society. Internationalism in an industrial society is predicated primarily on nationalism. Characteristically, the maintenance of national boundaries is an absolute necessity in all industrial societies. In agrarian societies, before the development of modern industry, agriculture was dependent on the labor of individuals, and produce found a market in a highly localized place. Such practices also characterized the feudal age, in which a feudal lord held fragmented fiefs under his rule. Later, as the Industrial Revolution brought a shift from agricultural to industrial society, the first task at hand was to enlarge the formerly limited market. Furthermore, development of mass-production industry resulted in the collapse of feudal society and promoted the birth of a large modern state with centralized authority. At this stage, the concept of national boundaries came to have different economic implications, as was true in Japan. Why was it that the Meiji government led the way in enforcing compulsory education aimed at infusing intense nationalism in children? It was because of their strong intention to carry out a revolution of ideals, the basic prerequisite for accomplishing rapid industrialization of the nation. The concept of a nation also underwent rapid change in Japan. Until then, a "country" used to mean to each his native place, but gradually it came to mean Japan as a whole. It seems that such a conceptual revolution, so systematically carried out, was largely responsible for the accelerated rate of industrialization of Japan.

Expansion of markets by the industrial society continued ceaselessly, and eventually they spread overseas. The home market remained intact and was indispensable as a stable market, however. It was in fact because the home market remained strong that many entrepreneurs could go abroad seeking expanded markets without restraint. When more than two industrialized countries emulate each other in their search for enlarged overseas markets, new rules governing bilateral or multilateral commercial transactions—that is, international trade—have to be formulated and put into effect. International settlement of accounts is another area where similar rules should be established. Ordinarily these rules are determined by mutual negotiations between interested parties in which nationalism—the foundation of the industrial society—plays a vital part, and extraordinary importance is attached to national interest. It follows, then, that thoroughgoing negotiations based on reason on both sides are a necessary ingredient in internationalism and that the national interest of one country can by its nature easily clash with that of another country. Consequently it is all too natural that nationalism and internationalism contain in themselves mutually conflicting elements. Educating people thoroughly to understand internationalism as a philosophy is necessary in order to forestall an outright clash with nationalism. Internationalism is good common sense, and it is beneficial toward the further development of industrial society, but many attempts to infuse this simple truth into the mind of man have encountered difficulties, as the present-day state of world affairs eloquently testifies.

Internationalism in an information-centered society is totally different than in an industrial society. The reason for this is the intrinsic difference in clique consciousness between them. In an industrial society, the national-interest-comes-first idea is basic to many people, including strong advocates of internationalism. The idea is a clear expression of patriotism from the viewpoint of clique consciousness. Patriotism is more instinctive than philosophical: two unrelated individuals can turn into two equal patriots simply because they share the same native country. In an information-centered society, however, the proliferation of information cannot help but greatly influence human consciousness. In Japan and elsewhere, twenty-three years have already elapsed since the end of the last war, and the immediate postwar generation has come of age. With their maturing, the world has entered a new historical age: the age of information. Television and a variety of other communication media made their first appearance riding on a sweeping tide of technological innovations. Still plagued by the one-way traffic of information, however, society continues to be deluged with all kinds of information which various communication media supply, regardless of public desire. Included in this flow of information is, naturally, a mass of information concerning things foreign. In particular, television is constantly providing visual information about foreign countries. The postwar generation has come of age under incessant exposure to and brainwashing by televized information. One result is that the postwar generation, unlike its prewar predecessors, does not regard things foreign as curious or peculiar. This is proof that the chauvinistic clique consciousness of the Japanese has been diluted and that a different kind of group consciousness has begun to be shaped. The existence of national boundaries is of gradually diminishing importance in their consciousness. In other words, what remains is clique consciousness as members of the *Homo sapiens* society, which far transcends the *raison d'être* of the other kind of clique consciousness, geared to family ties and ethnic background. This new and unique clique consciousness is not peculiar to Japan but is prevalent also in other countries where an information revolution is in progress. The phenomenon, however, is more pronounced in the advanced industrial countries of Europe and in the United States. Special note should be taken of the current worldwide trend toward the widening of a large gap not so much between different races and nations as between different generations within a race or a nation.

The world today abounds with seemingly insoluble problems. They appear fantastically difficult to resolve. For instance, there is the problem of finding an effective means for international settlement of accounts that can lead to materialization of a truly cashless global organization. Consider also the problems of the economic disparity between North and South, the ideological conflict between East and West, the Arab-Israeli racial strife, the plight of Negro Americans, religious conflicts, and many others.

These problems may appear quite insurmountable from the prewar point of view. From the postwar generation's point of view, however, the prospects for solution may be entirely different. The Tokyo Olympiad held [in 1964] offered some encouraging possibilities for the future. Viewed through the window of the International Olympic Commission (IOC), the Olympiad seems to have harbored within itself a number of knotty problems, but in the eyes of competing athletes, the Olympiad offered a bright, hopeful picture diametrically opposite to the view held by the IOC. The scene at the closing ceremony of the Tokyo Olympiad, in which all participating athletes joined hands to bid farewell, oblivious to differences in race, religion, and nationality, could not help but leave a powerful impression on the minds of young Japanese. Some oldsters held that the parting scene was sacrilegious because of the supposedly sacred meaning of the closing ceremony. In fact, some of the same observations may apply to other international events and conferences. The big difference between the Olympic games and ordinary international conferences is that the latter are almost invariably attended by those of the prewar generation and are seldom followed up with action by the younger, postwar generation as in the case of the former. The young postwar generation tends to picture existing international organizations and conferences at which they are not represented in the same way the IOC views the Olympics through its own special window.

Thirty and some odd years hence, the twenty-first century will arrive, and the present younger generation will by then form the nucleus of society both in name and in reality. All the problems now considered insoluble will then be resolved without any difficulty. If all men can be united in their sense of community with society, an ideal blending of internationalism and nationalism will become inevitable. For this reason, hopefully, I dare say that what appear to be major problems today in the areas of racial and ideological conflict are only transitory.

Attainment of new ideals in the future can become possible through comprehension of internationalism not as logic but as a sense of mission. Internationalism evolved from a new consciousness, in which foreign things shown on television are no longer held as curious, cannot conflict with nationalism.

At the very least, the revolution of consciousness poses an important problem for future education. Hitherto, the methodology of education has been predicated on one-dimensional receipt of information. This methodology is likely to prove less acceptable to future generations. In recent years, the importance of audio-visual education has been emphasized with little thought for the need for a revolution in human conception. Audio-visual education is taken up only as a technique for the purpose of teaching logic, and no attempt has been made at basic analysis of a new area of understanding through perception.

The dissemination of the computer eliminates the need to preserve past records in books or other forms of publications. It will not be long before all records are fed to computers; when needed, only the necessary information will be freely extracted. If and when a system of this sort is perfected, man may be able to live in a letterless society, but even then the person who comprehends information only in one-dimensional terms will find such a system difficult to live with. To avoid this, a revolution in human awareness is necessary. There is an urgent need to reflect now on this revolution of human awareness which is already in progress.

The Future
as Present
Expectation

Daniel Bell

In the mid-sixties, when worldwide interest in
futurism began its upswing, sociologist Daniel Bell
helped organize a distinguished panel of
researchers, government officials, and professors
to give it scholarly underpinnings. At a time when
campus traditionalists still regarded classroom
discussion of the future as either trivial or
academically improper, the Commission on the
Year 2000 not only probed significant problems of
the future, but also helped make it respectable for
other academics to do so. This short statement
explains the commission's rationale.

Time, said St. Augustine, is a three-fold present: the present as we experience it, the past as a present memory, and the future as a present expectation. By that criterion, the world of the year 2000 has already arrived, for in the decisions we make now, in the way we design our environment and thus sketch the lines of constraints, the future is committed. Just as the gridiron pattern of city streets in the nineteenth century shaped the linear growth of cities in the twentieth, so the new networks of radial highways, the location of new towns, the reordering of graduate school curricula, the decision to create or not to create a computer utility as a single system, and the like will frame the tectonics of the twenty-first century. The future is not an overarching leap into the distance; it begins in the present.

This is the premise of the Commission on the Year 2000. It is an effort to indicate now the future consequences of present public policy decisions, to anticipate future problems, and to begin the design of alternative solutions so that our society has more options and can make a moral choice, rather than be constrained, as is so often the case when problems descend upon us unnoticed and demand an immediate response.

But what began a few years ago as a serious academic enterprise . . . has been seized, predictably, by the mass media and the popular imagination. The Columbia Broadcasting System has revamped its documentary program, "The Twentieth Century," into "The Twenty-First Century," to depict the marvels of the future. *The Wall Street Journal* has been running an intermittent series on expected social and technological changes. *Time* has published a compact essay on "The Futurists: Looking Toward A.D. 2000." The theme of the year 2000 now appears repeatedly on lecture circuits and newspapers. . . .

All of this was probably to be expected. Much of the attention given the year 2000 is due, clearly, to the magic of the millennial number. Men have always been attracted by the mystical lure of the *chiloi*, the Greek word for a thousand from which we get our religious term *chiliasm*, the belief in a coming life free from the imperfections of human existence. . . .

A good deal of today's interest in the future arises also from the bewitchment of technology and the way it has transformed the world. *Time* writes portentously: "A growing number of profes-

sionals have made prophecy a serious and highly organized enterprise. They were forced into it by the fact that technology has
advanced more rapidly in the past fifty years than in the previous
5000." And most of the images of the future have concentrated on
dazzling technological prospects. The possibility of prediction, the
promise of technological wizardry, and the idea of a millennial
turning point make an irresistible combination to a jaded press that
constantly needs to ingest new sensations and novelties. The year
2000 has all the ingredients for becoming, if it has not already
become, a hoola-hoop craze.

All of this has its good side and its bad. What is bad, to begin
with, is that a serious and necessary effort is in danger of being
turned into a fad, and any fad trivializes a subject and quickly wears
it out. A second evil is that many more expectations are aroused
than can be fulfilled. There do not exist today any reliable methods
of prediction or forecasting (even in technology), but some spectacular predictions are often encouraged or demanded in order to
enhance the game and attract attention. . . . The serious effort is
devoted not to making predictions, but to the more complicated and
subtle art of defining alternatives. The third drawback in all this is
that our major attention, reflecting an aspect of our culture, becomes concentrated on "gadgets," and breezy claims are made that
such gadgets will transform our lives. . . . But the startling claims of
yesterday quickly become the prosaic facts of today. Twenty-five
years ago the technology magazines were filled with the coming
wonders of "fractional horsepower," which would lighten all our
burdens and transform our lives. And although small motors with
fractions of horsepower have been developed, they have also
resulted in such things as electric toothbrushes and carving knives.

The simple point is that a complex society is not changed by a
flick of the wrist. Considered from the viewpoint of gadgetry, the
United States in the year 2000 will be more *like* the United States
in the year 1967 than *different*. The basic framework of day-to-day
life has been shaped in the last fifty years by the ways the automobile, the airplane, the telephone, and the television have brought
people together and increased the networks and interactions
among them. It is highly unlikely that in the next thirty-three years
(if one takes the year 2000 literally, not symbolically) the impending changes in technology will radically alter this framework. Super-

sonic transport will "tighten" the network and bring the world more directly into the domestic frame. The major challenges and problems already confronting our society, however—a livable physical environment, effective urban planning, the expansion of postgraduate education, the pressures of density and the reduction of privacy, the fragility of political institutions beset by many pressure groups—will extend to the end of the century. . . .

This is not to say that substantial changes will not take place as they have been doing in the past thirty-three years. But one has to be clear about the character of such changes. In general, there are four sources of change in society, and they can be charted with differential ease. The first source of change is technology. Technology opens up many possibilities of mastering nature and transforming resources, time, and space; it also, in many ways, imposes its own constraints and imperatives. In the next thirty-three years we are likely to see great changes growing out of the new biomedical engineering, the computer, and, possibly, weather modification. Biomedical engineering, particularly its possibilities of organ transplant, genetic modification, and control of disease, promises a substantial increase in human longevity. Previous steps, principally the control of infant mortality, raised the average life expectancy; now the prolongation of life by the control of aging may be at hand. This may accentuate a tendency, already visible, in which the chief concern of a person (particularly in middle age) is not death from disease but staying young, thus strengthening the hedonistic elements in our culture. The impact of the computer will be vast. We will probably see a national information-computer-utility system, with tens of thousands of terminals in homes and offices "hooked" into giant central computers providing library and information services, retail ordering and billing services, and the like. . . .

The second source of change, one of the most powerful engines in American society, represents the *diffusion* of existing goods and privileges in society, whether they be tangible goods or social claims on the community. This, in effect, is the realization of the promise of equality which underlies the founding of this country and the manifestation of Tocqueville's summation of American democracy: "What the few have today, the many will demand tomorrow."

When diffusion begins to take rapid sway (as has recently been seen in higher education), it changes the size and scale of the servicing institution and, consequently, that institution's character. Dealing with such problems of size and scale and planning for the kind of institution we want become the urgent task of *anticipating*, not predicting, the future; for example, the university should not become a corporate entity because of the pressure of size.

A third kind of change involves structural developments in society. The centralization of the American political system in the last thirty years has marked an extraordinary transformation of American life. It is the result, in part, of our becoming a national society through the new transportation and the mass media. But it also grew out of the need for central instrumentalities first to mediate the conflicts between large functional groups and later to mobilize the society because of the demands of war. A different, more subtle structural change has been the transformation of the economy into a "postindustrial" society. The weight of the economy has shifted from the product sector to services; more importantly, the sources of innovation are becoming lodged in the intellectual institutions, principally the universities and research organizations, rather than in the older, industrial corporations.

The consequences of such a change are enormous for the modes of access to place and privilege in the society. They make the universities the "gatekeepers" of society. They make more urgent the husbanding of "human capital," rather than financial capital, and they raise crucial sociological questions about the relationship of the new technocratic models of decision-making to the political structures of society.

The fourth source of change—perhaps the most important and certainly the most refractory to prediction—is the relationship of the United States to the rest of the world. In the last twenty-five years, our lives have been transformed most drastically by our participation in World War II, by our military and political posture in the cold war, and by our relationship to the extraordinary number of new states that have emerged since 1945. The problem of *détente* in a nuclear age, the gap between rich and poor nations, the threatening role of "color" as a divisive political force, the changing balance of forces—both technological and moral—are all questions that reach from the present into the distant future.

We have begun to realize—and this is the positive side of the current interest in the year 2000—that it is possible to direct some of this change consciously. . . . Looking ahead, we realize that the rebuilding of American cities, for example, entails a thirty-five-year cycle, and one can rebuild cities only by making long-range commitments. In the process we are also forced to consider the adequacy of our political mechanisms, since Congress neither has a capital budget nor budgets money for long-range commitments. Furthermore, one must question whether a national society can sensibly be structured according to the present crazy-quilt pattern of fifty states and thousands of unwieldy municipalities.

In short, what matter most about the year 2000 are not the gadgets that might, on the serious side, introduce prostheses in the human body or, on the lighter side, use silicones to lift wrinkles, but the kinds of social arrangements that can deal adequately with the problems we shall confront. More and more we are becoming a "communal society" in which the public sector has a greater importance and in which the goods and services of the society—those affecting cities, education, medical care, and the environment—will increasingly have to be purchased jointly. Hence, the problem of social choice and individual values—the question of how to reconcile conflicting individual desires through the political mechanism rather than the market—becomes a potential source of discord. The relation of the individual to bureaucratic structures will be subject to even greater strain. The increasing centralization of government creates a need for new social forms that will allow the citizenry greater participation in making decisions. The growth of a large, educated professional and technical class, with its desire for greater autonomy in work, will force institutions to reorganize the older bureaucratic patterns of hierarchy and detailed specialization. The individual will live longer and face the problem of renewed education and new careers. The family as the source of primordial attachment may become less important for the child, in both his early schooling and his emotional reinforcement. This will be a more mobile and more crowded world, raising problems of privacy and stress. The new densities and "communications overload" may increase the potentiality for irrational outbursts in our society. Finally, there is the growing disjunction between the "culture" and the "social structure." Society becomes more functionally organized, geared to knowledge and the mastery of complex bodies of learning. The culture becomes more hedonistic, permissive, expressive, distrustful of authority and of the purposive, delayed-gratification of a bourgeois, achievement-oriented technological world. This tension between the "technocratic" and the "apocalyptic" modes, particularly among the intellectuals, may be one of the great ruptures in moral temper, especially in the universities.

The only prediction about the future that one can make with certainty is that public authorities will face more problems than they have at any previous time in history. This arises from some simple facts: Social issues are more and more intricately related to one another because the impact of any major change is felt quickly throughout the national and even the international system. Individuals and groups, more conscious of these problems as problems, demand action instead of quietly accepting their fate. Because more and more decisions will be made in the political arena than in the market, there will be more open community conflict. The political arena is an open cockpit where decision points are more visible than they are in the impersonal market; different groups will clash more directly as they contend for advantage or seek to resist change in society.

For all these reasons, the society of the year 2000, so quickly and schematically outlined, will be more fragile, more susceptible to hostilities and to polarization along many different lines. Yet to say this is not to surrender to despair, for the power to deal with these problems is also present. It resides, first, in the marvelous productive capacity of our system to generate sufficient economic resources for meeting most of the country's social and economic needs. It is latent in the flexibility of the American political system, its adaptability to change, and its ability to create new social forms to meet these challenges—public corporations, regional compacts, nonprofit organizations, responsive municipalities, and the like. The problem of the future consists in defining one's priorities and making the necessary commitments. This is an intention of the Commission on the Year 2000.

Futurology—
The New Science
of Probability?

Ossip Flechtheim

The founding father of modern futurism, if there is
one, may well be a mild-mannered German professor
who, as early as the mid-1940s, began speaking and
writing about the need for what he termed
"futurology." Almost thirty years ago, Flechtheim
argued that universities ought to teach about the
future. In this essay, he refers to "futurology" as a
new "science." Even if systematic forecasting did
no more than unveil the inevitable, he asserts, it
would still be of crucial value.

Man's concern with the destiny of his tribe, city, or nation is perhaps as old as his preoccupation with the future of his soul and
body. Many primitive peoples were fully absorbed in the problem of

death and after-life. Of the ancient Egyptians we know that they attempted to preserve the bodies of their rulers for eternity. The hope of the early Christians for the Millennium is no less known. However, as part of the secularization of Western thought the theological conception of human history as a brief chapter in the eternal book of God's creation, beginning with the Fall of Man and ending either with the Millennium or the Last Judgment, has long since been replaced by the this-world theory of progress. Divine perfection and human salvation were transplanted from the realm of a transcendent Heaven to a future Kingdom of God on Earth, toward which the historical process was aiming. This Millennium was no longer to be reached through death and salvation, but rather through the striving of mankind for improvement in time and space. What Carl L. Becker calls "The Heavenly City of Eighteenth-Century Philosophers" was built with many earthly bricks.

If proof is needed, we have the enduring testimony of the Marquis de Condorcet who, when in 1793–1794 facing death, proclaimed his undying faith in both "the future progress of mankind" and the predictability of the "future destiny of mankind from the results of history":

The friend of humanity cannot receive unmixed pleasure but by abandoning himself to the endearing hope of the future. . . . If man can predict, almost with certainty, those appearances of which he understands the laws; if, even when the laws are unknown to him, experience of the past enables him to foresee, with considerable probability, future appearances, why should we suppose it a chimerical undertaking to delineate with some degree of truth, the picture of the future destiny of mankind from the results of history? . . . In short, as opinions formed from experience, relative to the same class of objects, are the only rule by which men of soundest understanding are governed in their conduct, why should the philosopher be proscribed from supporting his conjectures upon a similar basis, provided he attributes to them no greater certainty than the number, the consistency, and the accuracy of actual observations shall authorize? Our hopes, as to the future condition of the human species, may be reduced to three points: the destruction of inequality between different nations; the progress of equality in one and the same nation, and lastly, the real improvement of man.

Condorcet's voice echoes the radical ideology of the period of the French Revolution, which in the nineteenth century gradually changed into the more sedate and scientific theory of evolution. To

Darwin and Spencer, the future appeared as gradually and un-
noticeably evolving from the past; and as the present became ever
more acceptable to the prospering middle-classes, the intellectual
spokesmen of the age conceived of the future as constituting but a
bigger and better present. Hence, the growing number of scientists
naturally limited their investigations to the past of man or to the
ever-recurrent present of nature. Though Comte might concern
himself with the future, most scholars of the positivistic century
consistently barred such concern from the halls of respectable
learning; and it was only natural that the future should come to
be monopolized by the "lunatic fringe" of the academic and literary
world.

With all its scientific and technical dynamism, the Victorian
period was an era of social stability when fundamental social
change occurred too slowly for most people to be aware of it. As
Whitehead puts it, down into the nineteenth century "the time-span
of important change was considerably longer than that of a single
human life." Small wonder then that the age-old view according to
which the past, present, and future of society constitute but so
many links in an unbroken chain, called human history, was slow to
disappear.

We who were born into the Atomic Age are living through an upheaval possibly surpassing in its impact the Neolithic and Urban
Revolutions which, some 6000 years ago, opened the chapter of
historic civilization. This is the first period in human history when
universal basic change occurs within less than one generation. The
rate of such change is increasing so rapidly that its effects have
already become extremely disquieting. At the same time science,
one of the revolutionary factors, has been forever expanding regardless of any signs of disintegration discernible in the social and
political sphere. Increased concern about the future combined with
the ability of science to deal with an ever-widening range of materials combine to create a condition generally favorable toward a
scientific study of the future.

To be sure, the gravity of the crisis which science itself has in
large measure produced is erecting new barriers of resistance
against objective and uncompromising forecasting. For in the face
of such uncertainty the average person is likely to repress his
curiosity and concern by withdrawing into supposedly safer though

probably illusionary shelters. Some retire, indeed, into what Walter Lippmann once called "the peace of human privacy"; others attempt to forget the present by burying themselves in the archives of a dead past. Again there are those who spend themselves in meaningless pursuit of an episodic present. Others who do look at the future view it through glasses colored by their own subjective expectation and desires.

Yet, the nature of science induces its disciples to continue their search regardless of the outcome. They have been conditioned by temperament and training to devote their lives to knowledge for knowledge's sake with the prime purpose of widening the area of human comprehension. Pure social science is becoming almost as self-propelling and accumulative as pure natural science. Consequently, the ever-increasing pace of scientific exertion of all kinds is resulting in the accumulation of an impressive body of material dealing not only with the present and the past, but also with the future. During the last hundred years, the birth and growth of a scientific natural history, sociology, and anthropology have yielded a series of significant and serious predictions. Still more recently, the development of a dynamic psychology with its application to the problems of society is removing another obstacle toward the understanding of the present and future of man and his world.

Naturally, the social sciences automatically reflect our general unrest and uncertainty. At the same time, the natural sciences are undergoing a crisis of their own. Inasmuch as specialization has led to contradictory conclusions, basic assumptions have become doubtful and are being re-examined. From the coincidence of these two crises, the need for a rigorous and thorough re-integration of all knowledge is felt more keenly than ever. To meet this need attempts in three directions are under way. First, we can discern a renewed interest in philosophy which, drawing upon the exact sciences, is once more attempting to integrate the universe *sub specie aeternitatis.* Second, a philosophically minded school of history is now using the past to focus upon the totality of all human endeavor. Third, philosophically oriented sociology and anthropology are laboring to encompass the entire human reality from the standpoint of the present. Closing the last remaining gap, "Futurology" will undertake to discuss man and his world in the hitherto forbidden future tense.

The question, of course, arises whether such an undertaking

should be characterized as a new science when it probably suggests to the reader only a congeries of claims, based upon broad generalizations and fragmentary findings, which lack the unity of content and method of organization of more established sciences. It is therefore imperative to examine the peculiarities of Futurology. While no attempt will be made to present those findings which already exist, the following basic issues are to be considered: What is the exact meaning of Futurology? What is its contents? What are its methods? How reliable is it? What function does it have, and what are its prospects?

The present author having suggested the term "Futurology," prefers to leave it up to the reader to think of Futurology either as a science or as a "prescientific" branch of knowledge. For much will depend upon our definition of the term "science." If we think of the term only in the original meaning of "exact science," Futurology will, no doubt, not qualify as a science. On the other hand, we may well accept J. H. Robinson's broad definition of science: "Science is nothing more or less than the most accurate and best authenticated information that exists, subject to constant rectification and amplification, of man and his world. . . . Science, in short, includes all the careful and critical knowledge we have about anything of which we can know something."[1] If we thus define science broadly as a system of organized knowledge concerning the facts of a particular subject, Futurology may pass as a science not so different from some of the humanities (for instance, musicology) or from the social sciences (for instance, history or political science).

But what distinguishes Futurology from the other disciplines? We know that the borderline between the various branches of knowledge is not a hard and fast one; it is subject to permanent change. In time new insights lead to new sciences. Sometimes the discovery of new material causes a branch of learning to split off the common tree. When information about the physical world began to increase, the sciences of nature separated from their mother discipline philosophy. Much later as a result of revealing investigations about the specific functions of the human mind, psychology emancipated itself from philosophy. Contrariwise, time and again hitherto dispersed findings are brought together and integrated into a new discipline which treats the same materials in a new way. Thus sociology, the generalized study of society, or history are younger than some of the more special sciences upon which they draw. Since Futurology does not so much deal with a new and special segment of knowledge, but rather represents a new synthesis of varied materials, it is closely related to history and could indeed be pictured as a projection of history into a new time dimension. In the absence of written or unwritten records, however, Futurology must make use of a different method of approach. It cannot work with the chronological sequence of detailed facts; instead it will avail itself of interpretation, generalization, and speculation to a considerably higher degree. In this respect, its kinship to cultural anthropology, theoretical sociology, and social philosophy becomes apparent.

Indeed, if the relationship between sociology and the other social sciences was better established, we could be tempted to think of Futurology as a division of sociology resembling that branch of sociology sometimes called "historical sociology" and summarized by Howard Becker as "an aspect of sociology in which data from the past, ordinarily defined as history, are utilized for predictive generalization rather than for the presentation of unique, particularized wholes." Historical sociology and Futurology differ, however, primarily in so far as historical sociology stresses retrospective and hypothetical predictions, whereas Futurology limits itself to actual prospective developments trying to establish the degree of their credibility or mathematical probability.

These two crucial concepts are defined by Bertrand Russell as follows:

. . . Two different concepts each, on the basis of usage, have an equal claim to be called "probability." The first of these is mathematical probability, which is numerically measurable and satisfies the axioms of the probability calculus; this is the sort that is involved in the use of statistics. . . . This sort of probability has to do always with classes, not with single cases except when they can be considered merely as instances. But there is another sort, which I call "degree of credibility." This sort applies to single propositions, and takes account always of all relevant evidence. . . . In some cases the degree of credibility can be inferred from mathematical probability, in others it cannot; but even when it can it is important to remember that it is a different concept. Though "degree of credibility" is a wider and vaguer conception than mathematical probability, it is not purely subjective . . . it is objective in the sense that it is the degree of credence that a rational man will give. . . . In relation to any proposition about which there is evidence, however inadequate, there is a corresponding degree of credibility, which is the same as the degree of credence given by a man who is rational.[2]

For an illustration of the difference between a prognosis with a high degree of credibility and an accidentally accurate prophecy, let us contrast two forecasts concerning the first and the second world wars. Frederick Engels ingeniously combined decisive trends in interrelated systems when, a generation before the outbreak of World War I, he predicted prolonged two-front trench warfare and a stalemate in the West as well as a Russian defeat and revolution in the East. On the other hand, H. G. Wells, who in 1933 prophesied the outbreak of World War II with only a few months' margin of error and quite correctly as an outgrowth of a German-Polish conflict about the Free City of Danzig, may have stepped beyond the limits of more or less reliable forecasting into the twilight of pure chance.

Mathematical probability is the tool used for the understanding of that segment of future social reality which, in its structure, resembles the world of nature. Wherever actions and relationships of relatively large numbers of analogous persons or groups are under investigation which are recurrent and unchanging over a certain period of time, the quantitative method typical of the exact sciences can be applied and the probability of future occurrences can be numerically determined. According to Professor Phelps, "predictions improve in accuracy when they are based upon trend-lines and probable error and reach their highest validity in the statistics of the insurance actuary."

More recently, trend predictions have been ventured with increasing accuracy in the fields of population movement and business fluctuation, and they are making headway in education, psychology, and criminology. With the help of statistics, changes in public opinion and election results are now forecast regularly.[3] In many instances, such mass phenomena can be correctly predicted by statistical means though the future behavior of the individual component of the mass may be completely unpredictable.

Nevertheless only part of the data concerning the future can be reduced to numerical series. In all social sciences, significant phenomena must be understood in their relative uniqueness, their complexity, and their interrelatedness with the whole fabric of culture. Wherever we deal with unique phenomena, we have to be satisfied with a qualitative statement of credibility which results from a combination of inductive and deductive reasoning.

"Objective (developmental) thinking," to use Harold Lasswell's term, "includes the evaluation of newly invented ways of moving toward the goal, and embraces the products of creative imagination about the ways and means of policy." Thus particular elements must be viewed in their functional relationship to the whole; specific qualitative regularities must be discovered that reveal the growth of a social phenomenon. In attempting to establish such patterns, the scholar constructs, within a relatively closed system, a pure type of the phenomenon under investigation, which shows both the enduring design of a social structure and its capacity for organic change.

The sociologist MacIver intimates that "all prediction . . . is based on the assumption of a relatively closed system," "the continuance of which we can reasonably predict on the assumption that no invading or eruptive factor breaks or thwarts the prevailing routine." "It is this type of prediction—not the prediction of sheer novelty—that belongs within the realm of science." Unquestionably, the anticipation of totally new single facts and isolated processes remains impossible as it is dependent on our sense perception which operates only in the present.

"Sheer novelty" is, however, less frequent than MacIver's statement might suggest. For what appears to be an erupting factor in one relatively closed system may be discovered to constitute an integral and, therefore, predictable factor in another connected system. Thus the organization and judicial policies of the United States Supreme Court, once explored, can be projected into the future, and a range of possible or even more or less probable changes can be deducted. We cannot, however, state in terms of mathematical probability who will sit on its bench or what particular decisions will be handed down a decade hence.

Our age is characterized by the beginnings of social and economic planning, undertaken more comprehensively than was possible in earlier periods of our civilization. Theorists of planning like the late Karl Mannheim have claimed that our society is about to become planned in all decisive socio-cultural aspects. In reality, however, planning is practiced not in all regions of the world and, in most instances, it does not cover all spheres of public life. As long as the world continues to be divided into a multiplicity of contending sovereign states, crucial complexes such as industry or agriculture, population or education are not yet subjected to world-wide planning. Hence, an all-inclusive science of global planning cannot yet develop. To the extent, however, that large segments of social reality are either partially planned or at least routinized, intelligent prediction can be ventured about the outcome of the interplay of the planned and unplanned complexes. In other words, while the world society of today is not yet subject to the universal unified control of any system, it is rationalized and stereotyped in sufficient areas to permit scientific prognoses that need not merely be guesswork or intuition.

Next the field to be covered by Futurology must be delineated. Because of its broadness, only the barest outlines can be drawn. Since Futurology encompasses the destiny of man, the future of his society, and the tomorrow of his culture, it must deal not only with his prospective biological and psychological evolution, but also with the entire range of his future cultural activities. Moreover, it includes all the natural (physical, geographical, etc.) factors and processes which will have a bearing on man and his culture in the times to come. In the exact sciences the bulk of investigations is concerned with quantitative determination of an infinite number of recurrent, and in that sense, "timeless" phenomena. Futurology can take in only the long-range hypotheses and theories concerning the prospects of the universe, the future evolution of the earth, the tomorrow of its climate, flora, and fauna.

Second, Futurology tries to answer, as objectively as possible, the problem of the destiny of our civilization within the next centuries. Ever since the writings of Marx and Nietzsche this set of topics has increasingly stirred the imagination of the general public. Ever more frequently the following issues have been raised: Can we anticipate an uninterrupted growth of Western civilization along lines firmly drawn throughout its millennial history? More specifically, will the history of the future corroborate the theory that the class structure, the cultural exclusiveness, the power pyramid of previous periods will be retained in our own development?

Or will our civilization be characterized by a new functional organization, by the elimination of power, and by the growth of an inclusive world culture? Will the so-called "Civilizational Process," i.e., the developments in science, technology, and industry, a process which in the past has proven cumulative and progressive, irreversibly persist until it will have, for the first time in human history, transformed the planet into a single rationalistic and technological world civilization?

Or will the so-called social and cultural lag, which has become so painfully evident since Hiroshima, stop or even reverse this civilizational process? Is our Western civilization irrevocably doomed to decline as the result of economic crises and social upheavals, of bloody revolutions and deadly wars, leading up to a complete relapse into another Dark Age of primitivism and ruralism, localism and bestialism? In other words, will war and want, hunger and servitude prove passing clouds on a bright horizon or will they reveal themselves as the long shadows of death?

. . .

Over and above the long-range forecasts of natural history and the middle-range prognosis of broad socio-cultural processes, Futurology is also interested in predictions of important short-term developments. Predictions of the growth of population in America or anticipations of the political trends during the next decades, analyses of business cycles and conditions during the coming months and years belong to the many themes of Futurology. Speculations about "The Dwarfing of Europe," "Whither France?," "The Prospects of Peace" are the inexhaustible topics of an age of rapid political change. A distinguished historian tried to answer the question: "How New Will the Better World Be?" while the director of a research institute discusses "The Future of Your Job and The Future of America's Classes during The Rest of Your Life." Conjectures concerning the "Religion of Tomorrow" or "The Future Independence and Progress of American Medicine" are as much a part of Futurology as a description of "What's in Store for Children."

It is evident that in this sphere of short-term forecasting the topics tend to become more numerous and more specific. In contrast to the more abstract and general speculations marking middle- and long-range developments, the immediate future in its concreteness and its nearness easily appeals to the public. At the same time, it is the fate of many short-term predictions to become outmoded before the scholar has had a chance to evaluate them in the light of more comprehensive and enduring trends. Under these circumstances all he can do is to verify retroactively the forecasts that had been made beforehand.[4] Unfortunately, material used in making short-range predictions is treated most unevenly. Some phenomena receive thorough and expert attention while others are left to sensation-craving journalists. Hence this area is at present the least integrated of all three segments of Futurology.

The function of Futurology will become fully evident only as it grows since its findings, even more than those of other social sciences, contain elements of considerable uncertainty. We do know that, in our utilitarian age when the utility of all rational knowledge is becoming increasingly doubtful, many will immediately question the need for a science of the future. Gone is the optimism of the Enlightenment and the Century of Science when the conviction prevailed that knowledge was power, and that it would in time enable man to become the master of his fate by giving him control over nature and society. In those days the findings of "pure science" no less than those of applied science were appreciated primarily for their contribution to the happiness and progress of humankind.

Today Ecclesiastes' age-old lament that "in much wisdom is much grief" and that "he that increaseth knowledge increaseth sorrow" sounds in our ears with renewed vigor. It becomes ever harder to prove that increased knowledge inevitably leads to greater happiness or goodness. The pure sciences, so we are beginning to realize, reveal not only our potentialities, but also our limitations. Thanks to the applied sciences we possess not only the tractor, but also the tank. And while we are sure that the latter is a bane, we are by no means certain that the former is an unmixed blessing. Hence all signs point toward the continued strength of the unscientific major ideologies of the day. Engaged in a gigantic struggle between institutions and systems, between ultimate valuations and ways of life, the great majority are likely to continue to interpret the present and future in terms of their parochial short-lived interests in wealth, power, and security.

True, it is theoretically possible that the total crisis will reach such proportions that the antagonistic forces—mass ideologies, social movements, and world powers—will be evenly and precariously balanced. In that unique constellation an authoritative prognosis could be imagined to turn the course of events in the predicted direction, transforming itself thereby into an active force in world history. But whereas in a therapeutic relationship the prediction of the psychiatrist will frequently be instrumental in producing the predicted result, the socio-historical scene is characterized by forces of such magnitude and complexity that a perfectly stable equilibrium can hardly ever be achieved.

Supposing then that it is beyond the power of Futurology to shape the future nearer to our heart's desire, we must proceed on the assumption that it will have to restrict itself to telling us what is in store for us. In so doing, it will base its forecasts among other things upon our fears and hopes, our omissions and actions. Still, if it were to show that our civilization was doomed, if it were to demonstrate that a new global war was inevitable, if it were to establish that a rejected ideology had the best chance of success, we would have no way of preventing these developments. Possibly many a friend of humanity will, under these circumstances, oppose a systematic attempt to lift the veil that hides tomorrow.

Concealing this truth would equal outright intellectual dishonesty, however. Moreover, even if it were true that complete ignorance is preferable to all knowledge, the fact remains that ours is not the choice between knowing and not knowing. There is no way of returning to a condition of "blessed innocence"—our real and only choice lies between less knowledge and more knowledge. And more knowledge about the days to come may, after all, help dispel some of the worst fears that are plaguing us. In this case, Futurology would on its part corroborate Pope's dictum that "a little learning is a dangerous thing." But even if Futurology were to confirm the gloomiest expectations of the pessimist, it could at least, like meteorology, serve the personal welfare of some favored individuals. As the weather forecast helps people to protect themselves against storms and floods, so futurological predictions might enable some to escape the social tempests, cultural deluges, and historical catastrophes. And if this lucky minority were to preserve not only their lives, but also some of the best social achievements and cultural values of the past, Futurology would have rendered some service to the future. By the same token, a knowledge of the future could help avoid disappointment which springs from vain and futile venture. Furthermore, a clear knowledge of the impending collapse of our society might be accompanied by the consolation that the Western civilization, in its disintegration, will become the seed of a new "higher" civilization.

To this future civilization and its intellectual equipment, Futurology would contribute its part, a part analogous to that played by the youthful sciences of nature in the Hellenistic world when, though unable to prevent the general breakdown, they nevertheless served as a foundation for the scientific advancement of subsequent civilizations. Finally, in our days a clearcut and unequivocal picture of the future could turn into a sublime personal challenge to those who are ready to withstand the inevitable with courage and conviction.

On the Nature
of the Future

Bertrand de Jouvenel

No book has had a more powerful philosophical
influence on today's futurists than *The Art of
Conjecture* by Bertrand de Jouvenel, the gifted
French political economist and philosopher. For
de Jouvenel, there is never a single tomorrow—the
future consists of a fan-like array of possibilities,
alternative futures that man can shape. *The Art of
Conjecture,* a book written in classic essay form,
is the source of this article.

There is a difference between the nature of the past and that of
the future. It should hardly be necessary to emphasize that I am
referring here to the difference that is perceived by the mind of an
active human being.

With regard to the past, man can exert his will only in vain; his liberty is void, his power nonexistent. I could say: "I want to be a former student of the École Polytechnique"—but this is utterly absurd. The fact is that I did not go to the École Polytechnique, and nothing can change this fact. Imagine that I am a tyrant and that my authority is sufficient to have the school records changed so that they show me as a member of the class of 1922. This would merely record a falsehood, not a fact. The fact that I did not go to the École Polytechnique cannot be changed. The fundamental impossibility of changing the past accounts for those very important moral sentiments—regret and remorse.

But if the past is the domain of facts over which I have no power, it is also the domain of knowable facts. If I claim to be a graduate of the École Polytechnique, evidence is easily assembled to prove me a liar. It is not always so easy to determine whether alleged facts are true or false, but we always consider that they are in principle verifiable. The impatience and irritation we feel when faced with conflicting testimony bearing on the same fact are signs of our deep conviction that this *factum* is knowable. And in such a situation we do not hesitate to say that one of the witnesses who presented testimony must have been lying or mistaken, even though we may not know which one was actually at fault.

. . .

On the other hand, the future is a field of uncertainty. What will be cannot be attested to and verified in the same way as an accomplished fact. When I say: "I saw Peter on my way here," I am testifying, but when I say: "I shall see Peter on my way back," I am making a supposition. If we are faced with two conflicting opinions regarding a past event, we try to determine which one is true; if we are faced with two conflicting opinions regarding a future event, we try to determine which one is more plausible. For, in the latter case, we have no way of arriving at certainty.

It seems, then, that the expression "knowledge of the future" is a contradiction in terms. Strictly speaking, only *facta* can be known; we can have positive knowledge only of the past.

On the other hand, the only "useful knowledge" we have relates to the future. A man wishing to display his practical turn of mind readily says: "I am only interested in facts," although quite the opposite is the case. If his aim is to get to New York, the time at which a plane left yesterday is of small concern to him; what interests him is the takeoff time this evening (a *futurum*). Similarly, if he wants to see somebody in New York, the fact that this person was in his office yesterday hardly matters to him; what interests him is whether this person will be in his office tomorrow. Our man lives in a world of *futura* rather than a world of *facta*.

The real fact collector is at the opposite pole from the man of action. One erudite scholar might spend years establishing the facts about the assassination of Louis, duc d'Orléans, in 1407, while another might devote his time to tracing Napoleon's itinerary day by day. Here are *facta* that could have no effect on our judgments concerning the future and on our present decisions.

For this reason these *facta* do not concern our practical man. If he is interested in certain *facta*, it is only because he uses them in presuming a *futurum*. For example, he may be worried about the departure time of his plane. Tell him that this flight has left on time for a long succession of days, and he will be reassured. He regards these *facta* as a guarantee of the *futurum*, which is all that matters to him. Now let us suppose that this man contemplates buying a business that holds no interest for him except as an investment. If the accounts show that sales have increased steadily every year, he will derive from these figures a strong presumption that this steady increase will be maintained in future sales.

The case of the business concern differs from that of the airplane in two immediately apparent ways: first, a much larger stretch of time is considered; next, and more particularly, the investor counts on the continuance of the same change, whereas the traveler counts on a simple repetition of the same phenomenon.

In both cases, however, the only use of the known *facta* is as *raw material out of which the mind makes estimates of futura*. The unceasing transformation of *facta* into *futura* by summary processes in the mind is part of our daily life, and thus the undertaking of conscious and systematic forecasting is simply an attempt to effect improvements in a natural activity of the mind.

The scrupulous student of fact brands assertions about the future as intellectual "adventurism": they are, he claims, the business of charlatans, into whose company the sober-minded scholar should not venture. Another, sterner critic admits that we must, perforce, divert some of our attention from intelligible essences to things as they happen to be, but proscribes speculation about their future aspects as too great a diversion. A third complains that our appreciation of the present moment is impaired when we cast our mind to the uncertainties ahead. In turn, a moralist warns against a concern with the future, lest the clear and immediate prescriptions of duty be supplanted by selfish calculations.

No doubt these objections have some foundation; but the representation of future changes is nonetheless a necessary factor in our activity. . . .

       .   .   .

Routines help to save us efforts of foresight: if I have an operational recipe, guaranteed to yield certain results, all I need do is follow the instructions faithfully. Who would be so foolish as to waste time trying out ways of cooking an egg or solving a quadratic equation? It is scarcely necessary to point out that the vast majority of our actions—at present, just as in the distant past—conform to recipes. Accordingly, it should not be difficult for us to imagine a society tied even more closely to recipes. At school, when we failed to do a sum, the teacher would say that we had not done it the right way, meaning the way we had been shown; similarly, we can assume that, in the past, failure and misfortune were readily attributed to departures from or breaches of the "right" practices.

Since we cannot live except in a social group, nothing matters more to us than our relations with other men, and nothing is more important to foresee than the way other men will behave. The more their conduct is governed by custom and conforms to routines, the easier it is to foresee. A social order based on custom provides the individual with optimal guarantees that his human environment is foreseeable. It is hardly surprising that the maintenance of a familiar social order has always been regarded as a Common Good whose preservation was essential.

Hence, aberrations of conduct were condemned, and change was feared and regarded as a corruption. The idea of the security afforded by the routine and familiar was so deeply ingrained that even extreme reformers appealed to this notion, saying they asked for no more than a return to the "good old ways.". . .

       .   .   .

Our positive knowledge of our social environment consists of knowledge of the present state of affairs (or, more precisely, it is a composite image of more or less recent past states of affairs). It would remain valid in its entirety, and for always, if nothing ever changed, but this is impossible. However, the fewer changes we anticipate, the more we can continue to rely on our knowledge for the future. If society tends on the whole to conserve the present state of affairs, our present knowledge has a high chance of being valid in the future. On the other hand, the future validity of our knowledge becomes increasingly doubtful as the mood of society inclines toward change and the changes promise to be more rapid.

We are in the position of a tourist who is planning a journey with the help of a guidebook that is already out of date. Under these conditions, it would be imprudent to trust the guidebook blindly, and we would be better off if we had the intellectual courage to figure out where it is wrong and how it needs to be revised. As foreseeability is less and less granted to us and guaranteed by an unchanging social system, we must put more and more effort into foresight. A saving of effort is possible in a society whose life is governed by routines, whereas the exertion of foresight must increase in a society in movement.

.   .   .

When we foresee or forecast the future, we form *opinions about the future.* When we speak of "a forecast," we simply mean an opinion about the future (but a carefully formed one). When we speak of "forecasting," we mean the intellectual activity of forming such opinions (serious and considered ones, but with an uncertain verification). This needs to be stated clearly and emphatically, particularly since aspirations the forecaster does not, and should not, have are often attributed to him.

More than anyone else economists have made forecasting into an important industry. They commonly use the term "prediction," which presents no drawbacks so long as it is correctly understood. My colleague N. "predicts" that the sale of automobiles will increase next year by so many thousand units: this means that after mature consideration of all the relevant factors he could find, he thinks this figure more likely than any other. But the strength of the term is suggestive, and there is a danger of misapprehension: the word seems to provide a completely certain verdict.

Any such misapprehension on the part of the forecaster's audience is, I think, very dangerous. The persiflage that sometimes
greets the forecaster's work may madden him, but he must fear
skepticism far less than credulity. In all ages men have gathered
about fortunetellers, and when these persons achieve a recognized
position and are able to back their pronouncements with figures,
they will attract a rash of customers who accept their words as
"what science says." The forecaster who takes care to give his
best opinion does not want to make others believe that there is a
"science of the future" able to set forth with assurance what will
be. He is apprehensive of letting this misunderstanding arise. . . .

.   .   .

Our actions, properly so called, seek to validate appealing images
and invalidate repugnant ones. But where do we store these
images? For example, I "see myself" visiting China, yet I know I
have never been there and am not in China now. There is no room
for the image in the past or the present, but there is room for it in
the future. Time future is the domain able to receive as "possibles"
those representations which elsewhere would be "false." And from
the future in which we now place them, these possibles "beckon"
to us to make them real.

.   .   .

. . . the future is the domain into which a man has projected, and
in which he now contemplates, the possible he wishes to make real,
the image that is and will be, as long as it subsists in the mind, the
determining reason for his actions.

.   .   .

An assertion about the future is a perfectly ordinary occurrence.
In the bus, I overhear a stranger saying: "I will be in Saint-Tropez
in August." He "sees himself" in Saint-Tropez, although he is now
in Paris, as I could testify; couched in the present tense his assertion would be an obvious untruth. But the future is available, allowing him to assert something that is not now the case, but is a
future possibility. In August, an observer will be able to determine
whether the assertion has been proven.

.   .   .

It would be naïve to think that over-all progress automatically
leads to progress in our knowledge of the future. On the contrary,
the future state of society would be perfectly known only in a per-

fectly static society—a society whose structure would always be identical and whose "Map of the Present" would remain valid for all time! All the traits of such a society at any future time could be foreknown. But as soon as a society is in movement, its familiar traits are perishable: they disappear, some more rapidly than others—though we cannot date their disappearance in advance—while new traits appear—traits not "given" beforehand to our minds. To say the movement is accelerating is to say that the length of time for which our Map of the Present remains more or less valid grows shorter. Thus our knowledge of the future is inversely proportional to the rate of progress.

.   .   .

Now let us consider public decisions. Suppose change is accelerating: that is to say, an increasing number of new problems arises in each unit of time (a year or a legislative session), and questions calling for decisions are exerting increasing pressure on the responsible men. It seems natural and even reasonable in such a case to take the questions in order of urgency—but the results show that this is a vicious practice. No problem is put on the agenda until it is a "burning" issue, when things are at such a pass that our hand is forced. No longer is any choice possible between different determining acts designed to shape a still-flexible situation. There is only one possible response, only one way out of the problem hemming us in. The powers that happen to be submit to this necessity, and will justify themselves after the event by saying they had no choice to decide otherwise. What is actually true is that they *no longer* had any choice, which is something quite different: for if they cannot be blamed for a decision that was in fact inevitable, they can hardly escape censure for letting the situation go until they had no freedom to choose. The proof of improvidence lies in falling under the empire of necessity. The means of avoiding this lies in acquainting oneself with emerging situations while they can still be molded, before they have become imperatively compelling. In other words, without forecasting, there is effectively no freedom of decision.

Crossing the Frontiers of the Unknown

Fred L. Polak

According to Fred L. Polak, the well-known Dutch political figure and social thinker, the future provides a hidden source of psychological power within us. In a masterful two-volume work called *The Image of the Future,* from which this poetic passage is drawn, he shows that what people *think* will happen has a definite impact on what *does* happen.

Since the dawning of time-consciousness, man has mostly seen the *future* rather than the *past* as holding the key to the riddle of his existence. Death itself, the one certainty of our future, is the chief inciter of our thirst for knowledge of what is to come thereafter. Man has never been able to accept *"ignoramus, ignorabimus"* (ignorant we are and ignorant we will remain) as his motto. Even the agnostic, in order to proclaim his not-knowing as wisdom, must first investigate the unknown and draw boundaries around it. The domain of the future is without boundaries. The audacious individual who unthinkingly crosses the River of Today runs a real risk of getting stuck on the other side without being able to find his way back. Many look in vain for The Key on the other side of the river, when they might have found it on this side. Perhaps that which is to come is already here.

That which is without boundaries and hence cannot be grasped is, for man, also without meaning. Only by drawing boundaries in the thought-realm can we produce a problem which can be grasped and worked with. All increase in knowledge, every advance in science, represents a redrawing of the boundaries of the unknown. No problem presses quite so hard on our intellectual horizons as the problem of the future, and no problem defies our skill at drawing boundaries so persistently. The most cynical definition of philosophy is not out of place: A blind man searching in a dark room for a black cat which isn't there!

Does this frighten off the philosophers? No, for the conviction of existence is stronger than the riddle of existence. The call of the unknown cannot be denied. Time is weaving the innumerable fine threads of what we now call the future. Or is it perhaps the future, *the pattern of the tapestry,* that chooses in advance the appropriate threads and works them into its preexistent pattern?* If . . . we can choose and trace the right threads, we may throw some important light on the remarkable interplay of Man and Time, which in its turn hurls the shuttle back and forth between present and future.

In the act of searching out the road into the future, man crosses the frontiers of the unknown and raises homo sapiens to a new level: the level of foresight and purposefulness. This represents a transition from the man of action, who performs on the basis of the momentary situation, to the man of thought, who takes account of the consequences of his actions and of events to come. The deliberations of the man of thought center about the future, about

* This suggestion is not to be confused with any kind of teleological or finalistic predestination doctrine, which implies that the future is already completely planned from the beginning of time. Dr. Polak is here thinking of the image of the future as determining the future and via this selected future as also determining the course of time starting from the past-present, but this image is itself susceptible to change by man in the course of time. (Translator's note.)

that which at present is not, but is yet to come. We might call it man's first great leap toward freedom. This shifting of concern from what is to what may be represents a tremendous spurt of the human spirit. In taking thought for tomorrow, man begins to create tomorrow. God*like,* he joins hand *with* God in creative partnership. Or if he is not actually a partner, he is at least an intermediary between God and human events, in the role of priest, magician or prophet.

Foresight presupposes a conception of time, duration, development, and continuation. Moving from the more concrete to the more abstract, man frees himself in spirit from the bonds of space and time, from the world's busy joys and sorrows. He leaves behind the familiar universe of sight and sound and charts the universe of the unseen and unheard, carrying his small candle bravely into the darkness. He is perpetually bringing small fragments of the unknown back with him out of this darkness and adding them to the known. Who knows whether this building up of the known diminishes the unknown? The future seems to be an ever-receding, ever-expanding entity, and the more we know the more remote and difficult the unknown appears. As we industriously master the "hows" of the universe, the "why" and the "whither" become increasingly obscure.

Man is not easily discouraged, however. Because of his unique gifts, the very existence of the unknown challenges him to bring science and philosophy into being to discover it. Everything drives man to accept this challenge of the unknown. The instincts of preservation and reproduction demand it. All economic activity is an answer to this challenge; the primitive nomad gathering fruits and nuts and the modern industrial magnate are alike answering the call of the unborn tomorrow; so are the men who chart the seas and the men who chart the heavens. No man, not even the suicide, can leave tomorrow alone. The suicide but hastens his tomorrow in his over-impatience.

In exploring his own future, man has always been haunted by the sense of doing the impossible and the forbidden. The Greeks knew well the sin of *hubris,* the sin of challenging the omnipotence of the gods. Any man who overstepped the bounds of permitted human activity was to suffer dreadful and never-ending punishment. And yet, through all the intervening centuries, man has never ceased to challenge these bounds. He has suffered, indeed, as a consequence, but he has also succeeded in pushing the bounds far out into the realm of what was once considered impossible. This spiritual overstepping of the bounds is the source of all human creativity and activity. If the time ever comes when the human spirit is content to stand still before its farthest limits, then the farthest limits of human history will at that moment have been reached.

In other words, man has always somehow realized that the impossible was absolutely necessary. The struggle for survival demands it, and every extinct organic species and every extinct civilization bears mute witness to this necessity of meeting the challenge of the future. Religion has always accepted this challenge, and bent every effort to the task of interpreting the foreordained will of God. Science, holding man and not God responsible for the future course of events, has concerned itself with causal relations in order to be able to predict their effects in a given situation. Bacon preached that such "knowledge is power." Finally, applied science has striven to eliminate the unpredictable from human life and to draw an orderly blueprint for the construction of society. The desire to eliminate the periodic social catastrophes which originate from the unleashing of the forces of blind nature or the forces of foolish man has been the driving power behind all our technical progress and the ratio for obtaining calculated future results by collective and responsible social action.

The boundary between the known and the unknown is never sharply defined or permanent. Man has not always been daring in approaching this boundary, however. History records a series of successive attacks on and retreats from this frontier. So far, the will to conquer has in the long run predominated. The longing for one's own home and hearth has always been countered by tremendous folk migrations and individual adventures of daring and discovery. The first small ships to brave the perils of vast stretches of unknown waters were launched by the same undaunted human spirit as is now endeavouring to launch rocket ships into space. Crossing frontiers is both man's heritage and man's task. The image of the future is his propelling power.

. . .

Once man knew that he *had* a future and had begun to dream

about it, it was but a step to wanting to know with some certainty what the future would bring. Since foreknowledge might prove to be foreknowledge of catastrophe as well as foreknowledge of blessings to come, the impulse to propitiate the powers of the future in order to avoid catastrophe and procure blessings may well have become part and parcel of the drive to *know* from its early beginnings. Both magic and religion probably arose at least in part out of this twin drive for certainty and for the power to alter a foreboded course of events through propitiation. For many centuries forward-looking man must have struggled to obtain a reliable reading of signs and omens, both in the heavens and in the world around him. Although we do not know, it seems likely that dependence on the direct inspiration of gifted and therefore specializing individuals, whether priests, prophets, sorcerers or clairvoyants, came somewhat later. Sometimes prophet and pro-pitiator were one and the same person, at other times the two functions were separate.

As Man the Maker embarked on the adventures of agriculture, navigation and his first large-scale engineering projects, such as pyramids and waterworks, the need to predict and control the future became of still more practical urgency. The beginnings of science grew out of this urgency, particularly the science of the heavens. Astrology and its more sober offspring, astronomy, alike served this need to know the future. We have already described . . . man's changing concept of his own role in relation to his future. The faithful transcriber of fore-ordained reality, in becoming slowly aware of his faculties to control part of that reality, finally emerged as the consciously emancipated humanist, determined when neces-sary to *alter* the course of events to the full extent of his supposed powers. Science during the last two centuries has been putting increasingly potent tools in his hand for that purpose.

In setting himself purposefully to control and alter the course of events man has been forced to deal with the concepts of value, means and ends, ideals and ideologies, as he had attempted to blueprint his own future. As long as the prophet-propitiator was acting as a divine transmitter of messages from on high, man felt that he was accepting his ethics ready-made, with no alterations allowed. In a later stage man staggers under the double load of not only having to construct his own future but having to create the values which will determine its design. To primitive man, his task of looking into the unknown must have seemed terrifying enough. As modern man gains an increasing understanding of the complexity of the interplay between attitudes and values and technological know-how in the process of social change at all levels of society from the primary group to the international community, the terrifying aspects of the unknown are scarcely diminished. However, between this initial period and modern times there has been a long series of attempts by man, accompanied by many ups and downs, to push back the frontier of the unknown farther and farther. This might be seen as a two-fold process: the development of ideas concerning the *ideal* future as it ought to be and the unfolding of the *real* future in history, partly as a result of man's purposeful intervention. Awareness of ideal values is the first step in the conscious creation of images of the future and therefore in the conscious creation of culture. For a value is by definition that which guides toward a "valued" future. The image of the future reflects and reinforces these values. The relationship between the conceptions of the time-dimension, "future," and the idealistic ethical objectives of mankind for that future has been a neglected one and offers a fruitful field for research.

The foregoing may, after due elaboration, throw new light on the emergence and development of culture. It becomes clear now that magic, religion, philosophy, science, and ethics might well owe their origin and further creative development largely to the basic need to get foreknowledge of the future. In other words, these fundamental fields of culture may have been developed at first mainly as ways and means of visualizing and influencing the future. The images of the future of mankind, viewed in this light, are historic landmarks and cultural mirrors of this process and its progress in time.

Faith in the Technological Future

John Wren-Lewis

Technology has been vitriolically attacked by humanists as the prime source of contemporary evil. Here a leading theologian, president of the British Association for Humanistic Psychology, takes a fresh look at the assumption that machines will dehumanize tomorrow. While Paul Ehrlich, in the opening essay in this volume, warns us that "Nature bats last," Wren-Lewis replies: Yes, but Man has the last laugh!

The most depressing thing I have come across in the last few years was a programme produced by the BBC in one of its series about science and the future, in which a number of children who will be the not-so-young men and women of 2000 were interviewed about what sort of a world they thought it was going to be. About fifteen or sixteen children were interviewed and only one was even remotely cheerful about it. All the rest saw a world in which "They" were going to turn us all into robots, a computer-planned society in which there was no room for individual initiative, a machine society in which there was no room for any artistic values; some also thought "They" were going to land us into world conflict or world starvation.

This was profoundly depressing because it seemed that the one thing which is absolutely certain to ensure such world catastrophe is precisely this pessimistic sense of the inevitability of catastrophe. If the young really believe there is no hope, they will have no possible incentive to work or struggle against the forces of inhumanity. Faced with such a situation, even dyed-in-the-wool technologists, who normally suspect prophets and missionaries profoundly, are faced with the need to become something very like missionary prophets, so as to help our society recover the faith that machines are made for men, not men for machines, that social systems and organisations are made for men, not men for them, and that there is at least some hope of winning the fight against the forces of destruction and depersonalisation. In general, there is a real duty for anyone who feels that there is the slightest hope for the future to try to analyse the grounds of that hope and to turn his analysis into some kind of mission.

When an analysis is made of the forces making for inhumanity, depersonalisation and mechanisation, the forces which stunt the sense of beauty and freedom and spaciousness and joy, it is found that these forces can quite properly be described as reactionary. To put it in another way, these evil forces of our time are not new things produced by the science and technology which take us into the future, as is widely supposed by pessimists of all kinds, including the inarticulate ones, but very ancient things which threaten us only because we are not allowing science and technology to take us into the future fast enough. The tendency for society to regiment people and deprive them of individual initiative is no greater today than it was in past ages, and if it grows worse in the future it will be because we use computers and robots too little rather than too much. If our society is in danger of being overwhelmed by materialism, war, or sheer multiplication of human numbers, it is not because control is being taken over by scientific and technological planners who have broken with mankind's age-old values, but because we are still far too bound by mankind's traditional values instead of taking really seriously the spirit of creativity and freedom which characterise science and technology.

The Threat to Individuality. Let us look at some of the problems of the modern world in a little more detail, and to begin with let us look at the phenomenon of totalitarianism, which is very often quoted as a distinctive evil of our own time. For example, in the Bishop of Woolwich's *Honest to God,*[1] there are many quotations from the German theologian Dietrich Bonhoeffer, notably his famous statement that today theology must change because mankind has "come of age," and the Bishop feels it necessary to remark that Bonhoeffer's optimism about the modern world was astonishing considering how that world was responsible for torturing him in a concentration camp even while he was writing. But in this it seems that the Bishop, for all his sympathy with Bonhoeffer, has failed to appreciate an important part of what he was saying. For the truth is that Bonhoeffer saw Nazism precisely as a reactionary phenomenon; he understood that Nazism was a deliberate attempt to recapture a kind of society which had existed in the ancient world and in mediaeval times but had been destroyed by that modern scientific thought which Hitler associated with the machinations of Jews and Communists. Hitler was trying quite consciously to recapture the glory of the First Reich in the Third: from his point of view, the world had lost, and needed to recover, the traditional "pre-modern" way of life in which the individual found his significance wholly in the tribe.

The psychology of totalitarianism is very beautifully and accurately analysed in George Orwell's novel *1984.*[2] The group can do far more than the individual, so it behooves the individual, even at the cost of accepting a regime of cruelty, to subordinate himself wholly and totally to the group. But where Orwell placed this in the science-fiction future, Hitler saw quite clearly that it was what all the older societies of the world did under the name of religion— specifically, in the name of the kind of mythology whereby the individual was seen, and was taught to see himself, as a limb or a cell in the body corporate. The particular Christian version of this mythology, whereby the individual is seen as a limb or a cell in the body of Christ, is simply a particular application of what everybody took for granted in Saint Paul's day, and that kind of vision of human life was common to every society in all the widely different civilisations of the world until the time of the scientific revolution.

Hitler believed it was the destiny of the German people to recapture this way of living, and he grasped intuitively what Orwell worked out by conscious logic, that the kind of individual self-consciousness which characterises the modern scientific/democratic world militates against group-consciousness unless it is systematically destroyed by organised tyranny and the infliction of pain. Hence Dietrich Bonhoeffer was being perfectly consistent when he proclaimed from the concentration camp that the modern world is "grown up" in a sense that the ancient world was not. He saw quite clearly that the thing which was killing him was not the modern world, but a deliberate attempt to go back on the most distinctive characteristic of the modern world.

This principle applies equally to the problems of overpopulation and violence. The problem of overcrowding is a product of science and technology only in the superficial sense that a man's sense of bewilderment on being released from prison is a product of his being released.

The real root of our modern problem of overpopulation is the fact that people are still, over a large part of the world, living by the traditional human pattern in which the human individual finds significance primarily in his breeding capacity. Women especially, in the traditional human pattern of thought, are seen as inadequate if they have no children. We shall overcome the problem of galloping population ("Plurisy of people" as the Elizabethan poet put it) only if we can break with the traditional patterns of thought and create a society in which people (of either sex) feel significant in their own right, without having to justify themselves by conforming to the supposedly greater plan of organic nature—in other words, a society in which people feel generally what scientists and technologists take for granted every time they perform an experiment —that the patterns of nature are made for man, not man for them.

There are no theological implications in the term "made," it is simply used to describe an attitude: but it is no mere coincidence that a phrase can aptly be used for this purpose that echoes what Jesus said about the Sabbath. On the contrary, there is a great deal in the Jewish-Christian religious scriptures which suggests the attitude to life advocated here: typically, it is suggested right at the beginning of our particular compilation of these scriptures— when the Book of Genesis declares that man's destiny is to have dominion over nature, to determine for himself the forms (the "names") of things instead of assuming, as the old nature-religions did, that everything is already determined by divinities hidden behind the scenes. Hence, it is supremely ironic that many Christians and Jews in the modern world should be opposing the use of human artifice to separate the expression of human love from its biological connection with reproduction, on the ground that the patterns of biological nature represent divine laws to which people should conform.

Manipulating the System to Desired Ends. It should be noted that the really distinctive feature of science and technology is the overall approach to the world in terms of which their calculation and manipulation have the distinctive modern scientific meaning, and this overall approach is profoundly humanistic. The experimental method means judging theories about nature by the way they work out in practical actions devised by human beings, and technology means using techniques to provide goods or services which people want. The attempt to conform human life to the supposedly greater plan of organic nature, as all the great traditional religious cultures did in their various ways, inevitably condones and encourages cruelty and inhumanity, for biological nature is full of cruelty and has no place at all for human values such as respect for individual feelings.

In fact the root cause of the population explosion is precisely the same as the root cause of totalitarianism—that individuals feel they have no intrinsic value in their own right as persons and so seek to lose themselves in the apparently larger stream of tribal and biological life. War is simply the reverse side of this coin; it is what happens when human beings, who have it in them to stand above nature and control nature, try to conform to the patterns of organic life in which aggressive drives are exercised in a kind of ritual and the individual is sacrificed to the collective. War was one of the traditional ways in which mankind prevented overpopulation by sacrificing humanity, and equally was one of the reasons why traditional social patterns encouraged people to breed as much as possible.

Our greatest hope of avoiding totalitarianism, overpopulation and war lies in the fact that over the past three centuries mankind has been breaking with these traditional patterns, and a new kind of attitude to life has begun to emerge, characterised by the scientist's and technologist's confidence in his right to assert his own experimental ideas against any kind of tradition.

The Question of Materialism. Fear of the technological future is epitomised in the fear that we are being driven into an age when purely materialistic understanding of the world will undermine human and aesthetic values. A correct analysis, however, will show that the dangers we face are not products of science and technology at all, but rather aspects of traditional culture which people fail to see because they have been encouraged to look at that culture through rose-coloured spectacles. Materialism, too, in other words, is a profoundly reactionary phenomenon, whether it be the philosophical materialism which regards everything in the world, including people, as mere by-products of the mechanical interplay of atoms, electrons and the like, or the practical materialism which expresses itself in the West by concern for refrigerators and washing machines and in the East by the philosophy which argues "I could not love thee dear so much loved I not my tractor more."

Materialism is commonly represented as the great enemy of religion, and those who fear materialism frequently urge a return to religion in order to safeguard essential human and aesthetic values.[3] The truth is, however, that generality of religion, far from preserving human and aesthetic values, has itself been their greatest enemy, in that it has taught people to see themselves as part of the Great System of the world rather than as creative persons of significance in their own right—and in this respect materialism, far from being opposed to religion, is actually a form of religion.

At the intellectual level, materialism takes the findings of a particular stage of science and erects these into a new Grand Design, in relation to which, it asserts, personal and aesthetic concerns are mere delusions. This is not a scientific thing to do at all: on the contrary, the essence of modern science and technology is the constant recognition that any theories and pictures we may form of the world as a system are merely intellectual tools to be evaluated by the creative action of experiment, with the corollary that some new experiment may be thought of tomorrow which will make it necessary to discard those pictures and theories completely. The essential procedures of both science and technology are psychologically closely related to the essential procedures of creative art, and also, to that prophetic strain in the world's great religions summed up in the declaration of Jesus that the Sabbath was made for man, not man for the Sabbath (a direct parallel to the characteristic assertion of modern science that theory is made for experiment, not experiment for theory). Materialism, on the other hand, is a reaction from the true spirit of modern science to the organised inhumanity of traditional religion which stoned the prophets and crucified Jesus.

It may at first seem paradoxical to describe materialism as a form of religion, but it does not take much imagination to see the essentially religious character of the materialistic totalitarianism which demands that individuals sacrifice themselves to the Process of History, while if we turn to one of the most famous statements of Western scientific materialism, Bertrand Russell's famous essay *A Free Man's Worship,* we find something remarkably like a hymn:

> Brief and powerless is Man's life;
> On him and all his race
> The slow, sure doom falls
> Pitiless and dark.
> Blind to good and evil,
> Reckless of destruction,
> Omnipotent matter rolls on its relentless way;

Real science knows nothing of omnipotent matter: on the contrary, the fact that every theory of real science has its meaning in terms of creative experimental action means that every theory, however impersonal in its detailed structure, implies the existence of Potent Man. Omnipotent matter, like the omnipotent God of traditional religion, is a fantasy into which people can retreat in order to escape from the challenge of taking themselves seriously as creative animals. It was because he saw religion in that light that Freud described it as something like a universal human neurosis, but the fact that modern science and technology have begun to emerge in the world over the last 300 years seems to be a sign that mankind is beginning to break out of that neurosis.

Recognition of this can give us the faith we need to face the future. It is an intensely humanistic faith, but not totally opposed to religion. Rather, it is a recovery of the prophetic faith which has always been found at the core of the world's great religions, but has hitherto been upheld only by a very small persecuted minority.

Technology and the Human Environment

R. Buckminster Fuller

Perhaps no futurist has been more energetic, more vocal, more popular, or more optimistic than a seventy-six-year-old engineer-visionary, poet-philosopher named R. Buckminster Fuller. Fuller's planetary perspective has won him zealous converts the world over. Even those who disagree with his technological transcendentalism share unbegrudged admiration for the world's youngest old futurist.

Your Senate hearing gives me a short but welcome opportunity to talk . . . about all that man has learned fundamentally from his two million years aboard our spaceship Earth, wherefore I wish to point out vigorously to you that we are indeed aboard an 8,000-mile-diameter spherical space vehicle. . . .

. . . Earth is a beautifully designed spaceship, equipped and provisioned to support and regenerate life aboard it for hundreds of millions of years, even until the time when so much energy of universe has been collected aboard Earth as to qualify it to become a radiant star, shortly before which man will have anticipatorially resituated himself on other planets at nonincineratable distance from the earth nova. . . .

Humans have high destiny, possibly the most important in the universe. And if the human team aboard space vehicle Earth does not make good at this particular occupation of this particular planet there are probably billions times billions of other planets with human crews aboard who will reboard Earth at some time to operate it properly. . . .

Humanity on this North American continent is the beginning of a world man. We are not a nation. Nations are tribes of people who have been isolated for a long time and have, of reproductive necessity, inbred—grandfathers with granddaughters—and have adapted themselves to exclusively local physical conditions.

We are not going to be able to operate our spaceship Earth successfully nor for much longer unless we see it as a whole spaceship and our fate as common. It has to be everybody or nobody. . . .

. . . We are going to have to find ways of organizing ourselves cooperatively, sanely, scientifically, harmonically and in regenerative spontaneity with the rest of humanity around earth. . . .

Considering our present dilemmas aboard our planet and earnestly seeking fundamental clues to both their cause and solution, we may note that we start our children off with a geometry whose lines and planes go (we say) to infinity. The little child says, "Where is that?" The teacher can't answer because she has never experienced infinity. . . .

I have been a visitor at 320 universities and colleges around the world and always have asked those university audiences "How many of you are familiar with the word 'synergy'?" I can say authoritatively that less than 10 percent of university audiences and less than 1 percent of nonuniversity audiences are familiar with the word and meaning of synergy. Synergy is not a popular word. The word synergy is a companion to the word "energy." Energy and synergy. The prefix "syn" of synthesis meaning with, to integrate and the "en" of energy means "separating out." Man is very familiar with energy, he has learned to separate out, or isolate, certain behaviors of total nature and thus has become familiar with many of the separate natural behaviors such as optics. But the only partially isolatable behavior is always modifyingly employed by the whole. If humans had to purchase their many separate organs, stomachs, livers, endocrine glands, tongues, eyeballs, and bowels and thereafter to assemble those parts into logical interfunctioning, they would never do so. All those parts had to be preassembled and unitarily skinned in and coordinately operated by multiquadrillions of atoms in the brain which after sixteen years of practical spontaneous coordination becomes so aesthetically acceptable one to the other that as it sings, dances, and smiles one is inclined to procreate with the other.

Synergy is to energy as integration is to differentiation.

The word "synergy" means "Behavior of whole systems unpredicted by behavior of any of the systems parts." Nature is comprehensively synergetic. Since synergy is the only word having that meaning and we have proven experimentally that it is not used by the public, we may conclude that society does not understand nature. . . .

Our school systems are all nonsynergetic. We take the whole child and fractionate the scope of his or her comprehending coordination by putting the children in elementary schools—to become preoccupied with elements or isolated facts only. Thereafter we force them to choose some specialization, forcing them to forget the whole. We start them off with planes and straight lines which run into infinity which no scientist has ever produced experimentally and therefore we defy the child to comprehend, and require that they accept and believe that it is logical to assume "infinity" and therefore to give up the child's innate propensity to learn by experiment and experience, recourse to which exclusively experientially informed reasoning made possible Einstein's epochal reorientation of all scientific theory. We stuff our children's heads with such nonsense as straight, continuous surfaces and solids paying no attention whatever to the fact that science has discovered no solids, nor any continuous surfaces. Science has found only discrete energy packages such as the atoms whose electrons and nucleons are as discretely remote from one another as is the Earth remote from the Sun. As a consequence of this theoretical mish-mash and our deliberate discard of the child's innate experimental techniques for self-teaching thereby, we find our world society looking askance upon its presently conjured, news-invented concept of its most prominent, inexorably developing fate with none of its predictions coming true and with all of the progenitors of the variously frustrated ideologies becoming progressively vindictive and intransigent. . . .

If the great design of the universe had wished man to be a specialist, man would have been designed with one eye and a microscope attached to it which he could not unfasten. All the living species except human beings are specialists. The bird can fly beautifully but cannot take its wings off after landing and therefore can't walk very well. The fish can't walk at all. But man can put on his gills and swim and he can put on his wings and fly and then take them off and not be encumbered with them when he is not using them. He is in the middle of all living species. He is the most generally adaptable but only by virtue of his one unique faculty— his mind. Many creatures have brains. Human minds discover pure abstract generalized principles and employ those principles in the appropriate special cases. Thus has evolution made humans the most universally adaptable, in contradistinction to specialization, by endowing them with these metaphysical, weightless invisible capabilities to employ and realize special case uses of the generalized principles. . . .

We know scientifically that all local physical systems are continually giving off energies. We call this entropy. Due to each of the local systems' unique periodicities, and so forth, the given-off energies are diffuse and randomly released in respect to other systems. Thus the physical universe is continually expanding and increasingly disorderly. Fundamental complementarity requires that there must be some phase of universe where the universe is contracting and increasingly orderly. . . .

All the biologicals are converting chaos to beautiful order. All biology is antientropic. Of all the disorder to order converters, the human mind is by far the most impressive. The human's most powerful metaphysical drive is to understand, to order, to sort out, and rearrange in ever more orderly and understandably constructive ways. You find then that man's true function is metaphysical. Man's physical function is the same as that of all other biological life; to impound and regenerate physical life, which means inherently to produce reconstructive order of every variety. The metaphysical, absolutely weightless function in universe, unique to humans, is that of continually looking for the generalized principles which are operative in all the special case experiences. Thus has humanity discovered that it could move and constructively rearrange multiton rocks that man's individual muscle could not move. He succeeded by his weightless mind's discovery of the generalized principle of leverage. Thus also did mind discover the principle of electron conductivity, whatever that may be, for electromagnetics, though discovered and used by man, is as yet a fundamental enigma. . . .

I find man utterly unaware of what his wealth is or what his fundamental capability is. He says time and again, "We can't afford it." For instance, we are saying now that we can't afford to do anything about pollution, but after the costs of not doing something about pollution have multiplied manifold beyond what it would cost us to correct it now, we will spend manifold what it would cost us now to correct it. That is a geometrical compounding of inevitable expenditures. (Originally sidestepped because we believed erroneously that we "couldn't afford" their correction.) For this reason I find that in satisfying humanity's vital needs, highest social priority must be assigned to the development of world-around common knowledge of what wealth is. We have no difficulty discovering troubles but we fail to demonstrate intelligent search for the means of coping with the troubles. This is primarily due to our misconditioned reflex which says that "we can't" afford to do the intelligent things. We discover with scientific integrity that wealth is simply the measurable degree to which we have rearranged the physical constituents of the scenery so that they are able to support more lives, for more days, at such-and-such standards of health and nourishment, while specifically decreasing restraints on human thought and action, while also multiplying the per capita means of communication and travel, all accomplished without increased privation of any human. Wealth has nothing to do with yesterday, but only with forward days. How many forward days, for how many lives are we now technically organized to cope? The numerical answer is the present state of our true wealth.

I find that our wealth consists exclusively of two fundamental phenomena: the physical and the metaphysical. The physical in turn consists of two subdivisions. One is the physical/energy associative as matter and the other is energy dissociative as radiation. After science discovered the speed of light, it went on to discover that when energy was lost from one system it was gained by another local system. It is never lost from the universe. Energy is inherently conserved, so the energy component of wealth cannot be depleted.

The other prime constituent of wealth, the metaphysical, is contributed by human intellect. Man's muscle has only a self-starter, button-pushing function. Man's mind comprehends and masters the energy of Niagara Falls. His muscle cannot compete with Niagara. Humanity's unique function is that of his mind's ability to discover generalized principles and to invent effective ways of employing those principles in rearranging the physical constituents of the scenery to ever greater metabolic regeneration advantage and metaphysical freedom of humanity. We discover that every time man makes an experiment, he always learns more. He cannot learn less. We have learned therefore that the intellectual or metaphysical half of wealth can only increase. The physical cannot decrease and the metaphysical can only increase, wherefore wealth, which results from the synergetic interaction of both the physical and metaphysical, can only increase. Which is to say—net—that wealth can only increase with each reemployment, and the more intelligently and frequently it is reinvested the more rapidly it increases. This is not disclosed in any books on economics. It is not recognized by the body politic.

So I say to you, man has acquired all the right technology within only sixty years to amplify from less than 1 percent to 40 percent the proportion of all humanity who are now economically successful with the possibility of elevating all of humanity in ever greater degree within another twenty-five years, all of which enabling technology humanity said it couldn't possibly afford until the military said, "This is the way your enemy is going to fight the war. You either acquire an equal or better technology or die." To which the people responded, "Though we think we can't afford it and though we don't know how we can pay for it, if we have the energy resources plus the know-how and human time to produce that technology we will go ahead and produce it and find out later how to pay for it," not realizing that in investing our time and know-how in producing it we were paying all that would ever be realistically required to pay for it. The constituents belonged in truth to no one. That physical phenomena which had originally been commandeered by illiterate sword and gun seizure and had been deeded thenceforth under guarantee of arms as property and that the paper equity had been loaned out at interest and compounded arbitrarily as a debt imposed by law on someone did not alter the fundamentals of this situation. . . .

These generalized principles were all found to be operating a priori to man. Man simply finds and employs. He does not put anything into the universe. We must realize that technology was not put into the universe by man. The universe is the comprehensive system of technology. Humanity is discovering and beginning to employ it. . . .

I would like to call your attention to a super piece of technology, the sailing ship. The sailing ship going through the sea is unlike a bulldozer. The sea closes behind the ship. The ship does no damage to the sea. The sailing ship employs the wind which is swirling ceaselessly around the earth without depleting any of the energy of the universe. This is a very beautiful piece of technology, no damage whatsoever to the environment. It is possible for all humanity to survive at higher standards than any have ever known while employing technologies that do no damage to the ecologically regenerative balance of the environment. It is possible for all humanity to prosper while employing only the natural energy income of wind, tide, sun, gravity as water power and electromagnetics of temperature differentials. We are not justified in using the energy savings account of fossil fuels where the energy-hour investment in their creation and storage would cost us today possibly as much as $1 billion a gallon figured at present kilowatt-hour generating rates. Having discovered that the function of man on earth is to impound and conserve energy, we find him operating antievolutionizarily in using the fossil fuel petroleum and coal for any other than minor self-starter functions when the rate of energy expenditure is negligible as compared to the rate of planet Earth's energy storing.

The kind of technology that endangers is that occasioned by the blinders of specialization where each of our various acts is executed without consideration of the others.

So I think we are in an historically critical state of humans aboard space vehicle Earth. I think we have been given adequate resources to absorb our many trial and error explorations for knowledge. We have been allowed to make a great mess of things —until now—in order that we might discover our great function. I identify humanity very much with the following analogy—as life is regenerated by the bird. The bird, in order to survive in flight, has to take on very small energy increments in order to avoid being too heavy to fly. For reasons of this same flight-maintaining capability, the bird does not gestate the new life inside its womb, because the mother bird would become too heavy to fly to reach the insects to get enough energy to keep both the mother and the new life alive. So the new bird embryo is put in the egg, with all of the chromosomic instructions of how to design the bird's progressive organisms. All of the nutrients are stored inside the shell. The only thing the embryo needs further is energy as heat given off by the mother sitting on the egg in the energy-insulating nest. This design keeps the temperature at exactly the critical level to permit the mother bird's swift, food-gathering sorties from the nested egg.

The little bird develops beautifully inside. The mother is freed to do her flying tasks to gain enough food energy to keep the critical metabolic regeneration balance.

Finally, the little bird develops completely within the shell, having had just enough nutrient to do so.

The new little bird, exhausting the nutriment inside the shell, impulsively pecks at the eggshell, it break open, and there is the little bird, suddenly moving about on its own legs, beautifully prepared to operate on an entirely new basis.

I see that all humanity thus far has been guarded by such an innocence-tolerating nutriment which could sustain all the trial-and-error-won ultimate discovery that our muscles are as nothing beside the power of the waterfall and that the power-comprehending and -employing mind which can harness the gravity force of the waterfall to generate electricity and discover how to conduct that power to drive motors to do work anywhere . . . is our unique faculty.

We discover that we are essentially the weightless immortal mind which can comprehend and communicate and invent words and codify them in a dictionary, to implement the integrity of communication by noncontiguously existing humans. I think we are at that critical historical moment in which we have just broken our shell of permitted ignorance and henceforth we can survive only by learning to operate in our universe in a very different way. If we do not comprehend and behave spontaneously with the highest, most unselfish integrity, I think man may readily not make it on this particular planet. . . .

. . . If you are going to be wise . . . you are going to have to look at things in these big ways.

Notes

Alvin Toffler, Introduction: Probing Tomorrow

1. *Typological Survey of Futures Research in the U.S.,* National Institute of Mental Health, Division of Mental Health Programs. Principal Investigator: John McHale.
2. See his essay in this volume, pages 257–263.
3. Mimeographed letter sent to various futurists.

John McHale, "The Plastic Parthenon"

1. E.g., after Buddha died in the fifth century, his body relics were divided up again and again, but there were still not enough remains to supply all the shrine in the land—so an elaborate system of "reminders" was set up. A "reminder" was a shrine that contained no actual relics—but was an exact replica of one which did. There are many traditions in which the image or replica of a sacred relic was no more than a "reminder," but also carried the same magical power as the original.
2. Sarkis Atamian, "The Anaktuvuk Mask and Cultural Innovation," *Science*, March, 1966, no. 3716.
3. Lewis Feuer, "A Critical Evaluation," *New Politics*, Spring, 1963.
4. Daniel Bell, "The Disjunction of Cultural and Social Culture," *Daedalus*, Winter, 1965.
5. Lawrence Alloway, "L'Intervention du Spectateur," *L'Architecture d'Aujourd'hui,* July, 1956.

Robert Jungk, "Evolution and Revolution in the West"

1. Erich Jantsch, *Technological Forecasting in Perspective,* Paris, 1967.
2. Olaf Helmer, *Prospectus for an Institute for the Future,* Santa Monica, 1967.

307

3. Erich Jantsch, *op. cit.*
4. Impact, UNESCO, Paris, 1968.
5. See the appendix to *China and the West: Mankind Evolving*, p. 128.
6. In *Analyse et Prévision*, Paris, 1967.

Arthur C. Clarke, "Hazards of Prophecy"

1. The dead weight of the rocket (propellent tanks, motor, etc.) would actually make the ratio very much higher, but that does not affect the argument.
2. In all fairness to Dr. Woolley, I would like to record that his 1936 review contained the suggestion—probably for the first time—that rockets could contribute to astronomical knowledge by making observations in ultra-violet beyond the absorbing screen of earth's atmosphere. The importance of this is only now becoming apparent.
3. Cherwell's influence—malign or otherwise—has been the subject of a vigorous debate since publication of Sir Charles Snow's *Science and Government*.

Theodore J. Gordon, "The Current Methods of Futures Research"

1. H. Wentworth Eldridge, "Teaching Futurism in American Colleges and Universities," presented to the Environmental Forecasting Conference, University of Texas at Austin, January 1970. According to Dr. Eldridge, forty courses are now being offered at various institutions (half at the graduate level), and forty-one other schools are considering such courses.
2. Bertrand de Jouvenel, *The Art of Conjecture*, translated from the French by Nikita Lary (New York: Basic Books, Inc., 1967).
3. S. C. Gilfillan, "A Sociologist Looks at Technical Prediction," in J. Bright, ed., *Technological Forecasting in Government and Industry* (Englewood Cliffs: Prentice Hall, 1968).
4. Nancy T. Gamarra, *Erroneous Predictions and Negative Comments Concerning Exploration, Territorial Expansion, Scientific and Technological Development*, Legislative Reference Service, Library of Congress (April 1967).
5. Theodore J. Gordon, *A Study of Potential Changes in Employee Benefits*, Reports R-1, R-2, R-3, Institute for the Future (April 1969).
6. Olaf Helmer and N. Rescher, "The Epistemology of the Inexact Sciences," *Management Science*, Vol. 6, No. 1 (October 1959).
7. Norman Dalkey, *The Delphi Method: An Experimental Study of Group Opinion*, Memorandum RM-5888-PR, The RAND Corporation (June 1969).
8. Theodore J. Gordon, Olaf Helmer, "A Report on a Long-Range Forecasting Study," *Societal Technology* (New York: Basic Books, Inc., 1966), pp. 44–96.

9. R. M. Campbell, *Methodological Study of the Utilization of Experts in Business Forecasting*, unpublished Ph.D. dissertation, University of California, Los Angeles (September 1966).

10. A. D. Bender, A. Strack, G. Ebrigh, G. von Haunalter, *A Delphic Study of the Future of Medicine* (Philadelphia: Smith, Kline & French Laboratories, January 1969).

11. C. Bjerrum, "Forecast of Computer Developments and Applications 1968–2000," *Futures*, Vol. 1, No. 4 (June 1969).

12. R. de Brigard, Olaf Helmer, *Some Potential Societal Developments*, Report R-7, Institute for the Future (December 1969).

13. Theodore J. Gordon, *A Study of Potential Changes in Employee Benefits*, Reports R-1, R-2, R-3, Institute for the Future (April 1969).

14. Theodore J. Gordon, Robert H. Ament, *Forecasts of Some Technological and Scientific Developments and Their Societal Consequences*, Report R-6, Institute for the Future (September 1969).

15. M. Adelson, "The Education Innovation Study," *American Behavioral Scientist*, Vol. 10, No. 7 (March 1967), pp. 8–12.

16. H. Q. North, L. Pyke, "Technological Forecasting in Planning for Company Growth," Institute of Electrical and Electronics Engineers *Spectrum*, Vol. 6, No. 1 (January 1969).

17. Dalkey, *The Delphi Method.*

18. Campbell, *Methodological Study.*

19. Colonel J. Martino, "Trend Extrapolation."

20. Gordon and Helmer, "Report on a Long-Range Forecasting Study."

21. Robert H. Ament, "Comparison of Delphi Forecasting Studies in 1964 and 1969," *Futures*, Vol. II, No. 1 (March 1970)

22. Gordon and Ament, *Forecasts of Some Technological and Scientific Developments.*

23. de Brigard, Helmer, *Some Potential Societal Developments.*

24. J. W. Forrester, *Urban Dynamics* (Cambridge, Mass.: The M.I.T. Press, 1969).

25. Portions of this section are drawn from T. J. Gordon and H. Hayward, "Initial Experiments with the Cross-Impact Matrix Method of Forecasting," *Futures*, Vol. I, No. 2 (December 1968); T. Gordon, "Cross-Impact Matrices: An Illustration of Their Use for Policy Analysis," *Futures*, Vol. I, No. 6 (December 1969); and R. Rochberg, T. Gordon, and O. Helmer, *The Use of Cross-Impact Matrices for Forecasting and Planning*, Report R-10, Institute for the Future (April 1970).

    Since the time when this section was originally prepared (early 1970), cross-impact techniques have undergone considerable further development, and the reader should be aware that the current approach to cross-impact differs in several important respects from the version described here. The latest discussions of cross-impact techniques may be found in Selwyn Enzer, Wayne I. Boucher, and

Frederick D. Lazar, *Futures Research as an Aid to Government Planning in Canada: Four Workshop Demonstrations*, Report R-22, Institute for the Future (August 1971).

And since this report was written there have been many contributions to the development of cross-matrix methods. Therefore, the reader should view this description of cross-impact methods in historical perspective and realize that research has added considerably to the scope of this early work.—T. J. G., Spring 1972.

26. Rochberg, Gordon, Helmer, *The Use of Cross-Impact Matrices.*
27. Otto Sulc, "Interactions between Technological and Social Changes," *Futures*, Vol. I, No. 5 (September 1969).
28. H. Kahn, A. Wiener, *The Year 2000* (New York: The Macmillan Company, 1967), p. 351.
29. P. Ehrlich, "Eco-Catastrophe!" *Ramparts* (September 1969).

I. Bestuzhev-Lada, "Bourgeois Futurology and the Future of Mankind"

1. V. I. Lenin, *Collected Works*, Vol. 21, p. 72.
2. *Ibid.*, Vol. 19, p. 389.

Kenneth E. Boulding, "The Economics of the Coming Spaceship Earth"

1. K. E. Boulding, "The Consumption Concept in Economic Theory," *American Economic Review*, 35:2 (May 1945), pp. 1–4; and "Income or Welfare?" *Review of Economic Studies*, 17 (1949–50), pp. 77–86.
2. Fred L. Polak, *The Image of the Future*, Vols. I and II, translated by Elise Boulding (New York: Sythoff, Leyden and Oceana, 1961).

Ossip Flechtheim, "Futurology—The New Science of Probability?"

1. James Harvey Robinson, *The Humanizing of Knowledge*, p. 57.
2. Bertrand Russell, *Human Knowledge*, 1948, p. 343 f.
3. The reader who has been discouraged by the failure of the public opinion "pollsters" to predict Truman's election should consult Louis Bean's *How to Predict Elections* (New York: Knopf, 1948).
4. This has been done by Dr. H. A. Larrabee and his students at Union College who, early in 1942, studied various authorities who had gone on record in print, prior to Pearl Harbor, with specific predictions concerning the prospects of a war between this country and Japan.

John Wren-Lewis, "Faith in the Technological Future"

1. J. Robinson, *Honest to God* (London, Student Christian Movement, February 1963).
2. George Orwell, *1984* (London, Lecker and Warburg, 1949).
3. A whole spate of books have appeared on this subject recently. They are usefully summarised in Theodore Roszak, *The Making of a Counter Culture* (London, Faber and Faber, 1970).

Fifty Books
About
the Future

The following is a partial list of recent or particularly influential nonfiction books about the future, most of which are readily available in libraries and bookstores. Many contain more elaborate bibliographies for the serious researcher.

Amalrik, Andrei. *Will the Soviet Union Survive Until 1984?* New York: Harper & Row, 1970.

Baade, Fritz. *The Race to the Year 2000.* Translated by Ernst Pawel. Garden City, N.Y.: Doubleday, 1962.

Baier, Kurt, and Rescher, Nicholas, eds. *Values and the Future: The Impact of Technological Change on American Values.* New York: Free Press, 1969.

Bell, Daniel, ed. *Toward the Year 2000.* Boston: Houghton Mifflin, 1968. (Book version of special issue of *Daedalus*, Summer 1967, based on work of the Commission on the Year 2000.)

Bell, Wendell, and Mau, James A., eds. *The Sociology of the Future.* New York: Russell Sage Foundation, 1971.

Boulding, Kenneth E. *The Meaning of the Twentieth Century: The Great Transition.* Evanston, Ill.: Harper & Row, 1964.

———. *A Primer on Social Dynamics.* New York: Free Press, 1970.

Brzezinski, Zbigniew. *Between Two Ages.* New York: Viking Press, 1970.

Calder, Nigel. *Technopolis.* New York: Simon and Schuster, 1970.

———, ed. *The World in 1984.* Baltimore, Md.: Penguin, 1965.

Clarke, Arthur C. *Profiles of the Future.* New York: Harper & Row, 1963.

de Jouvenel, Bertrand. *The Art of Conjecture.* Translated by Nikita Lary. New York: Basic Books, 1967.

Drucker, P. F. *The Age of Discontinuity: Guidelines to Our Changing Society.* New York: Harper & Row, 1968.

Ehrlich, Paul R. *How to Be a Survivor.* New York: Ballantine Books, 1971.

———. *The Population Bomb.* New York: Ballantine Books, 1968.

Esfandiary, F. M. *Optimism One*. New York: W. W. Norton, 1970.

Eurich, Alvin C., ed. *Campus 1980: The Shape of the Future in American Higher Education*. New York: Delacorte, 1968.

Ewald, W. R., Jr., ed. *Environment and Change: The Next Fifty Years*. Papers commissioned for the American Institute of Planners' two-year consultation, 1966. Bloomington, Ind.: Indiana University Press, 1968.

Flechtheim, Ossip K. *History and Futurology*. Meisenheim am Glam: Verlag Anton Hain, 1966.

Fuller, R. B. *Operating Manual for Spaceship Earth*. Carbondale, Ill.: Southern Illinois University Press, 1969.

Gabor, Dennis. *Inventing the Future*. New York: Knopf, 1964.

————. *Innovations: Scientific, Technological and Social*. New York: Oxford University Press, 1970.

Gordon Theodore J. *The Future*. New York: St. Martin's Press, 1965.

Hayashi, Yujiro, ed. *Perspectives on Postindustrial Society*. Tokyo: University of Tokyo Press, 1970.

Helmer, Olaf. *Social Technology*. New York: Basic Books, 1966.

Jantsch, Erich. *Technological Forecasting in Perspective: A Framework for Technological Forecasting, Its Techniques, and Organization: A Description of Activities and Annotated Bibliography*. Paris: Organization for Economic Cooperation and Development, 1967. (Also available from OECD Publications Center, 1750 Pennsylvania Avenue, N.W., Washington, D.C.)

Jungk, Robert. *Tomorrow is Already Here*. New York: Simon and Schuster, 1954.

Jungk, Robert, and Galtung, Johan, eds. *Mankind 2000*. Papers presented at the 1967 1st International Future Research Conference, Oslo. Oslo: Universitetsforlaget, 1968.

Kahn, Herman, and Wiener, Anthony J. *The Year 2000: A Framework for Speculation on the Next Thirty-Three Years*. New York: Macmillan, 1967.

Kostelanetz, Richard, ed. *Beyond Left and Right*. New York: William Morrow, 1968.

————, ed. *Social Speculations: Visions for Our Time*. New York: William Morrow, 1971.

McHale, John. *The Ecological Context*. New York: Braziller, 1970.

————. *The Future of the Future*. New York: Braziller, 1969.

McLuhan, Marshall. *Understanding Media*. New York: McGraw-Hill, 1965.

Marek, Kurt W. *Yestermorrow*. New York: Knopf, 1961.

Mead, Margaret. *Culture and Commitment*. New York: Doubleday, 1970.

Meadows, Donella H.; Meadows, Dennis L.; Randers, Jorgen; and Behrens, William, III. *The Limits to Growth*. New York: Universe Books, 1972.

Mesthene, Emmanuel G. *Technological Change.* New York: New American Library, 1970.

Michael, Donald N. *The Unprepared Society: Planning for a Precarious Future.* New York: Basic Books, 1968.

Peccei, Aurelio. *The Chasm Ahead.* London: Collier-Macmillan Ltd., 1969.

Platt, John. *The Step to Man.* New York: John Wiley & Sons, 1966.

Polak, Fred L. *The Image of the Future.* New York: Oceana Publications, 1961.

————. *Prognostics.* New York: Elsevier, 1971.

Schon, Donald A. *Beyond the Stable State.* New York: Random House, 1971.

————. *Technology and Change.* New York: Dell, 1967.

Stevens, L. Clark. *Est: The Steersman Handbook.* New York: Bantam, 1971.

Theobald, Robert. *An Alternative Future for America.* Chicago: Swallow Press, 1968.

Toffler, Alvin. *Future Shock.* New York: Random House, 1970.

Waskow, Arthur I. *Running Riot.* New York: Herder and Herder, 1970.

Wolstenholme, Gordon, ed. *Man and His Future.* A CIBA Foundation volume. Boston: Little, Brown, 1963.

*   *   *   *   *

For information about futurist activities and additional literature see also: *The Futurist,* a monthly, and *Futures,* a quarterly.

Index

About the Author

Alvin Toffler has been an editor of *Fortune,* a Washington correspondent, and a contributor to scores of periodicals ranging from *Life, Horizon,* and *Playboy* to the *Annals of the Academy of Political and Social Science.* Mr. Toffler is the editor of the prize-winning volume *The Schoolhouse in the City* and the author of *The Culture Consumers* and *Future Shock,* which was a nominee for the National Book Award and the winner of the 1971 Prix de Meilleur Livre Étranger. Mr. Toffler lectures widely and includes many campuses in his travels; he has been a Visiting Scholar at the Russell Sage Foundation and, at the New School for Social Research, the teacher of "the sociology of the future"—one of the first such courses in the world. He has been a Visiting Professor at Cornell University, where he conducted research into future value systems, and is a member of the board of directors of the Salzburg Seminar in American Studies.